Romanticism and Marxism

American University Studies

Series I
Germanic Languages and Literature

Vol. 51

PETER LANG
New York · Bern · Frankfurt am Main · Paris

Marcus Paul Bullock

Romanticism and Marxism

The Philosophical Development of
Literary Theory and Literary History in
Walter Benjamin and Friedrich Schlegel

PETER LANG
New York · Bern · Frankfurt am Main · Paris

Library of Congress Cataloging-in-Publication Data

Bullock, Marcus Paul
  Romanticism and Marxism.

  (American university studies. Series I, Germanic
languages and literature; vol. 51)
  Bibliography: p.
  1. Criticism—Germany—History. 2. German literature—
History and criticism—Theory, etc. 3. Schlegel,
Friedrich von, 1772–1829—Aesthetics. 4. Schlegel,
Friedrich von, 1772–1829—Knowledge—Literature.
5. Romanticism—Germany. 6. Benjamin, Walter, 1892–1940—
Aesthetics. 7. Benjamin, Walter, 1892–1940—knowledge—
Literature. 8. Marxist criticism—Germany. I. Title.
II. Series.
PT74.B84 1987   801'.95'0943   86-21028
ISBN 0-8204-0317-2
ISSN 0721-1392

CIP-Kurztitelaufnahme der Deutschen Bibliothek

Bullock, Marcus Paul
Romanticism and Marxism : the philosophical
development of literary theory and literary
history in Walter Benjamin and Friedrich Schlegel
/ Marcus Paul Bullock. — New York ; Bern ;
Frankfurt am Main : Lang, 1987.
  (American university studies : Ser. 1, Germanic
  languages and literature ; Vol. 51)

ISBN 0-8204-0317-2
NE: American university studies / 01

© Peter Lang Publishing, Inc., New York 1987

Printed by Weihert-Druck GmbH, Darmstadt (West Germany)

TABLE OF CONTENTS

INTRODUCTION

THE IDEA OF TRANSLATION

The words Romanticism and Marxism have both been so ravaged in the various storms of polemic and invective through which they have passed that it would be quite wrong, and certainly quite historically uninformed, for it to be assumed by anyone that they knew what was meant simply by the mention of either term. Words like these always carry a strong connotation of where the speaker wishes to identify his or her own position in the history determined by what they denote. This goes beyond the simple question of whether one approves or disapproves of the directions things take within such movements. It also means that there is no settled agreement on what those bodies of ideas really are. With terms like these, there will be a growing collection of different contents with every instance they are used violently or creatively to add a new force in the turbulent current of historical dispute. It follows as well that all of these accretions in meaning are part of the importance of the words themselves.

An important aspect of my own attempt to establish an understanding in these questions can be seen at once in the project of bringing Romanticism and Marxism together. By undertaking to discuss them as connected rather than alien or antipathetic to one another, I have already indicated a concern with changing a very widespread preconception about them. At the same time, I should make it clear that I do not intend to construct a relationship between those two domains as totalities, exploring and accounting for connections in all the elaborate variations they show as global entities. That would inevitably bring me into a level of overblown scale and sweeping generalization which would contribute little to real knowledge of the matter in hand. Nor will I even try to map out the full variations and versions in which each domain appears. Were I to make that the methodological prerequisite of my task, I could never reach its beginning. At the same time, even though I have had to select strategic points of focus between which my arguments may be set out, I do not intend any claim that the positions so chosen have some specially privileged standing. They are not more representative of the whole than many others, but were selected because they were particularly well suited to my purpose. I hope I can show why, and justify this choice, in the course of my analysis.

Even within the writings and career of Karl Marx himself, there is a constant strain between what is meant by his philosophical thinking, and his proposals for action in the political sphere. Since his time, the idea of a unitary "Marxism" able to reconcile that tension has burst open in every direction, and in the gaps and spaces which expand to receive them, a hundred ancillary developments of analysis, insight, program, opportunism and synthesis multiply and compete. Similarly, the literary and philosophical period we designate "Romantic" has no clear beginning or end, except for those who pick on dates in the crassest spirit of territorial division. Romanticism also follows a profoundly different development in every national tradition where it may be identified, and within the several phases it passes through in each, a challenging variety of different outlooks and attacks emerges.

In order to avoid the unending problems involved in attempting to define and describe these historical abstractions, I focus my efforts on two specific individual figures, Walter Benjamin and Friedrich Schlegel, to exemplify Marxist and Romantic thinking respectively. My strategy rests on the advantage of a discussion which is restricted in scope, but capable yielding some definite positions, as against the disadvantage of navigating through two such unrestricted bodies of material, and becoming embroiled in debates which lead without hope of resolution to points lying out of view beyond every horizon. I do not suggest—indeed it would be absurd to do so—that these men might adequately represent domains so large and complex, nor do I even assert they are in some way at the central point of each. I would suggest, on the contrary, that there are no central points to be sought here.

The appropriateness of these two figures lies partly in the subtlety and open-textured quality of their particular treatment of the issues which are common to any valid point at all in the two terrains covered by the general terms of Marxism and Romanticism. Of equal importance are the factors which link the two men, and make their work commensurable in a vivid and fruitful constellation. I refer here not only to the way they both stake out an unusual combination of ground on the boundaries between literature, history, philosophy, criticism and theology, but also to the most helpful factor of Benjamin's early study of Schlegel, and the evidence of continuing influence in his later work. The result is that between them, they open up a field of thought whose usefulness in understanding our own situation in our own times is not hampered by narrow and exclusive dogmatic claims to truth, but is conducive to continued flexible and responsive inquiry into the quality of all knowledge.

While Romanticism may not, like Marxism, be the issue in a vast conflict of propaganda and power, general usage of the expression "romantic" to mean lost in the unreality of personal private fantasies has tended to generate a great deal of distortion in the way texts linked with the word are read. Although this prejudice is completely unscholarly, it is not really surprising that it is so widespread, since perhaps the one thing one could say about all the phenomena one would wish to designate with the term "Romanticism" is that they do treat the sphere of personal experience with a concentration and complexity which we now reserve only for questions of "objective" knowledge modeled on that scientific approach which, from the Romantic era to the present, appears to have scored such startling successes in every domain. I will suggest in the argument pursued through this book that our ability to understand the Romantic era depends on changes in our own era regarding the character of scientific knowledge. The field of scientific study itself also has an interesting and still somewhat neglected history of its own among the Romantics, which I shall discuss as well.

The concept which links Marxism and Romanticism is that of revolution. The historical inheritance passed on from the Romantic period and taken up in its own form by the socialist political movements of the nineteenth century undoubtedly centers on this principle of change and discontinuity. At the same time, it is no less true to insist that while the Romantics understood revolution as the manner in which an **idea** enters and transforms the world, Marxist revolution is understood to be a change first of all in the material relations and conditions of society. Yet these positions are not absolutely opposed. They differ only in emphasis when considered from a philosophical point of view.

The conception of revolution that enlivens Schlegel's thinking, especially in the early years of Romanticism, circulates about the idea of an unlimited and dynamic subjective freedom. The concept Benjamin took from Marx envisions an end to community divided up by property, a division which is taken to be the violation of all the possibilities that community could offer. In either case, the issue centers on the way that individual existence can be expressed and represented in the collective context of a social world. If historical materialism ascribes priority to the conditions in the world, and Romantic idealism looks first to the dynamic subject, this does not mean that either of these could or did overlook the philosophical implications of separating those two spheres. As I hope to demonstrate, Schlegel and Benjamin show acute and continuing awareness of this distinction from their respective standpoints. In Benjamin's work that is especially evident in his rejection of "vulgar-Marxism" or "scientific socialism" which inclined to treat political change as a simple matter of exercising power in a perfectly transparent causal system. The impulse behind revolutionary change in history, the desire for justice and authentic expression of individual potential in objective life, involves a transferral of personal and collective force from one medium into another. The desire for change and the course of action to bring it about lie athwart a point of discontinuity across which an extremely complex refraction takes place. The transformation of one into the other by no means occurs in a singular and transparent medium, but via a dialectical process.

For Schlegel, the revolutionary work of bringing the Romantic idea of change into human life depends on the development of different and appropriate forms of human association which support and empower individual thought or imagination. This is the basis of all his positions on politics. In Marxism, political change is consummated when the individuals who make up a class identify the collective interest which each one embodies. It is this consciousness which mediates the collective power and the collective purpose of a revolutionary class. Although the importance of differences in priority should not be overlooked, there is a comparable sense of the complex relations between these two interlocking opposites, consciousness and society, running through significant parallels in each one's corpus of writing.

Just as this fundamental philosophical complication is essential to Walter Benjamin's constantly shifting perspective within dialectical materialism, so too it generates a fluid, highly demanding use of language in dialectical Romanticism. It is the difficulties encountered in Friedrich Schlegel's writings which offer the most telling indications of how he is to be—and how not to be—read. The issues he confronts are mysteries and paradoxes, and just as he can only come to grips with them in full recognition of their ultimate impenetrability, so we too can only deal adequately with his work if we acknowledge the place and function of that resistance to interpretation which is an essential part of it. As he observes in Lyceum Fragment number 10: "Man muß das Brett bohren wo es am dicksten ist"[1] ('One must drill the board where it is thickest'). Following this admonition, my attention will be focused on the phase of Schlegel's work from 1796-1801, the Jena or Athenäum period of German Romanticism. This is not necessarily the time at which his writings take in the most abstruse questions or present the most convoluted theories, but, because those are the years when he was able to take the most radical stand with regard to traditional views on ontology and theology, it is the period in which his method of exposition is at its most uncompromising and most paradoxical.

The materials to be considered from these years are pre-eminently series of fragments. Even where Schlegel appears to make a clear and concise point in one of these, no single statement may be taken in isolation as the indication of his position. He is always in the process of building up a picture which is constantly modified by each new line on it. This is the way he pursues the logic or sequence of his own thoughts, and it is also the way he speculates the universe is constituted—not as a fixed structure waiting to be uncovered, but something in infinite transformation which can never be apprehended directly or finally, and only approached in the endless process of representation. To follow the direction he takes, and render it into a form more easily grasped and compared to other figures in the tradition of Western thinking, one has to keep a maximum of differing utterances in play at one time. By this often trying but necessary feat of juggling, one can suspend final judgement on what is meant until these contradictory elements can be put together and used to plot the curve of a complex line of thought, or mark strategic points on a configuration too intricate and variable to portray in its entirety. This patient style of interpretation has proved its value in some surprising degrees of coherence in what have hitherto seemed the most recalcitrant of texts.

What Schlegel is most at pains to avoid is the léger de main through which a reality which cannot be comprehended is hidden by an image of simplicity, and we should similarly be wary of this in the expectations we bring to his work. In reading him, one should always look for the last ramification of contradiction which defers comprehension, not the solution which would most rapidly bring the problem to a close. Occam's Razor, the principle of explanatory parsimony, will not be of great help here. The appealing concept of a world constructed as though by a divine providence which has made it intelligible in full, even if only ideally, has no place in Schlegel's thinking during these years. The order of certainty appropriate to that traditional and tempting presumption into which one can fall so easily, is a delusion and a danger, and it is precisely the spell he does **not** want to weave.

As he wrote in a notebook of 1799: "Zauberworte sind wie Gifte für die Unvorsichtigen" (KA XVIII p. 300 #1266, 'Words with magical power are like poisons for the unwary'). For the careless reader who becomes its thrall, and forfeits his or her judgement in the haste to confirm received prejudices, such obscure and "profound" writing can become a form of black magic. At the same time, Schlegel was in no doubt that there was an esoteric capacity in the written word which would liberate understanding. The question of how to read carefully, therefore, and use the magical power of words in a positive form, is the central concern in my attempt to elucidate his work in this book.

Of all the things Schlegel knew, it was the written text which had the capacity to touch his own numinous intuitions and transform them into some other kind of entity that he could elaborate and make accessible outside their special sphere, observing: "Der Buchstabe ist der wahre Zauberstab" (KA XVIII p. 265 #846, 'The letter is the true magic wand'). If the process of writing was a magical act, so was reading in its turn also. The reader performs a complementary thaumaturgy which reverses the process to produce something out of the text which is as different from it as whatever preceded it in the act of writing: "Buchstabe ist fixierter Geist. Lesen heißt, gebundnen Geist frei machen, also ist auch eine magische Handlung" (p. 297 # 229, 'The letter is spirit in fixed form. To read is to set bound spirit free, and so is also a magical act'). The relationship between Geist and writing is thus the obvious crux of all our interest in this matter. Without writing, thought or spirit will elude us, since it is not "fixed," but with writing it eludes us too, except within the limits of care, since it is a delusion to mistake "fixed" spirit for spirit itself.

The fixity of the letter is alien to thought, which Schlegel regards as essentially free, and the freedom of thought is alien to the fixity which is necessary to the letter. Care in reading means, first of all, recognition of the alienation which is an inescapable part of the text itself. The letter must be read with an index or reminder that it is absolutely distinct from what it fixes or represents, and cannot offer that other sphere through its own self-evident presence. Despite this contradiction, all the knowledge we have of Geist which has come through reading and writing obviously depends on signifying forms, and those forms also have no significance without thought. Therefore the fixed form of the expressive medium has to be interpreted in the consciousness of where the process began. Truth in reading is not a perfect return to that beginning to uncover the precise origin "in" the text. The origin is not in the text. But truth in reading does involve completing the task of moving from the letter back to the domain or quality of that beginning: "Ohne Buchstabe kein Geist; der Buchstabe nur dadurch zu überwinden, daß er fließend gemacht wird" (p. 344 #247, 'Without the letter there is no spirit; the letter can only be overcome by making it fluid'). Nevertheless, it is a kind of fetishism of the letter to expect meanings in the domain of thought to be available in ways which resemble the tangible presence of writing.

Schlegel could see, as can anyone, that the requirements of social life give a person the characteristics of a written word. One's public role and function is fixed, visible, consistent according to a body of rules. This is incompatible with the fluid quality of thought, which can therefore have no public existence. In one's identity as a thinking being, one enjoys a contrary domain of fluidity and freedom, but one is also constrained within the frailty and ephemeral isolation of that enclosure. In one's identity as a public or social being, one benefits from the support of a stable and enduring general order, but that benefit is only extended to meanings which reflect the qualities of the letter. A person therefore lives in two domains of meaning, and cannot choose but to translate constantly between them.

Each aspect is born from the other and in this interdependence each must carry the weight of the other with it in its own sphere.

The translation or transmutation of one into the other is not simply a change in the outward garment by which the soul, as it were, remains the same while the body changes. It is a radical, exclusive difference which must be comprehended as such. The common justification of translation that it carries the sense of a text intact from incarnation to incarnation in different languages is therefore a deception. The practice which claims that "thought, if it be translated truly, cannot be lost in another language"[2] is, by this criterion, a black art. The real justification and value of translation must be sought within an understanding of the larger issue of textual representation in general. All writing which attempts to make that magical transsubstantiation from intuition to text, and the further transformation from the text to its correlative in the reader's mind, is subject to an absolute discontinuity between modalities, and the mystery of what is made accessible to the reading of a translation is only an extension of the same question applied to the original text.

The sense that writing itself is a form of translation is so widespread that it may be regarded as a commonplace of our tradition. The difference between the imaginative forms which the author is aware of, and the visible expression into which it must be wrought, is felt to correspond to the image of two languages. D. H. Lawrence, for example, complained in a letter: "I am doing a novel, a novel which I have never grasped. Damn it's eyes, there I am at p. 145 and I've no notion what it's about. . . . It's like a novel in a foreign language I don't know very well—I can only just make out what it's about."[3] The text is, consequently, not the "original," but only the result of an origin in intuition which can never be taken out of its own realm. There is a distressing, but unbridgeable, contradiction between them. Virginia Woolf wrote:

> I believe that the main thing in writing a novel is to feel, not
> that you can write it, but that it exists on the far side of a gulf,
> which words can't cross: that it's to be pulled through only in a
> breathless anguish. . . . A novel, as I say, to be good should
> seem, before one writes it, something unwriteable: but only
> visible; so that for nine months one lives in despair, and only

when one has forgotten what one meant, does the book seem tolerable.[4]

What one can express as writing goes out into the world and is carried forward in the traditional inheritance of history, but whatever was present in the writer's consciousness is banned from passing the threshhold of its own sphere. Its existence, no matter how we imagine it to be conditioned by what is exterior to it, is its own, and cannot be otherwise. The expressed form finds recognition by a potentially vast readership, it is saluted as a vivid exposition of whatever it is thought to carry within it; it may set new chains of response in motion and change the way generations think. But it is not the writer's thoughts. They are sealed off. They cannot act in their own name, but only send a representative out into the alien sphere, and this is true whether thought produces writing, or some other activity. In both cases it will be an alien representative whose character and capacities, and whose language, enter the distant turmoil, while the intuition itself fades and vanishes. The world of action can never know it.

Friedrich Schlegel writes: "Die Süßigkeit des Ruhms liegt darin, daß es ein historisches Daseyn giebt" (KA XVIII p, 87 #690, 'The sweetness of fame is that it gives one a historical existence'). Yet it is also clear that such a historical existence would not be at all identical with what one is for oneself, or even to those who know one personally, with whom a single existence is shared. The exterior image which is produced in the medium of history is created by visible acts; the interior sphere is their opposite. Pure thought and reflection are out of history. They are situated in a spere of inactivity, to which Schlegel accordingly ascribes enormous value. In his novel, _Lucinde_, he exclaims: "O Müßiggang, Müßiggang! . . . du heiliges Kleinod! einziges Fragment von Gottähnlichkeit, das uns noch aus dem Paradiese blieb" (KA V p.25, 'O idleness, idleness! . . . thou sole fragment of divine nature still left to us from Paradise'). This unmoving central spark is the home of the individual's primal identity in consciousness itself, and therefore the source of philosophy: "Die Begeisterung der Langeweile ist die erste Regung der Philosophie. Alle

Langeweile die man hat, macht man eigentlich sich selbst" (KA XVIII p. 87 #689, 'The inspiration of boredom is the first stirring of philosophy. All the boredom one has is actually one's own creation').

The juxtaposition of these two ideas, history and conscious existence, depends on the concept of representation. Language, or signification of any kind, is what both joins and separates them. It is this join or break which permits us to generate the visible and transmissible token or image that somehow originates with something else in whose place it stands, and which, through what we know as history, will then survive as reminder and replacement after the source is gone. Yet while the acts which live on in history seem only to persist by virtue of the thoughts which lived in the moment of their birth, these latter are not present in them.

The relationship is one of translation, of the global transformation from one medium to another in which the original is irremediably excluded. The otherness of a representation always implies this quality of an irreversible step away from a prior mode, so that Schlegel notes: "Die Mimik ist offenbar eine übersetzende Kunst"[5] ('Mimicry is clearly an art of translation'). When one reads or interprets the transmission of history, and becomes conscious of the acts which make it up, the original, a-historical thought is in no way redeemed, any more than retranslation of a text back into its mother language will produce the original. One would never hope to recover Shakespeare's dramas by translating A.W. Schlegel's or Tieck's German versions back into English. On the other hand, it is possible to think in theoretical terms of something else being gained. The existence of the "original" already present in the language is of only relative importance. One naturally responds sceptically to this idea, because in language, and between languages, one does normally think of something being "lost" rather than gained. Nor is this ordinarily wrong, but the reason depends on the element of translation already inherent in the original text.

The literary work is an act in the history of its mother language where the thought of which **it** is a translation (i.e. representation), marks and changes the medium which it cannot enter, but against which it exerts a modifying influence. The reader also lives in two domains, that of history and language, the public dimension, on the one hand, and the dimension of personal experience on the other. Each is equally dependent on its counterpart. As Schlegel observes, spirit is not possible without the letter. Historical change or development in the realm of public expression brings the potential for equivalent development in individual experience. Reading, making the letter fluid, means realization of this change to produce historical renewal of one's own thought. And that development in the mode of spirit or experience, in turn, then brings the possibility to manifest this response in the alternate mode of acts (or a new text). Where the reader does this by reproduction in a different language, this is a translation in the common meaning of the word.

This line of argument removes translation between language and language from paradigm status in the way we usually to see the term employed, and in fact brings it closer to Schlegel's more extended application. Translation considered as a representing function moving from medium to medium will be more clearly exemplified where it is more radical, where the media are more contradictory in nature. The distance between language and language is surely a far narrower one than that from the medium of thought to an act, or between consciousness and history, or that separating the person from his "fame." Nonetheless, translation in the commonplace sense **also** has the potential to add something new to the recipient language in a comparable manner to that in the production of the original, albeit almost always to a lesser degree.

The reason, furthermore, I want to consider ideas of gain rather than loss in translation stems from the universality of this distance. There is nothing in human life that is not subject to it, from the most private issues to the largest collective realm of political power and decision. The degree of authenticity or reality at every point along this spectrum depends on the manner in which the existence in one modality is able to project itself across an absolute boundary to generate an impression corresponding to it in another. If the measure of success in this projection is to be measured by the fidelity with which a change, an addition, is registered in the recipient medium, then the element of loss is always essential. If the interdependence of the two sides of the process is understood as I suggest, however, then all growth and development in each sphere comes out of that essential contradiction between them.

The appearance of a systematically (i.e. "grammatically") coherent new meaning or image in a given medium indicates the latter's orderly growth and development. Whatever remains behind in the prior sphere from which the image is drawn is of no significance to it. That may be regarded as "lost" in this sense, but the recipient medium cannot be regarded as losing what it never had. The gain begins when a tension or contradiction is registered in the process of imitation, and is a function of what is difficult, not what is easy. Only to the extent that translation in the commonplace use of that word is a measure of the gap between one language and another, and the foreignness leaves its mark on the new representation by virtue of this, does it produce that change, that gain. It is by virtue of this incompleteness that the process is in principle endlessly renewable. At the same time, however, the gain is ordinarily much slighter than that which occurred by the writing of the work itself. Only very exceptionally will translation between languages equal the historical dynamism, in the recipient medium, of a major original in its own tongue.

Though the separateness of the individual translator's consciousness guarantees the distinctness of each new attempt, the labor which carries one text over into another is quite circumscribed as an inventive practice. What one good translator produces is determined quite closely, and must resemble within quite close limits, what another would have produced. His situation in the salient where one language approaches another is restricted by the firm approximation with which the speech of one history may match what is voiced in the contours of another. The narrow band of territory between these two fronts allows much less freedom than in the production of an "original" text. The mysterious and unpredictable possibilities are expanded far beyond this in the writing of an original, where the "translation" operates between a reading of the multidimensional "text" of a historical situation in the alternate mode of consciousness, and the resultant text in language. Whatever is "pulled through" across that "gulf" to make a novel can take many forms depending on where in the given landscape of language and literature the labor of reconstructing an experience is begun.

The variability of outcome in such a project will be determined by the difference between any language or "objective correlative" and the experience to which it is to correspond. No single solution is perfect, and the equality between many imperfect solutions separates the significance of the work from its particular content. Content which can be recognized as reflecting things and facts outside the novel in the everyday world does not indicate what the text is "about" in the way that the identifiable original of a translation indicates what the translation is "of." On the other hand, the informational accuracy of a literary translation is not what distinguishes an excellent from a mediocre piece of work. The element of truth or value in a novel and literary quality in a translation both go beyond, respectively, subject matter and informational content. Their specific value rests with what they have brought into the medium, language, whose substance is their substance.

History and language are both created or extended through the mark thought makes on them by disruption, not by intentions which pass into expression without resistance. It is the element of incommensurability which is of concern here, not information. A million acts for which the historical inheritance is already able to account in full, and which are not in tension with it, will not produce the smallest vibration in its course. This form of "content" is taken up and leaves no trace, like the superimposition of a million shadows which will not darken the first. The accumulation here will neither constitute personal consciousness as in the magical process of reading, nor produce a development in history, as in the creation of new literary writing. It is a pure repetition of the same. The neutrality of what circulates in the dimension of information is a function of the commensurability of medium and content. Within this singular, one-dimensional domain thought and act move indifferently from one to the other. The system holding them both is continuous, and there is no difference like that between the fixity of the letter and the fluidity of the spirit which requires a process of innovative transformation.

Because the truth of literary expression is never perfect, just as the image of the person in his fame is always inauthentic, these are both always only provisional. Each effort to renew them may relieve the tensions surrounding what had gone before, but the continued demand of life for the "sweetness" of fame, the desire to be represented in a historical form, and not be lost with the passing of time, reveals the bitterness of an inevitable limitation and falsehood. That which lives on is not oneself, and that which is oneself remains bound within its own enclosed circle of life, in secrecy, obscurity and mortality. The struggle to represent oneself in history is renewed again on the basis of all that has been achieved in previous struggles, and the process goes on both despite and because of its ultimate impossibility. This is in fact the productive process of human life itself in both domains. It is productive in both the public domain of culture, and the private one of experience. The transmission of information and the translation of information are both quite different in this respect. With them, repetition has the reverse configuration—it is redundant, because it is adequately achieved each time, so that the **information** contained in one of Shakespeare's scenes might be passed from language to language, and return home after circling the globe, but have gained and contributed nothing in its travels.

Each age not only must write its own great dramas and stories in order to find itself represented, and is able to fulfill this task to the extent that it is **able** to believe itself represented, in the forms of literature; it also requires its own translations of the most canonical of its texts written in foreign languages. Each stage in the Western tradition needs its particular versions of the Bible, the Greek classics and so on, which reflect the changing ways it inhabits the landscape of its own language. In just the same way, the rewriting of history is necessary for each generation too. Schlegel was not only one of the very first to see that literature exhibited a history of its own, he also saw that the **writing** of history itself had a history as well. As early as 1797 he observed in a notebook: "Eine **Geschichte der Historie** müsste eins der interessantesten, lehrreichsten Werke sein können" (KA XVIII, p.115 #1032, 'A history of history would be one of the most interesting and instructive of all works'). The intrinsic connection between what is involved in history and translation is made explicit in the way Schlegel applies the term translation to characterize what defines and limits truth in historiography: "Je ähnlicher historische Historie einer **Uebersetzung,** je vortreflicher" (KA XVIII p. 211 #181, (The more historical history resembles a translation, the better it is').

The distinction between authentic and informative translation is also clearly in play in his criteria of value for such works: "Jede **Historie,** die sich nicht auf die . . . Uebersetzung der Menschheit bezieht, ist nur ein Essay. Fast alle historischen Werke, die nicht Urkunde sind sind **diaskeuastische Uebersetzungen**" (p. 204 #88, 'Every history which is not conceived as a . . . translation of humanity, is just an essay. Almost all historical works which are not simply documents, are **interpretive translations**').

A very similar principle to this which enables us to establish a systematic basis for pursuing speculations along essentially the same track in Walter Benjamin's work also occurs in an early essay of his, The Task of the Translator, published in 1923 as the introduction to his translations of Baudelaire's poetry. Benjamin puts forward the view here that the literary tradition, the history of writing, is one of living organisms. This is not a mere sentimental expression of vaguely perceived significance for our own life, but, on the contrary, a serious contention that the essential structural features of organic life are repeated elsewhere in a manner which can both be rendered explicit, and contribute to the clearest and most reasonable comprehension of all such manifestations. As Benjamin states: "The idea of life and afterlife in works of art should be regarded with an entirely unmetaphorical objectivity."[6] The possibility of doing this is not always taken seriously, and it is seldom pursued in a philosophical spirit. For Benjamin, however, there is no question that it is a valid undertaking: "The concept of life is given its due only if everything that has a history of its own, and is not merely the setting for history, is credited with life" (Illuminations, p. 71).

It is the persistent identity which bestows coherence and organized connections on the otherwise disparate constituents of an organism—like the material elements which a body takes up and relinquishes—that is characteristic of life. A work of art performs the same function through the medium of its history in the organic relationship between the varied and transitory experiences for which it is the factor of structural unity. The endless multiplicity of translations (representations or readings) is contained within the growing life-form of the work as its historic identity, whose persistent individuality transcends an unlimited area of change. That continuation in "fame" corresponds to the growth or survival of the vital entity, whereas its birth is the appearance of the original act or work from the womb of consciousness in which it was conceived. This special mode of identity generating diversity and continuity in its coherence both reflects Schlegel's view of history, and supports Benjamin's own claims with respect to translation:

> And indeed is not the continued life of works of art far easier to recognize than the continual life of animal species? The history of the great works of art tells us about their antecedents, their realization in the age of the artist, their potentially eternal afterlife in succeeding generations. Where this last manifests itself, it is called fame. Translations that are more than transmissions of subject matter come into being when in the course of its survival a work has reached the age of its fame (*Illuminations*, p. 71).

The shift in emphasis to the historical domain which is evident here is central to everything I will argue in comparing Friedrich Schlegel and Walter Benjamin. In place of the continuous interdependence of two spheres between which no meaningful order of priority can be established, Benjamin searches for a simpler dialectical ascent. The process of history for him resembles the revelation of the true nature of a work, and clearly transcends any personal or individual experience in it or of it. This is the way he uses the vital reality meant by the term "life," which here is the life of the species, fulfilled in the uncurtailed development of historical time, and thus distinct from that of the individual, which is circumscribed, unique, and irretrievable. In pursuing this, I shall take my distance from Benjamin's Messianic concept of a defining purpose in life where all aspects are directed towards a final redemption in one life. While accepting the importance of historicity as a concept of integrity in change, and a manifestation of reality at that level of extension, I also maintain that the constituent elements of this general or extended level are not <u>aufgehoben</u>, or negated, in order to participate in history, but continue to exist at their own level simultaneously and equally.

It follows, too, that when I attempt to analyze a stratification of life within society and especially according to the relations of class, I will differ from Benjamin by endeavoring to treat these primarily as abstractions or generalizations derived from the individuals categorized in each particular way. The reason for this is not to dispute Benjamin's picture of the economic structure of class-society where he builds it up according to a Marxist model. The objection I wish to bring to bear in the political analysis of literary texts is not meant to detract in any way from his critique of the oppressive nature of industrial capitalism or the falsehood of its ideology. The difficulty I see in his position lies in the image of a perfect translation—that is, an alternate society in which a general order will represent perfectly the existence of those who participate in it.

I will argue that there is no change in society, no revolution, no matter how correct and just the social order it brings about, which can abrogate the distinction between the collective domain and the personal, even if it narrows the distance and the contradiction between them. A truly just and humane order must begin and end with recognition of that difference. In the same way that literature and translation continually fret away at the limitations of a language at all times, so the constant complaints and objections of individuals are required to generate an unsteady but ultimately unfailing pressure against oppressive or unresponsive social forces which are not human or personal, and thus create conditions which are alien to personal human life. It also follows that as these objections are converted into power in order to become effective, and are developed into collectively organized movements in order to manifest themselves as power, their character changes. They are translated into political action which is both a representation of individual impulses, and also an alienation from those origins.

A retranslation of those impulses will be required by every age, every generation, in order to renew the language of public action which is always false to a degree, yet always indispensable, and also always inclined to decay into greater falsity if it is not constantly reappropriated. No history can be written which does not take its place in the history re-written after it. No revolution can bring to an end the need for revolutionary change in subsequent generations. No language can absorb all the differences in languages, and, transcending the inadequacies of individual manifestations of language, bring to an end all the changes which register its vitality as the continuing redress of its inadequacy. Precisely the same thing applies to the discourse of political change. A political movement represents true human interests in the task of resisting and destroying an alien and oppressive imposition of power. Where it has to draw on the highly effective tactic of representing itself as the end of politics, the ultimate and immutable image of truth and justice, it has already fallen into a mythology which excludes criticism from the quarter of human freedom and authentic life.

In developing the Messianic idea in politics, Benjamin writes of Language itself, as opposed to concrete languages. He suggests that this is not just a utopian image against which a particular historical discourse may be criticized, but a locus of absolute authority. Similarly, his concept of the revolution and the classless society which it is to usher in have a theological finality about them. My own terminology is not meant to imply any such claim. I adhere to the non-Messianic idea that none of these modalities can ever be perfectly incorporated in a single manifestation, any more than a work could be perfectly expressed in one single translation.

I do, however, want to treat the invocation of life in his discussion of cultural and political history as an invitation to apply a kind of critique to his arguments which is not usually attempted. Although there are many striking parallels in the terminology and imagery which Schlegel and Benjamin use, a simple documentation of these correspondences yields only limited understanding of their work and its relationship. Both bodies of work are so complex and often obscure that the conceptual similarities to which one might draw attention may produce intriguing and even elegant matching patterns, but these are likely to owe much to looser connections in their use of a common idiom, rather than convey a picture of deeper conjunctions in their thought. In consequence, I intend to build my analysis on the fundamental questions of system and organization common to all entities which both change and maintain continuity. That is to say, I begin with characteristics essential to two domains which are otherwise entirely different— living matter and the phenomena of history.

The principle of my argument is that all culture, all history and all life forms exist alike in a systematic stratification between whose levels certain definite principles of organization hold which can be described quite succinctly. The individuals at each level arise by the combination of elements existing in a stratum of lower organization, and that expresses a relationship which has significant constant features. Such a construct accounts systematically for the dimension of language which constantly exceeds precedent, notably grammatical precedent, and from which we determine degrees of "literariness" both in original texts, and of translations from them.   In considering life-forms as historicity, the model to examine first is that in which the term has its commonplace meaning, the form of organism in the natural world.   From this we can describe the distinction between matter at the molecular and animate or vegetative levels as a paradigm case for the structure in question, and express it in terms sufficiently generalized to establish its visible and equal recurrence elsewhere.

The condition of matter prior to the appearance of organic life is that there is no center from which any regularity among material entities could be measured. This may be a rather obscure concept, but it is simply an extension of the commonplace notion in history as such by which a connection between events which does not spring from the mediating agency of human experience is disallowed as a historical occurrence.   There is a corresponding distinction at the most primordial level of the nature of things, for without something functioning in the role of an observing agency, all events, or all conditions, are absolutely unique and separate. There is neither time, nor distance, nor number.

The dependable patterns of constancy in the past and confident predictions for the future which we know as physical laws depend on our ability to repress the differences, the disparity in every instant and position in the cosmos. We are able to do this to the extent that we remain constant ourselves, and will respond with a coherent series of impressions to events even though they may be different with regard to time and space and the totality of accompanying conditions. They will be registered as repetitions of the same phenomenon because there is a singular feature which recurs for us.   But this is not only a matter for human consciousness and scientific laws, which already imply an array of complexities far beyond the minimal pattern we need to establish the general principle we are seeking.

The simplest organism is all that is required to provide the first continuity by which the disparate instants are linked to establish time, because it has a singular and constant response to series of molecular individuals. This constancy transcends the incommensurable aspects of instant, position and surroundings in the molecular condition.   The living entity as such bestows a quality with regard to itself which all members of a given series of particles will have in common; a chemical element or compound becomes a set, or an identity, to which its molecules may potentially all conform. That qualitative constancy allows the possibility of quantitative distinctions, temporal, ordinal and spatial, which are all relative and comparative.

It is, as it were, "written" in the coherent identity of the organism that certain materials must appear to it, fulfill a role predetermined by it, and be recognized as proper to it. By these distinctions, it also sets a structural rather than material boundary or discontinuity between itself and all that is foreign to it, so that it can extend itself by annexing and adding. Its material constituents are altered, but that which determines its identity stands separate from them, a stability which does not lose what it was at the instant of change. Chance itself is encompassed in its identity, and it is this structure which is able to reproduce itself by the complete suppression of difference in its material substance. Non-living chemistry cannot duplicate itself because its units are instantaneous, surrendered in the moment of alteration. Its separate instances are open, wholly identical with their substance, and therefore not individual in the vital conception of enclosure indicated when Schlegel notes: "Wo Einheit ist, da ist auch Bewußtsein" (KA XVIII p. 164 #491, 'Where there is unity, there is consciousness also.')

The transformation which the organism has imposed on its surroundings is the production of its own individuality by the negation of the subordinate individuality of those entities which it has organized into collective functions of its various material ingredients. The molecular mode of existence, in other words, has been translated "upward" into generalized forms constituting the "outside" which marks, and masks, each member of a series with the same qualitative identity as the others. That may be regarded as its "significance" as opposed to its "being" or its uniqueness, which vanished to a lost "inside." The sense in which a molecule, or any particle, is a unity **in itself** cannot, consequently, appear to that outside. Its theoretical particularity gives way to a phenomenality vested in a separate and superordinated unity.

This figure of repression of interior unity to constitute an imposed aspect centered outside, is observed for the individual person in relation to the collectivity of mankind in the same fragment as that quoted above: "Ein Zeitalter der Menschheit ist ein Gedanke der Menschheit. Hier auf diesem Standpunkt verschwindet die Freiheit des Menschen" ('An age for mankind is a thought by mankind. This is the point where freedom of the individual person disappears'). A person is contained and constrained within a historical thought he cannot himself think. This is the relationship which expresses the transformation from personal experience to the condition of "fame," and this corresponds with precision to what has been established as the defining structure of life also.

The thought of mankind, or the historical consciousness of an age, is thus a denial or exclusion of the inner unity of personal consciousness. But equally, personal consciousness also illustrates this pattern in its own dimension. Here, memory creates time out of a series of states of being by a consistent "outside" which can be repeated in and above the absolute uniqueness of every experienced instant in itself. This will be an aspect which both appears as the factor of equality between each lived moment and its recollections, and similarly establish an equivalence between the recollections themselves. Different situations become commensurable by this agency, and so the very principle of repetition itself is founded for this level. A higher order of time emerges in this higher order of continuities, but this is still not historical time. That arises with what we know as "symbols."

The meaning of a symbol, for example a word in language, is its power to suppress the absolute particularity of individual consciousness. It is the outer aspect which is made common to all the interior phenomena in the subordinated continuity of personal perceptions/recollections. It is, once again, a suppression of disparity, and the possibility of organization. No-one is ever quite the same as he or she was before, nor like anyone else. Nor is any state of affairs one might experience exactly like something comparable in the past, or the way it would be experienced by another person. The repetition of words that applied in one situation, and then in another, has created a dimension where there is return and equivalence in things. A word is the condition of a repetition between consciousness and consciousness, and the continuity which that generates in the superordinated intersubjective medium is historical time. That negates the enclosure of experience to produce the outer aspect of historical identity in significant acts which figure for other historical subjects—that is, live in "fame."

These systems of gain and loss are always irreversible in the way that translations are. That is, at each step, what precedes and is incorporated into the new structure is lost, in its own particularity and prior structural identity in the lower level, to the one superordinated over it. One cannot deduce the condition of matter prior to its incorporation in a living organism from the creature itself; one cannot reproduce in oneself a state of consciousness from the legacy of fame in which another person's thoughts live on. The separation acting here is not like that between languages, or "systems," but between temporalities. Each stratum has its own characteristic order of continuity, and its own discrete mode of time.

The passage of translation between them is made radical by the cancellation of what is prior or below. In order for the higher level to "know" events in the lower, to "recognize" them, it must exclude that perspective which obtains between them among themselves, by which each is always met with as a first instance. The state of organization that this implies is liable to the second law of thermodynamics at each specific level, because transformations within these strata are equivalent to the transferral of information. Thus, the bad kind of translation which does not build its recipient medium, and is not renewable the way literary translations or literary representations of the same phenomenon are, is liable to degradation in its precision. The content of the scene which could be translated around the linguistic globe and back would in the end be severely impaired by that entropic effect, according to information theory. The sublation of temporal strata, however, raises their constituents into higher levels of organization, and thus reverses entropy.

It would be interesting, albeit not part of our present concern, to speculate whether the relationship between field and particle in microphysics is not also an expression of this pattern. Since a particle may be regarded mathematically as the sublation into a mode of continuity and identity of the absolutely disparate and mutually unknowable positions throughout a field, this could yield an expressive figure between these two also. The possibilities of pressing further with this idea seem very intriguing. At the other end of the scale, also, the theoretical potential of a supra-historical mode of time, an esoteric temporality beyond conventional signification, cannot be dismissed.

The existence of an individual organism ends in death because its orderly genetic structure lives only as information, and cannot change. The species persists and evolves, however, since it is the medium in which the "translation" from generation to generation is able to add to itself by the progressive response to the material environment. This is the form in which all readings and representations within their tradition which register the uniqueness of individual experience, and respond to it in their outward or symbolic face for history, add to the growing degree of order in the culture. That is, by examining the question of order at its most fundamental point, we can establish the principle which may be found in Friedrich Schlegel's entire opus, and especially during the period 1796-1801, when he was the leading philosophical spirit of early Romanticism. This argues that the nature of the human cultural heritage is created by its constant redefinition and continuous re-production. Only when it is the object of an unrelenting critique from the "disorder" below, the subjective enclosure of individual a-historical intuitions, can its orderliness survive. Entropy, or the decay of language, culture and tradition, results from the defence of its coherence before the chaos of individual imagination and individual freedom. Rigidity and conformism therefore lead to death; cultural conservatism is in fact the opposite of its claim, and proves to be more ravaging than revolution.

Translation, where it alters the existing state of the medium, renews or rejuvenates the life of the entity it changes: "Jede wahre Uebersetzung muß eine Verjüngung sein" (KA XVIII p. 204 #87, 'Every true translation must be a rejuvenation'). Moreover, the only source of renewal of a system of representation is from outside, by this same means: "Jede Uebersetzung ist eigentlich Sprachschöpfung. Nur der Uebersetzer ist ein Sprachkünstler" (p. 71 #513, 'Every translation is actually linguistic creation. Only the translator is an artist in language').

The great danger in history is that any manifestation should be elevated to the standing of an ideal or perfect representation, or the definitive translation of the human condition which eliminates all rivals. Human beings live as historical subjects as essentially as they do in the role of personal subject. These cannot be separated. On the other hand, the categorical distinction between them means that each is absolutely "out of context" in the other, and they can never be brought together. The personal experience of history is never history "as it is," the representation of experience in a collective modality is never conscious existence "as it was." These are translations. And just as the real translation which is more than a presentation of information is the representation of the historical work as it passes through the personal subject, the historical subject can only "reproduce" through the agency of its alternate, and sustain its life by constant adaptation with regard to the latter's demands. The translation of this basic and universal text of history must go on forever, for nowhere can there be a finally authoritative version.

Reading, the making of meanings of any kind other than as information, is always a process of drawing the text out of its context, and the reading can never be authentic if this is not realized in that process. But at the same time, history has a tendency to overwhelm existence and to appear as authority, to encircle itself as both text and context so the reader's own sphere of experience is expunged. No space for freedom is then left. The result of this situation is monstrosity—conformity, reaction, persecution, violence and sterility—and there is always a pressing urgency for the reader to focus his energy against it. Schlegel's theory of New Mythology, in which contradictory representations, or "myths" in the singular form of authority, are brought together to purge them of their claim to truth, is one formulation of that concern.

Yet the record shows that history has not proved susceptible to such an enterprise. It is in the nature of history to remain beyond the grasp of unaided human velleities. Even though its fabric is woven out of mankind's acts and achievements, it persists as impenetrable and unpredictable precisely because it is a "life-form" superordinated above the sphere of the will. Therefore the tendency to produce itself as integral finality is uncontrollable by the means of philosophical thought or exhortation. History has the power to sweep aside the kind of critique we find in New Mythology, so that the vast mass of humanity, perhaps even the isolated writer himself in another moment, is unable to resist the images which it presents.

The analysis here does not conclude that we are then necessarily condemned to passivity and pessimism. On the contrary, a remedy is perceived in the ongoing process of history itself. The changes which technical developments have brought to the means of representation are extremely influential in altering the picture which the inheritance brings. This is the changing element through which the very possibility of Schlegel's overcoming of old myth as the principle of a singular image of permanent truth is considered here to have come about. The basis of multiple reading of history is indeed historical itself, but the indication of diminished autonomy for the personal subject is lightened by the judgement that a deep and immensely significant resolution of the dangers of myth, of singular reading or interpretive methods, has in fact been brought into being.

If the criterion of success, i.e. survival, in cultures and traditions which are the particular instances of the historical life-form, depends on their responsiveness to the subordinated ingredient out of which it constructs itself, it follows that there is an intrinsic weight in history overall, to preserve a positive and harmonious relationship between the historic entity and the personal subject. The consequence where this does not occur is failure, or dissolution of the tradition. Thus, the tendency of a culture to impose itself as a fixed content, or overwhelm individual consciousness as an integral finality in the role of information and authority, runs counter to the larger demand of a power also vested in history itself. Though individual cultures may age and die where they arrest change, the continuity which transcends them is an evolving one. To escape entropy and dissolution, that power must by the nature of things elaborate the responsive media of representation.

In the beginning of historical time, there was only speech, ("Die **Sprache** ist die älteste Urkunde der Geschichte" KA XVIII p. 301 #1279, 'Language is the oldest document of history'). At the period when Schlegel wrote, described in the Gespräch über die Poesie ('Dialogue on Poetry') as "das Zeitalter der Bücher" (KA II p. 332, 'the age of books'), the widespread availability of printed texts had added a notable range of possibilities which found expression in his theory of prose. The vastly heightened sense of the relativity of historical production illustrated in his New Mythology was therefore conditioned by the historical advent of new technical possibilities for representation. It is a familiar and widely acknowledged principle that the unitary character of traditional myth is not compatible with the multiplicity of viewpoints which may be collected in the medium of the novel. Yet the most established or classical manifestations of the genre certainly **do** appear compatible with a lesser degree of allotropy than that proclaimed in New Mythology. Consequently, Schlegel's own attempt at a novel-form in Lucinde did not prove to be the model for 19th century narrative genres, nor did his epistemology win much of a following.

I consider Schlegel's writings from the period of early German Romanticism at each point together with those of Walter Benjamin because the latter's work takes place against the explicit background of a further transformed technology of representation. In Benjamin's time, the techniques of photography, film, sound recording, and the mechanical reproduction of all works of art, generated a renewed awareness of the way texts of any kind figure in the often aggressive and paradoxical march of history. The interpenetration of these polymorphic "translations" tends to introduce a greater and greater sense of the inadequacy of a canonical tradition to personal existence, which in turn implies a development of the historical sphere itself as a self-conscious and therefore critical and responsive medium. Thus the revolutionary change from the rigid stability of old myth to New Mythology does not stop with Romanticism, but advances rapidly to the contemporary situation in which the enormously intensified activity of representation through electronic technology generates a leap in the degree of diversification as great as that first diagnosed by Schlegel.

The circumstances this has introduced are now much more favorable to the broad acceptance of a critical attitude modeled on his. By combining his work with the appropriate aspects of Benjamin's analyses, and also with Paul Feyerabend's critique of scientific knowledge, we arrive at some additional conclusions which go beyond Schlegel's thoughts in the direction indicated above. For this approach I apply the term New History.

That basic idea, expressed here in a few broad strokes, obviously could be expanded in almost any direction and used in the analysis of the widest variety of texts. At the same time, it requires to be tested and demonstrated far beyond the degree possible in the present undertaking. For the moment, however, the concern has only been to bring forward those resources available to an exposition of this issue in Friedrich Schlegel's literary and philosophical notebooks from the period 1796 to 1801. Although only a small portion of the immense span of material contained in them has been drawn into the argument here, this still offers some substantial support for the principle I have endeavored to propose.

These notebooks are a very unusual body of writings. They were not intended for the eyes of anyone outside his immediate circle of friends and associates. Many of his published ideas can be traced back to antecedents first commited to paper in these pages, and there is a very real sense in which one can take them to be the most uninhibited or undissimulated evidence of his developing views. Rediscovered little more than a generation ago, they have shown themselves difficult to penetrate without a willingness to depart from the conventional image of reading, but this is, of course, also their great strength and promise. They demand **not** to be imposed on their subject matter in a singular, self-content interpretation. They do not require acceptance of an integral content or methodology, but generate continuous revolutionary movement between thought and text.

The aphoristic form is a constant reminder that each principle enunciated is derived from a moment of consciousness as distinct as the fragment correlative to it. Though each has survived for more than one hundred and eighty years beyond its original time, the inconsistent texture of the whole shields it from the abysmal eminence of a venerable claim to truth. Incomprehensibility, in the sense that the authority of a united front can never be attained in its reading, is the greatest guarantee that this text will support the purpose of renewed interpretation, not bring it to a halt. The terrible danger manifest so often in the past, where a historical image has become the agent of destruction of anything that contradicts or opposes it, receives no support here. The balance is secured by the "ewige Dualität" ('eternal duality') of thought and realization, whose dignity is expressed in the endlessly projected contradictory harmonies and harmonious contradictions of these notes. This frequently astonishing, and sometimes baffling, approach to writing is an indication of a possible maturity in the still young phenomenon of history itself.

The sense of this self-conscious stage of historical development is the masterful achievement of Friedrich Schlegel, further enhanced by the more recent works which I examine together with it and through which I bring it into the context of the present age. The task I set myself is to add what clarity and accessibility I can to that achievement.

At the same time, it is important to remember that this approach to epistemology and to the significance of the literary and artistic tradition was only a stage, and a relatively short one, in Schlegel's career. It would be unjustifiable to set it above the later period in which a transcendental basis is looked for in the revelation of Catholic theology, as though the latter were only evidence of a failure of the intellect, an aberration of character or symptom of personal flaws of biographical rather than philosophical importance. The conundrum posed by a choice between a wholly immanent or human account of all meaning, and a transcendent or theological one remains. We can avoid, but not solve, questions expressed by the image Benjamin introduces in the first of his Theses on the Philosophy of History, in which dialectical materialism figures as a chess-playing automaton which wins its games because it is operated by a dwarf who is a master-player concealed in the mechanism, and who represents its now hidden theological component.

The critique of Benjamin's Messianism which is used to give a focal point to this investigation of Schlegel, treats the theological category as a mythic element which attempts to protect itself within an immanent structure of meaning by a false claim to transcendence. It is considered as an ideology only, and one which has, moreover, grave attendant dangers. There is a further possibility which is not confronted here, but should not be ignored. The opposition of an immanent concept of history and language to a mythic structure of transcendence may not enclose the full universe of phenomena and experience, and the inescapable foundation of a theological origin of meaning may remain. How this might be dealt with intellectually is the question to which I have made no approach or reference, but it must be acknowledged. The idea of revelation, or of truth restored by a Messiah, are both ideas for which workable language and readiness of thought have now disappeared. As Benjamin says, the dwarf "today, as we know, is wizened and has to keep out of sight" (Illuminations p. 253). Whether the apparatus of the kind of account I have attempted here will wear out and collapse, so that the theological carrier of understanding is forced to return to view, is an issue whose outcome simply may not be foreseen.

?

NOTES

[1] Kritische Friedrich-Schlegel-Ausgabe, Hrsg. Ernst Behler, (München: Schöningh, 1967), Bd. II p. 148. Quotations from this edition hereafter cited as KA with volume number. In the case of fragments, the editors' numeration is included also.

[2] From the preface to John Dryden's translation of Ovid's Epistles, quoted in T. R. Steiner, English Translation Theory 1650-1800 (Assen: Van Gorcum, 1975), p. 71.

[3] Quoted by Aldous Huxley in his introduction to D. H. Lawrence, Letters, selected by Richard Aldington (London: Heinemann, 1950), p. 1.

[4] Letters of Virginia Woolf, Vol.III 1923-1928, Ed. Nigel Nicolson and Joanne Trautmann (New York: Harcourt Brace Jovanovich, 1978), p. 529.

[5] Friedrich Schlegel's Literary Notebooks 1797-1801, Ed. Hans Eichner (Toronto: University of Toronto, 1957), p. 167 #1671. This collection is henceforth indicated in the text with the abbreviation LN.

[6] From "The task of the Translator" in Illuminations, Trans. Harry Zohn, Ed. Hannah Arendt (New York: Schocken, 1969), p. 71. This source hereafter indicated as Illuminations.

CHAPTER I

ECLIPSE OF THE SUN—MYSTICAL TERMINOLOGY,

REVOLUTIONARY METHOD AND ESOTERIC PROSE

Feuer muß überall unsichtbar vorhanden sein wo Erde ist—das ist
der Sinn des Centralfeuers. Feuer ist das Esoterische, Erde das
Exoterische. (Friedrich Schlegel, Philosophische Fragmente)[1]

Pflanzen und Thiere laufen um den Menschen, wie Planeten und Monden
um die Sonne. Alles lebt nur durch und für den Menschen, er is die
Centralsonne des Organismus auf Erden.
(Johann Wilhelm Ritter, Fragmente)[2]

Wie Blumen ihr Haupt nach der Sonne wenden, so strebt kraft eines
Heliotropismus geheimer Art, das Gewesene **der** Sonne sich zuzuwenden,
die am Himmel der Geschichte im Aufgehen ist.
(Walter Benjamin, Geschichtsphilosophische Thesen)[3]

The Parabola

There are two prose works which are generally considered to exemplify the
narrative ideas of early German Romanticism, Heinrich von Ofterdingen by
Friedrich von Hardenberg, better known as Novalis, and Lucinde by
Friedrich Schlegel. The two men were intimate friends, but even Novalis
expressed doubts about Lucinde when he read it in 1799. Although
Heinrich von Ofterdingen does contain some esoteric allegorical passages
and undercurrents, it strikes the reader more by the eloquent
"yonderliness" of its sensibility than any radically innovative form.
Schlegel's novel, on the other hand, caused something of a literary scandal.
This was partly occasioned by some sections which were not only rather
erotic, but quite obviously drawn directly from his own life with his
companion Dorothea Veit, whom he would later marry after her divorce.
That was, however, only part of the scandal. It was also a quite
shockingly strange piece of writing.

Conceived as a digressive novel in the tradition of <u>Tristram Shandy</u> or Diderot's <u>Jacques le Fataliste</u>, a work which Schlegel very much admired, it layers narratives within narratives in such obsessive complexity that at the end one really does not know if the story has reached a point in time after the beginning or before it. The writing passes through or parodies various familiar forms and tones on the way, insisting as it does so on the author's perfect right to all arbitrariness. There are philosophical allegories, domestic scenes, epistolary interludes and a sort of brief counter-<u>Bildungsroman</u>, in which the main figure learns to withdraw himself from society, rather than integrate his life into it. The baffling result combined a deliberate exposure of private existence with a labyrinthine indifference to the formal principles of public exposition. It shows no interest in hiding anything, but an odd lack of interest in presenting it either. In short, the novel mocks the very idea of a content present in fiction which is available to the reader as anything but a fascinating and provocative chimera.

One result was that Schlegel came to be thought of for a time as something of a danger, and was followed about by the police. Eventually, the nineteenth century decided that the book was a playful, innocent story of Romantic love and domestic intimacy, and so it matured into a period of acceptance, reprints, and indeed "fame." How Schlegel himself had thought of it is another matter. An intriguing clue is given by the first mention of it we know, which was in a letter written to Novalis in October of 1798. He mentions the plan "einen leichtfertigen Roman leicht zu fertigen" ('to write an unserious novel without serious effort'). What is striking about this is the immediate context, for right before that line, he announces his intention of writing a Bible. This causes some excitement in the correspondence, as it turns out Novalis has been speculating, by coincidence, along very similar lines. Despite the enthusiasm this evidence of "Symphilosophie" elicited, distinct and significant differences emerge in subsequent discussions. Nonetheless, in Schlegel's case a connection between the project of an intentionally unserious or frivolous novel, and the writing of what is traditionally the most serious of all texts, can be deduced quite simply.

If an individual writes a Bible as an explicit act, he or she transforms the unique status of Biblical writing as singular and authoritative beyond the standing of any personal author. A novel in which the narrator insists on his own irresponsibility, and fragments himself into an impenetrable system of different voices, is an equally clear attempt to overthrow the dominion of the most common form this genre took among its broad readership. That meant, for Schlegel, the turgid and usually quite pompous works whose task was to confirm and shore up a solid moral structure for the bourgeois world. One should remember that the German tradition is quite poor in examples of what can be done at the highest literary level in the "classical" novel of social life, as represented in figures like Fielding or Laclos. The novels which Schlegel did not like oppressed the freedom and autonomy of personal life by representing, or rather misrepresenting, it as a function of a rigid public domain, conventionalizing images of life in the language of this set and unresponsive writing. They were a very bad, very disrespectful, very incomplete translation of private life into the alien transparency of a rigid public discourse. One might say something similar of the exclusive claims of the Bible to represent the whole of spiritual experience within a single written authority.

What Schlegel rejected in the theory of the novel which produced Lucinde, was the idea that the text fully reflected the essence of a determinate moral reality, and that life could circulate about this essence and derive its truth or substance in the secondary process of reading. For Schlegel writing was to be the secondary process, a response to the experience of a fluid life whose vitality its imaginative productivity shared in fully, but which as a reproduction or representation in language, it could never do more than reflect in part. His views on the foremost genres characteristic of various historical stages of development in the means of textual production suggest this is also the basis of his view of a general frame characterizing literary history. He looks at the principal narrative genres of each age in the way they impose a simpler and more determinate picture of existence in their own image on the complexity of life. The epic world, because it is drawn from a stage of development that precedes writing, reflects the relative frailty of an oral tradition by unifying all experience within a single system of mythology. The Bible and metaphysical philosophy, using the more solid medium of writing, can allow a more complex system with multiple levels of being. The forms of the encyclopaedia, the compendium and the journal in his own time, draw on the yet more powerful potential of printing. They can advance beyond the limits of general descriptive and prescriptive principles, extending their domain into a world of facts and information.

Yet it was the novel which interested him most. The novel, der Roman, was central to the very idea of Romanticism from the outset. This was to be the foundation of a new literature and a new age. The nature of the Romantic novel, the romantischer Roman, is constantly discussed in his criticism and in his notebooks. For this reason, his comments on his own novel are of especial interest. For this reason, too, it is a little surprising to find in entry 2071 of his Literary Notebooks the apparently paradoxical observation by this major founder of Romanticism that Lucinde is not a true Romantic work. Clearly, his position on the nature of Romanticism and Romantic literature was complex, speculative and constantly developing.

Earlier he had noted: "Eigentlich ist alle Poesie = Romantisch![4]" ('Actually all poetry = Romantic!'). Paradox and contradiction are of course, as I noted in my introduction, not unusual in Schlegel's writings. Examples are easy to find, and the idea itself defended. Since the principle of inner organization, the organic whole, is also propounded throughout his career, however, as it is indeed in the fragment on Lucinde where that comment occurs, the contradictions are often regarded by those with a positive attitude to their progenitor either as deferments of a meaning which may be elucidated by the study of further contexts, or as experimental stages on the path by which such a position is developed. The option of experiment also has ample support here: "Meine Notizen über den Roman sind chronologische und zwar experimentierende Fragmente" (LN 1367, 'My notes on the novel are chronological and indeed experimental fragments'). Those less patiently inclined—of which there have always been many, even among his friends—will find confirmation here of that well-established vulgar notion of Romanticism as confused, incomprehensible and nonsensical.

"Gefahr übermütig zu werden, weil das Gesindel mich so sehr verabscheut" (LN 1941, 'Danger of becoming filled with overweening pride because the rabble loathes me so much'), is the response entered in the Literary Notebooks to the hostile reception of his novel. That hostility lives on. Two of the most distinguished and enthusiastic Schlegel scholars active today agree, in introductory comments to their magnificent critical edition of his work, that it falls far short of those achievements for which he takes his place in the history of German and European letters. Hans Eichner remarks on the scandal it provoked, "so liegt das zum Teil an den ästhetischen Schwächen des Werkes, die ja gelegentlich das Mißverständnis geradezu herausfordern"[5] ('that is partly to be blamed on the aesthetic weaknesses of the work, which at times do really provoke misunderstanding'), while Ernst Behler, in a later volume, says "Die Vorlesung sollte der Ersatz für den mißlungenen Roman werden"[6] ('The lecture was to compensate for the failed novel'). From the historical point of view, these judgements are incontestable. Nonetheless failure, and failure to be comprehensible, are highly contingent in their significance, and difficulties in being understood were an integral part of Schlegel's situation from the begining to the very end.

In a letter to Friedrich's brother, August Wilhelm Schlegel, written on the occasion of Friedrich's death, Ludwig Tieck comments that the lectures interrupted by that event were so peculiar "daß nicht allein ich, sondern auch andre Freunde, denen er sich mehr als billig entdeckte, oft eine Verstandeszerrüttung zu erkennen glaubten. Mit solcher kühlen Sicherheit sprach er von Dingen, die uns als Aberwitz erschienen.— Welch ein Genius hat sich zerstört!"[7] ('that not I alone, but also other friends with whom he had shown himself to be more than fair, believed what they were hearing was a deranged mind. He spoke with such cool assurance of things that struck us as madness. What a genius has destroyed himself!') And of course incomprehension was not a strange birth in those late days of seperate paths and divergent views. It was the subject of his essay Über die Unverständlichkeit ('On Incomprehensibility') in the journal Das Athenäum, during the early years. And if he was a disappointment to his friends, he is also frustrating to his apologists today. Among Eichner's introductory comments to the first edition of the Literary Notebooks, we read: "A part of Schlegel's theoretical considerations is pedantic in the very worst tradition of the Greek writers on rhetoric, others are based on wild generalisations. A part of the notes are inspired by a philosophy of nature that, plausible as it may have appeared at the time, tends to strike the modern reader as faintly absurd, and some entries are incomprehensible" (LN p. 7).

The distance between the defenders and detractors of Schlegel's theoretical thinking is a small and relative quantity, for the criterion of value is essentially the same. To friend, as to foe, there is a first impression of "utter chaos," and this fault is only redeemed by its limitation: "Closer inspection, however, soon reveals a suprising degree of coherence" (LN p. 7).

But there is reason to believe that "coherence" in the sense of lucid exposition, is not the most fruitful way to read Schlegel, whether surprising or not. That is to say, the polarities within which acts of reading are performed as the regular and correct procedure of contemporary academic practice are not those within which these texts are written. The inconsistencies and obscurities may be found neither to register flaws to be healed, nor to be rhetorical flourishes of a somewhat scurrilous kind, nor even experiments in any simple sense. In a letter dated July 26th 1799, Henrik Steffens, the Scandinavian writer and scholar who would later introduce Romantic ideas to Denmark, wrote to Schelling, under whom he had been studying philosophy in Jena: "In Berlin lernte ich Schlegel kennen. Ein Mensch, der behaupten kann, die Menschen sollen nicht consequent sein, der bloß von Gedanken, und, wie er sich ausdrückt, unmittelbaren Anschauungen lebt"[8] ('In Berlin I met Schlegel, a man who insists that people should not be consistent, who lives only in thoughts and, as he puts it, immediate intuitions'). With these points of caution in mind, we should now consider how Schlegel continues in the note on Lucinde alluded to above: "Die revolutionäre Poesie und die romantische noch ganz getrennt. Die Romantische auch chaotisch aber in sich organisirt. Die revolutionäre durchaus ⊂. Lucinde nur Uebergang aus der revolutionären in die romantische" (LN 2071, 'Revolutionary and Romantic poetry still quite separate. The Romantic also chaotic, but organized in itself. The revolutionary entirely ⊂. Lucinde is only a transition from the revolutionary to the Romantic').

The aspect to examine first is the curious symbol ⊂. This is described in the concluding remarks to his essay on Lessing:

> Mann nennt das Paradoxe zu Zeiten exzentrisch. Es ist überhaupt eine löbliche Maxime, die Aussprüche des Gemeinsinns mit Absicht buchstäblicher zu nehmen als sie gemeint sind; und grade hier ist es ganz besonders der Fall.

Gibt es wohl ein schöneres Symbol für die Paradoxie des philosophischen Lebens, als jene krummen Linien, die mit sichtbarer Stetigkeit und Gesetzmäßigkeit forteilend immer nur im Bruchstück erscheinen können, weil ihr eines Zentrum in der Unendlichkeit liegt? (KA II, p. 415)

('One sometimes calls a paradox eccentric. It is a most excellent principle deliberately to take commonplace expressions more literally than they are meant, and here especially it is to be recommended.

Is there a more delightful symbol for the paradox of philosophical life than those curved lines which, stretching away in clear constancy and regularity, can only appear as a fragment because one of their centers lies in infinity?')

The parabola, an ellipse whose closure is only a theoretical or mystical concept because its second focus is infinitely removed from the first, indicates a meaning which can never be completed in the lower realm of the visible world. What August Wilhelm first referred to as his brother Friedrich's "mystische Terminologie" ('mystical terminology') will, in the same way, ever evade or exceed the consistency of ordinary language, because it is always "out of context," not signifying a meaning in the determined, finite world in which it is uttered, but invoking an absolute beyond it.

Yet, as the figure suggests, the character of this absolute is not that of being. Its only determinate or knowable quality is its infinite separation from the phenomenal world, which removes it from the situation of characteristics altogether, or, conversely, its pure negativity vis-à-vis the fixity of character is what constitutes its separation. And since it is not being, its representations in the visible realm are not grounded in any stability of correspondence or parousia. When considered philosophically, all being on the visible plane is consequently undermined also—if there is nothing beyond appearances to sustain it, it is only illusion, and the concept of world altogether breaks down. As Schlegel writes in a philosophical notebook of 1798: "Nicht der Tod ist Gegensatz des Lebens, sondern die Welt" (KA XVIII p. 319

#1527, 'It is not death which is the opposite of life, but the world'), or, as he expands this in his literary notebooks: "Welt ist Verwicklung der kleinlichen Verhältnisse, Furcht, Schwäche, Krankheit, Vernunft, Unvernunft alles zusammen. . . . Allerdings eine nothwendige Bedingung aller immanenten (i.e. nicht mythischen) Poesie. . . . Welt=Gemeinheit" (LN 2178, 'The world is the entanglement of petty relations, fear, weakness, sickness, reason and unreason all together. . . . Nevertheless a necessary condition for all immanent, i.e. not mythical, poetry. . . . World=Meanness'). The writing of "mythic" poetry, however, freed of the concept of world, of its constraints, its "meanness," is no longer absorbed into its interests or its needs. Nor is it constrained by the necessities of temporal order, consistency or causality. It enjoys a different life.

Lucinde is precisely an instance of that "mythic" poetry in Schlegel's special sense. A quite extreme and "ex-centric" instance. The hostility to this novel, whose venerable and varied history takes in such luminaries as Hegel, who regarded it as a satanic abomination for its arbitrariness and its wilfully self-sufficient "subjectivism,"[9] and Kirkegaard, who was equally appalled that "along with the enjoyment of the flesh it also enjoys the negation of the spirit,"[10] can be centered at just this point. The metaphysical views of spirit as true or absolute being, whether rational or theological, are no less excluded along with the concept of "world" than the naive reality of the ordinary citizen. A metaphysical reality like this which Schlegel endeavors to overcome is simply the recuperation at a higher and more refined level of an entity which stands above all as the limitation of imaginative freedom. Schlegel opposes the "truth" based on such affirmations for reasons very similar to those of Friedrich Nietzsche's essay Von Wahrheit und Lüge im außermoralischen Sinn. That idea of truth runs through the various strands of our tradition as an inequality in what may be thought. It encloses us always within the restrictive boundary that distinguishes between the permissible and the derogated thought.

The narrative structure of Lucinde reflects a determination not to allow such a concept, or such a distinction, to assert itself in the composition of this fiction. Development in a traditionally shaped novel is, of course, not restricted to a literal truth since it relates imaginary events. It is, nevertheless, restricted to a particular kind of "literary" truth in that it strives to mimic the world as it is understood according to a particular and restrictive form of metaphysical truth.

What we expect of a traditional novel is the unfolding of imaginary events according to an intrinsic logic so as to arrive at a unified and explicit form. This may be built out of particular viewpoints, particular conceptions of personality and action, which generate a consistency echoing that without which we could not think or grasp the idea of a world. _Lucinde_ neither arrives at a unified form, nor sustains the unified image of a world. The incoherence or inconsequence of the work offends because the philosophy on which it rests is entirely opposed to the ideology in which virtually all our tradition is enclosed. That body of Schlegel's theoretical writing which could as easily be called the non-metaphysics as the metaphysics of his Jena period, substantially eliminates the idea of a truth or Being which is an ordering, determining constituent of the "world", or to use what is for us a more contemporarily enlivened word, the concept of "presence."

From this point of view, the hostile readings have in general been better informed and better grounded methodologically than the apparently more favorable ones. Neither respect for the author's great name as a critic and founder of modern literary scholarship, nor approval by a somewhat different brand of romantic enthusiasm for the personal and emotional dimension of existence, are adequate veils for what is at stake in this book. Its concern to fray and unravel the texture of a stably formulated world is indeed satanic from the perspective of a coherent metaphysics, and the concomitant expectation that a text be ultimately cohesive in reflection of it. Schlegel perceived the evil principle elsewhere— precisely in the fixity of a world or the foundations which made it possible. Only by negating this could a positive writing be set free. For that reason, the freely inventive, productive speculations of theory are defended as indivisible in status from the empirical, both constituting an undivided reality as equals (KA XII, p. 98, p. 102). The alternative constraint on the sufficiency of theory is evil itself: "Für die Theorie ist eben alles ein heiliges Spiel, da ist das Böse nur Täuschung, nicht so für die Praxis. Und also ist das absolut Böse . . ." (KA XVIII p. 370 #593, 'For theory, everything is just a sacred game, and so evil is merely illusion; but this is not the case for praxis. And therefore that is absolutely evil').

I want to demonstrate in this chapter that the theoretical work of contemporary criticism, where it has exorcised the element of onto-theology from its grasp of textuality, and separated itself from the metaphysics of presence, is indeed the new light in which _Lucinde_ may be read adequately. It is not simply to be taken as yet another text to "deconstruct," but has, rather, a very special relationship to present developments, becoming legible in its constellation with our time after generations of misapprehension. I intend, therefore, to read the insightful hostility of the past as a helpful indication of what was truly innovative in the work. That the text has had to wait so patiently for the subsequent steps in its elucidation to be embarked upon, is partly the fault of its apologists. Those analyses which supplant a full reading of the novel by approaching its morphology merely as a manifestation of the Romantheorie of its author turn reading into a process where the reader effaces the critical demands of his own position. This simultaneously closes out the potential range of the theory, and the possibilities awaiting realization in this revolutionary text.

Such accounts as Michael von Poser's in his Der abschweifende Erzähler (Bad Homburg v.d. H.: Verlag Gehlen, 1969), or even Hans Eichner's "Friedrich Schlegel's Theory of Romantic Poetry," PMLA, 71 (1956), thorough though they are, do not open the work into the situation of readership now. They do not treat this novel as an active literary text, as opposed to an intriguing historical document. The approach represented there is really of a piece with the not-so-inexplicable silence surrounding Lucinde in many works tracing the development of the German novel where the canonical texts we read, and from which we learned to read, are assembled as a continuous series. Benno von Wiese's Der deutsche Roman, for example, has no discussion of it, nor does E. K. Bennett even include it in the list of dozens of titles at the end of his History of the German Novelle. And one must concur—truly it does have no place among them. The development traced through the books which are named is exactly what blocked that Progression by which Schlegel expected to see the illusory fixity of being overwhelmed. It is the urgency of that which, in the fragment LN 2071 quoted above, even defers "the Romantic" itself insofar as, in the usage of this instance, there is a distinction between it and the necessity of constant revolution.

It is into the concept of revolution that a reader of this novel must look most deeply to grasp its life, and from its quality as a revolutionary novel that the most spirited readings can be drawn. It is also at this point that ultimately its limitations will be most justly weighed.

The Exoteric Esoteric

The negation of "world" as the complement of language, as being which is in stable or penetrable contact with language, is the fundamental feature of Schlegel's writing altogether during this period. In the lecture series delivered at Jena University, the theory of mystical terminology makes this break with truth and communicable meaning or comprehensibility quite explicit, but a tradition still wedded to another modality of language has continued to treat it as a puzzle to be unlocked by the old key, rather than an adamant refusal to remain under that law. Brilliant and exhaustive studies of items in Schlegel's terminology have been published, notably Raimund Belgardt's Romantische Poesie (The Hague: Mouton, 1970) and Karl Konrad Pohlheim's Die Arabeske (München: Ferdinand Schöningh, 1966), but despite scrupulous scholarship taking in virtually all instances of their use, the terms continue to elude determination and remain at large, untamed and unbranded.

It is they, in the end, which have exhausted the resources of all the lines brought up to contain them. This parabolic language obviously presents real problems to the very basis of the means of discussion, because it reduces the realm of meaning itself, in the public and visible sense, to secondary status. Meaning, and the being of what is meant, are for Schlegel only an allegory of the Real, which is non-being (and also absolute freedom). Every word is a potential parable, for not only can it mean something in being adequate to a "signified" in the visible world, but it may further be an indication of the invisible, the absent, in its inadequacy, its shortcoming. This allows it to break out of the orbit of the mundane, and function as an indicator of the ultramundane, to be "ex-centric." In giving up its claim to fixed and full meaning, it becomes progressive, and free: "Jeder Satz, jedes Buch, so sich nicht selbst widerspricht, ist unvollständig" (KA XVIII, p. 83 #687, 'Every sentence, every book, which does not contradict itself, is incomplete'), or again: "Alles, was sich nicht selbst annihiliert, ist nicht frei und nichts werth" (p. 82 #628, 'Everything that does not annihilate itself is not free and is worth nothing').

Simply to gather up an elaborate concatenation of cited passages to generate a "complete" picture of this theory, however, to show its "coherence," is precisely to lose it completely. The idea of a stable, comprehensible body of meaning corresponds to the geometric form of the circle about a fixed enclosed center, not the parabola. In Schlegel's view of history, this was the condition of antiquity, when the agency of mythology in classical Greece made all poems part of one poem, and all meanings joined in one world. But this was an extraordinary natural phenomenon. Only there "Wandelt die Gottheit in irdischer Gestalt" ('the Godhead wanders abroad in human form'), only in that unique situation could "das Beschränkte vollständig, das Endliche vollendet, das Einzelne allgemein-gültig seyn" ('the limited be perfect, the finite be complete, the singular be universally valid'), or works appear "in denen das Gesetz der Ewigkeit sichtbar wird"[10] ('in which the law of eternity becomes visible'). Nor can this be restored. The modern condition is the striving for "unendliche Realität" ('infinite reality') after the loss of that "endliche Realität" ('finite reality'). Even the new mythology called for in Gespräch über die Poesie reflects this, abandoning the simplicity of the antique model. It aims at producing unity by universal extension and inclusiveness, quite the opposite of the traditional feature of national exclusiveness and enclosure.

Like Nietzsche, who attacks the "verwöhnte Müßiggänger im Garten des Wissens" ('spoilt idlers in the garden of knowledge') in Vom Nutzen und Nachteil der Historie ('On the Benefit and Detriment of History'), Schlegel does not write in order that his words should be taken up idly as learning, to be accumulated like things possessed. The very essence of his work, developed into a philosophical system in the Transzendentalphilosophie and the Köln lectures of 1804-05, is that there is no real being of things, and the possession of knowledge which partakes in that fixity, is error. In fact, the only error. The sign by which real learning may be grasped is not acquisition, but change. It is Bildung, formation, and also transformation, the idea of revolution. He notes in his Philosophical Fragments: "Bildung ist antithetische Synthesis, und Vollendung bis zur Ironie.—Bei einem Menschen, der eine gewisse Höhe und Universalität der Bildung erreicht hat, ist sein Inneres eine fortgehende Kette der ungeheuersten Revolutionen" (KA XVIII p. 82 #637, ('Learning is antithetical synthesis, and perfection to the point of irony.—When a person has reached a certain peak and universality of learning, his interior will be a continuous chain of the mightiest revolutions'). But this continuous revolution, the principle of progressivity, is also named as religion because it is the will away from the empirical world of things, the element of Beharrlichkeit, fixity, and towards absolute freedom, the absolute non-determination of fully realized consciousness. In the later lecture cycles, this is developed into a system of metaphysics, transcendental psychology, theology and cosmogony, but it is important to remember that even here the first principle of being as allegory of the unbounded and invisible Real still holds. The description of being is always made with the explicit caveat that it is not a primary reality, but a secondary manifestation of an ultimate which is necessarily distinct from its self-representation. Only when such manifestations are perceived in the correct form, that is as allegorical representations of an eternally undeterminable Real, can there be true meaning, not Täuschung.

Real meanings are paradoxical in the everyday world because they are out of context. Their function is not wholly taken up between visible terms, but refers also from the visible to the invisible: "Paradoxon ist ein exoterisch gemachtes Esoterikon" (KA XVIII p. 104 #896, 'A paradox is something esoteric which has been made exoteric'). The real, the absolute freedom of consciousness, the object of absolute longing in the human spirit, is not wholly out of reach where this modality is embraced:

> . . . wäre dieser Wunsch wirklich unerreichbar, wie uns jene
> Sophisten glauben machen wollen, so möchten wir nur lieber das
> nichtige und verkehrte Beginnen ganz aufgeben. Aber er ist
> erreichbar, denn er ist schon oft erreicht worden, durch dasselbe
> wodurch überall der Schein des Endlichen mit der Wahrheit des

Ewigen in Beziehung gesetzt, und eben dadurch in sie aufgelöst wird: durch Allegorie, durch Symbole, durch die an die Stelle der Täuschung die Bedeutung tritt, das einzige Wirkliche im Dasein, weil nur der Sinn, der Geist des Daseins entspringt und zurückgeht aus dem, was über alle Täuschung und alles Dasein erhaben ist (KA II p. 414).

('. . . if this desire were really unattainable, as those sophists would have us believe, then we should rather give up this pointless and mistaken undertaking at the very outset. But it is not unattainable, for it has often been attained, and by the same means whereby the appearance of the finite is brought together with the truth of the infinite and thus dissolved away in it: by allegory, by symbols through which the place of delusion is taken by meaning, the only reality in existence, because only the sense, the spirit of existence arises from and returns to that which is set above all delusion and all existence.')

This is the route of a revolution in which consciousness pursues absolute freedom in a state of insurgency against all being considered as exoteric. That being in its entirety is of negative value until returned to allegorical status, tied to meaning as its esoteric aspect. There is indeed something in the vision of this process of change which is reminiscent of Rilke as he expressed himself in the often-quoted letter to Witold von Hulewicz, where he says "Wir sind die Bienen des unsichtbaren"[11] ('We are the bees of the invisible'). The role of man described there is esoteric transformation of the external world to the higher vibration of interiority, the visible to the invisible. Reading, also, is not an acquisitive act, but part of this alchemy. As he concludes his poem "Archaischer Torso Apollos:" "Du mußt dein Leben ändern" ('You must change your life'). But whereas Rilke's vision, in addition to being weighed down with a limp, cloying nostalgia, is one of self-denial, asceticism, enclosure and isolation, Schlegel burns with the light of an enormous expansion, association, a vast, unlimited affirmation of all human joys and desires, and in the erotic emphasis of Lucinde, an elevation of physical love and sensuality to vehicles of the highest realization. The natural goal of religion in Schlegel's sense includes the orgy. In fact LN #2063 explicitly equates the orgy with the symbol $\subset$.

In the Philosophische Fragmente he observes: "Orgien entstehen durch die Enthüllung von Mysterien" (KA XVIII, p. 314 #1450, 'Orgies are brought about by the uncovering of mysteries'). The revelation of the esoteric nature of the Real as the unconditioned, recasts all conditions, all laws and infringements of freedom by the (deceptive) principle of fixity as oppressions of realized existence. All such divisions and exclusions are appropriate only to the letter of being, not to its fulfilled spirit. Accordingly, in poetry the ideal is Universalpoesie, the fusion of all forms, not only of literature, but of all branches of writing—science, philosophy, and criticism as well. The fragment has a special place as a "genre" in early Romantic writing because it does not partake in an illusory completeness, but refers, like the incomplete figure $\subset$, to the esoteric harmony of the infinite. The greater the range of elements which it brings together by the ars combinatoria of Romantic wit (Witz), the greater the reflection of that esoteric unity belied by exoteric distinctions based on fixity or Beharrlichkeit.

The combinations produced by wit do not depend on the false continuity of the world of things, but are divinations, prophecies of an ex-centric completeness. The universality of the Romantic novel is a reflection of the same progressive impulse, the suspension of divisions based on fixity, the revolutionary achievement of an absolute inclusiveness, the unrestricted, orgiastic intercourse of all genres, all disciplines, all regions of thought. Thus Lucinde, as the transition or point of entry into the Romantic condition of prose, is to be read ex-centrically, to revolutionize the reader, to carry him or her over the boundaries of experience and the oppression of the comprehended world of things.

Time and Memory

Progressivity (Progression, Progressivität) is opposed to progress (Fortschritt) as expressed in this unifocal exoteric world. "Alles Gute ist schon da; gegen das unbedingte Fortschreiten" ('Everything good is already at hand; against unrestricted progress'), he comments in LN 1508. Similarly, there is a false and a true universality, the former being purely cumulative, that of a bad dictionary, as stated in Athenäum Fragment 447,[13] (even dictionaries should be witty, he says in LN 480). True universality is "Wechselsättigung aller Formen und aller Stoffe" (AF 451, 'The mutual saturation of all forms and all contents'), just as "In der ächt romantischen Prosa müssen alle Bestandtheile bis zur Wechselsättigung verschmolzen sein" (LN 585, 'In genuine Romantic prose all the constituents must be melted together to the point of mutual saturation'). The Romantic novel is not a mixture, in which the elements are set side by side, but a fusion. In this respect, the opinion expressed by Erich Heller in The Ironic German, A Study of Thomas Mann (London, 1958) that it is Mann's panoramic novels which, introducing the issues of philosophy, psychology, and history together with topics of art, social questions, and politics, truly exemplify the Romantic theory, cannot be sustained. If anything, it corresponds more nearly to Schlegel's idea of critical prose, a more detached perspective: "Die kritische Prosa muß von allem haben wie die Romantische, nur in entgegengesetzter Zusammensetzung. Jene gemischt, diese verschmolzen" (LN 609, 'Critical prose must have something of everything, like the Romantic, only in the opposite style of combination. The former is mixed, the latter fused').

The panoramic assembly of events and views in this false universality is precisely what Walter Benjamin terms "Historismus" ('historicism') in his Theses on the Philosophy of History. Moreover the ideas associated in that text show close and very important parallels with Schlegel's, allowing a communication to be established between the Marxist image of revolution represented in Benjamin's work, and that of Romanticism. Although a comparative procedure bringing Romantic idealism into a close relationship with historical materialism might appear strained to an uncritical glance, there is of course no lack of foundation here. Both were born under a similar dialectical star. The old formula that Marx stood idealism on its head should not obscure the sense in which both are opposed to the atomistic, linear materialism of a mechanical causality of events. As Benjamin stresses overwhelmingly, a metaphysical priority of the material does not reduce dialectical history to the singular and continuous mode in which causal events are assembled like scientific facts.

This concept of knowledge produces a vision of history in which the past is spread out before a fixed and universal panoramic gaze. Time is empty and unvarying, so that the events of history can be understood with the same objectivity as phenomena in the domain of natural science. For Benjamin, on the other hand, history is always a part of the active concerns of the present, inextricably bound up with the way people understand their own situation, and the fulfillment of their desires in the present. The view of the past is therefore fundamentally transformed by the particular concerns and interests of whoever explores the record. What is seen, and how it is interpreted, depend on the motivation of the historian. It is a knowledge mediated by the experience of people in society, and is therefore always political in character. It cannot be reduced to a singular, unchanging universal view, unlike historicism which "culminates rightly in universal history" (Thesis XVII, Illuminations p. 262).

The historical materialist, says Benjamin "stops telling the sequence of events like the beads of a rosary" (Thesis XVIII A), in contrast to that historiography for which the connections are restricted to the causal: "But no fact that is a cause is for that very reason historical. It became historical posthumously, as it were, through events that may be separated from it by thousands of years." The truncation of the chronological continuum by which this articulation of events is effected, implies an alternate, a dialectical temporal mode. In like manner, the temporality of historicism reflects the cumulative nature of what Schlegel identified as false universality, for, writes Benjamin: "Its method is additive; it musters a mass of data to fill the homogeneous, empty time" (Thesis XVII). The medium of history is the human condition, which the dialectical historian makes conscious in comprehending "the constellation which his own era has formed with a definite earlier one. Thus he establishes a conception of the present as the 'time of the now' which is shot through with chips of Messianic time" (XVIII A).

The weight of priority in the Messianic sphere as a transcendent other, which is marked by the manner of that penetration of Messianic time into the historical moment only as "chips," is a point of important contrast in the status given autonomous human life in Schlegel's and Benjamin's thinking. This is true both for the radical idealism of Schlegel's Jena period, and for later developments such as the Köln lectures, where he begins to permit a more properly distinct transcendent origin for the phenomenal realm (which would, later still, culminate in a rapprochement with Catholic theology). The being of Bedeutung (meaning) which is the mode in which the Real, for Schlegel, emits itself into the visible, is a relationship which makes up the fullness of all nature. The site of signification, the being outside of Being, is consciousness, which is also a fully integrated element in the unending process of becoming which constitutes the universe. It is through the awareness of our constitutive involvement in this harmonious, organic entity—the universe as individual—that we discover "daß wir nur ein Stück von uns selbst sind" (KA XII p. 337, 'that we are only a part of ourselves'), and therefore the standing of the lower domain of experience before the higher domain of the 'invisible' is not an absolute privation of mankind. This, again, is reminiscent of the letter by Rilke quoted earlier, where the transforming poetic activity is pursued "Nicht in ein Jenseits, dessen Schatten die Erde verfinstert, sondern in ein Ganzes, in das Ganze" ('Not towards something beyond us whose shadow darkens the earth, but towards something whole, towards the whole'). This distinction might define the activity of the Romantic religious, as opposed to historical Messianic, revolutionary.

He is spared the ban by which Marx separates the pre-revolutionary from the post-revolutionary condition, and, as "der Gehülfe der Götter" (KA XII p. 43, 'the helpmeet of the gods') is a direct agent of the Real: "Wissen wir aber, daß die Welt unvollendet ist, so ist unsere Bestimmung wohl, an der Vollendung derselben mitzuarbeiten. Der Empirie wird dadurch ein unendlicher Spielraum gegeben. Wäre die Welt vollendet, so gäbe es dann nur ein Wissen derselben, aber kein Handeln" (ibid., 'If we know that the world is incomplete, then it is our task to work also on its completion. The empirical realm thus offers an unlimited field of play. If the world were complete, there would only be knowledge of it, but no action'). For Benjamin, however, "Only the Messiah himself consummates all history in the sense that only he redeems, perfects and creates its relationship to the Messianic. For this reason nothing historical can relate itself on its own account to anything Messianic."[14]

The role of historical man and his freedom are limited here. He brings to birth the disruptive historical moment when he "recognizes the sign of a Messianic cessation of happening" (Thesis XVII), but he cannot set in motion its finest process. In realizing "the time of the now" (Jetztzeit) he interrupts progress, for "The concept of the historical progress of mankind cannot be sundered from the concept of its progression through empty, homogeneous time" (Thesis XIII), but this bears only traces, or chips, of Messianic time. The true vein can move only of itself, and is not "the Telos of a historical dynamic." On the other hand, Schlegel writes: "Der revolutionäre Wunsch, das Reich Gottes zu realisieren, ist der elastische Punkt der progressiven Bildung, und der Anfang der modernen Geschichte. Was in gar keiner Beziehung aufs Reich Gottes steht, ist in ihr nur Nebensache" (AF 222, 'The revolutionary desire to realize the Kingdom of Heaven is the elastic point of progressive learning, and the beginning of modern history. Anything that has no bearing on the Kingdom of Heaven, is only of secondary concern to that history').

The correlative in Benjamin's theory of historiography to true Romantic Universalität is "the following truth: nothing that has ever happened should be regarded as lost for history" (Thesis III). This will only arise for a "redeemed humanity" however, for only in that condition "has its past become citable in all its moments. Each moment it has lived becomes a citation à l'ordre du jour—and that day is Judgement Day." Such a redeemed history of the infinitely full moment of an infinitely foreshortened Messianic time finds its equivalent in the "wahre, volle Mitte" (KA XII, p. 414, 'true, full middle') which for Schlegel is the completion or perfection (Vollendung) in eternity of the fragmented time of past, present and future. This is arrived at when "man die beiden entgegengesetzten Kräfte, die äußersten Endpunkte des Lebens sich verbinden und durchdringen, sättigen läßt, wo denn etwas Neues, ein Drittes entstehen kann" ('one allows the two opposing forces, the extreme termini of life, to join, interpenetrate and saturate one another, so that something new, a third element, can arise').

This new, third thing corresponds to Benjamin's Jetztzeit or "present which is not a transition" (Thesis XVI), though only to the extent allowed by the contrasting concepts of a singular Messianic redemption, and the continued, "elastic" trans-formations of permanent revolution. In each case, it is a full time, unlike the empty chronological time of historicism—"keine Zeitleere, sondern eine Zeitfülle" (KA XII, p. 145, 'not an emptiness of time, but a fullness of time')—yet that fullness clearly also exceeds the content of chips of Messianic time in the privileged moment of Jetztzeit. The correspondence is more adequately found in the redeemed time of Judgement Day as Benjamin represents it, rather than the paler historical foreshadowing marked only by "chips" of redeemed temporality.

The idea of eternity as empty of time is, in Schlegel's view, an erroneous construction derived from the present as "falsche, leere Mitte" (ibid., p. 414, 'false, empty middle') in which the extremes are excluded. This also matches the panoramic model of history whereby "Historicism gives the eternal image of the past" (Thesis XVI) from a vantage point out of time altogether—illustrated by the abstract irony of Thomas Mann in contrast to the active, productive irony of Romanticism. The negative eternity, the universality of the panoramic, empty present is "das Tote, das Fesselnde, und steht in der nächsten Beziehung auf den Begriff der Beharrlichkeit, des Dings" (KA XII, p. 414, 'that which is dead, that which fetters one, standing closest to the concept of fixity and the thing'). In this false form, history figures as progress, proper to a materialism not dialectical, but atomistic, frozen, within which man becomes passive, bound, patient. This dead dimension, by which consciousness is locked into an alien straitjacket, is negated for Benjaminian history by a process exactly equivalent to the wit or "kombinatorischer Geist" ('combining spirit') of inventive, creative genius in Romanticism.

Benjamin describes how the spirit of inventive correlations in history is directly productive of revolutionary critical and active power in revolutionary politics:

Thus, to Robespierre ancient Rome was a past charged with the
time of the now which he blasted out of the continuum of history.
The French Revolution viewed itself as Rome reincarnate. It
evoked ancient Rome the way fashion evokes costumes of the
past. Fashion has a flair for the topical, no matter where it stirs
in the thickets of long ago; it is a tiger's leap into the past . . .
the same leap in the open air of history is the dialectical one,
which is how Marx understood the revolution (Thesis XIV).

Historical truth is the truth of the situation of the historian himself,
his own highly charged present moment: "It means to seize hold of a
memory as it flashes up in a moment of danger" (Thesis VI). This approach
does not begin by separating itself from the past in order to make its
content into a determinate object of abstracted contemplation, for "to
articulate the past historically does not mean to recognize it 'the way it
really was' (Ranke)" (ibid.), and the historical materialist, motivated by a
full present "leaves it to others to be drained by the whore called 'once
upon a time'" (Thesis XVI). The dialectical tiger's leap which produces
the true configuration or "monad" (Thesis XVII) in which the historian can
grasp his understanding of past and present requires the negation of the
empathetic approach identified with historicism. The origin of this process
of empathy, characterized by the recommendation quoted from Fustel de
Coulanges that "to relive an era . . . historians blot out everything they
know about the later course of history," is condemned by Benjamin as the
"indolence of the heart, acedia, which . . . Among medieval theologians was
regarded as the root cause of sadness."

The equivalent locus in Schlegel's metaphysics also shows a necessary
distinction here, for in place of the moment of danger corresponding to
immediate historical contingency, the motivation which retrieves full time
for him is founded in the interiority of consciousness. The perfected
temporality of man in Schlegel's theory presented in the Köln lectures is a
reflection of an absolute time, just as it is for Benjamin, but it is not

mediated by the separate and indirect agent of concrete material exigency. The connection is ultimately a direct one, and the motivation is a directly ascertainable sense of loss. The derivation of the knowledge of time is expressed as a function and counterpart of an "original time" in which absolute consciousness, having expanded to establish the spatial basis of the universe, reestablishes contact with itself: "Dieses Wiederfinden ist die Erinnerung; diese Erinnerung muß aber mit Schmerz und Reue verbunden sein; über den wo nicht gänzlichen, doch teilweisen Verlust der ursprünglichen Einheit, über den innern Zwiespalt und Kampf. . . . Auf dieser . . . Stufe der Erinnerung entsteht die Zeit, als Zurückgehen in den Anfang, mit dem Bewußtsein, daß es der Anfang ist" (KA XII, p. 435, 'This rediscovery is memory; the memory must, however, be accompanied by pain and regret over the loss of the original unity, even though this is not complete but only partial, and over the inner conflict and struggle. . . . On this . . . plane of memory time arises as a return to the beginning in the consciousness that it is the beginning').

The idea of memory, especially one born in pain and regret, as an esoteric procedure opposed to an exoteric contrary, is developed by Benjamin in his essay on Proust. He explores it in the Proustian opposition of voluntary and involuntary processes. "What was it that Proust sought so frenetically? What was at the bottom of these infinite efforts?" he asks, and finds it to have been "the hopeless sadness within him (what he once called 'l'imperfection incurable dans l'essence même du présent')." (Illuminations, p. 203). This is the present not of Jetztzeit, but of acedia. It is the experience of inner loss, the void present which is only "transition," reduced and obliterated as real presence of lived life for which "there is never enough time." The true center of Proust's work, Benjamin writes, lies in the recovery of that loss:

> Cocteau recognized what should have been the major concern of all readers of Proust and yet has served no-one as the pivotal point of his reflections or his affection. He recognized Proust's blind, senseless, frenzied quest for happiness. It shone from his eyes; they were not happy, but in them there lay fortune as it lies in gambling or in love.

The recovery of lost times is not the gathering up of past incidents in the manner of historicism. No such accumulation can redeem the author's present. On the contrary, it is precisely what lays that experience bare as a bleak gap between what has been and what will have been, a future equally unredeemable as it falls prey endlessly to the past:

> For the important thing for the remembering author is not what he experienced, but the Penelope work of recollection. Or should one call it, rather, a Penelope work of forgetting? Is not the involontary recollection, Proust's memoire involontaire, much closer to forgetting than what is usually called memory? (Illuminations, p.202).

It is like the opposition of day and night, for the purposeful activity of day ordinarily wipes away the inner coherence, the nether realm of experience. But it is this, in its obscure existence, which yields the perfect stamp, the precise tone, of its own truth and particularity. Here, protected from the harsh glare of a sunlit world in which acts and thoughts are brought together in the continuum of history as conformism, progress, agreement, is a hidden demesne. Labors of clarity and the bourgeois will are "the counterpart to Penelope's work, rather than its likeness. For here the day unravels what the night has woven." The power of the day, the clear, bright world of public men and women, must be neutralized, overcome, denied. ".This is why Proust finally turned his days into nights, devoting all his hours to undisturbed work in his darkened room with artificial illumination, so that none of those intricate arabesques might escape him."

Politics and Reflection

It might be thought that such a picture lies far from the Marxist image of class struggle. The isolated writer, locked away in a room shielded from every penetration of light and sound, is not a figure conjured up by the idea of a class-conscious revolutionary. Yet the insurgency of night against day, of the hidden against the visible, is the most absolute of revolutionary motivations, and a quest for the redemption of happiness the most universal and human. If Benjamin, in straining against the "vulgar-Marxist" notion of progress, of moving "with the stream," which "already displays the technocratic features later encountered in Fascism" (Thesis XI), has struck against a real historical weakness in what we are told is Marxist theory and practice, then its criticism through the close passage he makes to Romantic thinking becomes all the more promising.

That is not to say that we should continue by looking for a social and political theory in Schlegel's writings, correlative to his idealist speculations, but rather consider the absence of such a direct method. Schlegel, who wrote fearlessly on every topic throughout his early years, alluding frequently to political concepts, still maintained a carefully managed restraint in that area, and long avoided any rigid commitment to an explicit programmatic position. There is a significance in that which may easily be misinterpreted. Though not bound by the systematic impediment wherein Marxist theory does not permit the characteristics of a post-revolutionary condition to be perceived from a pre-revolutionary perspective, Schlegel does prove to observe a corresponding principle. What is involved here is not an absolute distinction limiting the accessibility of a knowledge which is nonetheless determinate, but rather the opposite. The possibilities of the political sphere, as understood in Schlegel's idealist construction of the concept, are not a matter of knowledge, but of invention or production. Freedom of the human present, when fully realized, changes the concept of knowledge altogether, so that what is known already is no longer incompatible in its quality or form, with a liberated or revolutionary existence. It is not a matter of what is known, but how.

Any notion is a fetter if it restrains the productive imagination. Thus it is not a question of revealing a particular truth which has been concealed, but of revealing the oppressive nature of any conception which demands absolute and unalterable acceptance. The exclusivity of any particular knowledge is the falsehood which must be broken through by revolutionary progressivity. What appears as knowledge produced on the other side of that revolutionary act of criticism, must remain open to the same process. What can be thought as a possibility, and presented for consideration to the motivations of desire in a particular moment of existence, should not be restricted by a tyrannical continuity and conformity with what is already known, or rather established as knowledge. If the division between the true and the false is imposed as a boundary of the possible in this way, it only ensures the continuation of whatever is once established as true. If that boundary is set only as what has been arrived at by a particular history, and open to movement with the changes of time, then it does not act as a screen excluding what lies beyond it. Nothing is hidden. Nothing which may also with time prove realizable within the privileged realm of experience and conviction. Nothing may thus be declared which has a pre-emptive force of a "natural" or "historical" law. The mark of freedom in time, is the freedom to change one's mind.

Among the truths which "flared up in the moment of danger" (Thesis VI) from the period when Benjamin wrote in the shadow of Nazi power, was the uncomforting revelation that help from a revolutionary counter-force was not to be found in the established socialist entities, for this was also a "moment when the politicians in whom the opponents of Fascism had placed their hopes are prostrate and confirm their defeat by betraying their own cause . . ." (Thesis X). What is clearer today, though already present as an irrepressible suspicion to Benjamin, was the corruption inherent in a revolution which did not disseminate itself as the freely committed work of all, but the singular, central authority of the few. In this sense, revolutions themselves have become fixed, like things, and capable of being possessed. They therefore approximate the very character he diagnosed for great achievements of the past as interpreted by historicism when they become "cultural treasures" (Thesis VII). They acquire the authority by which the past, and an image of the future impressed by the past, drains reality from the present. Revolution itself may fall as a spoil to the victors like other cultural treasure, and so, as we can now see in Moscow each May and October, be "According to traditional practice . . . carried along in the triumphal procession," and become, like other such treasures in tradition, both in itself, and the process of its transmission, "not free of barbarism."

For this reason, the concept of revolution presented in Schlegel's writing, precisely because it stands outside almost every aspect of political debate on the subject, holds out the possibility that it harbours the vital force of new life to move our thinking out of the present desolation and deceit. A legislative revolution, an adjustment conceived as final, a singular transferral of power which is not also a transformation, remains tied to the laws of the causal, the technocratic world of "inevitable" progress by historical mechanism to the future goal. This cannot be equated with a real change. A revolution produces a new situation only where it sets human thought and lived understanding free over the conditions of collective life, and does not merely shift around within the particular conditions which rule over human existence. To give priority in political acts to the mechanical image of change in this way is to see them lost, no matter how well meant, in the devouring rush of a progressing continuum.

For Schlegel, in whom, as we have seen, not even the principle of consistency is permitted to subvert the autonomy of the human spirit, there is no place for any kind of hegemony: "Auch die Universalhistorie wird sophistisch, sobald sie dem Geiste der allgemeinen Bildung der ganzen Menschheit irgendetwas vorzieht, wäre auch eine moralische Idee das heteronomische Prinzip, sobald sie für eine Seite des historischen Universums Partei nimmt . . ." (AF 223, 'Even universal history becomes sophistry as soon as it sets anything above the general cultivation of humanity in its entirety, and that applies as well even if the extraneous principle should be a moral idea, as soon as it takes sides in the historical totality'). There is, in other words, no principle or law which is given a privileged status to draw attention from the goal of perfect and universal freedom. Moreover, the implication of the symbolic figure " ⊂ " is that as a process it is never complete, so that no point can be set beyond which everything else may be excluded as alien.

There is no "Judgement Day" here, no Messianic end in which the task of redemption is finished. The invisible continues to project itself dialectically in its self-representation as the visible, and man pursues his task of its Aufhebung through art/religion/Bildung, for "Der Mensch ist der schaffende Rückblick der Natur auf sich selbst" (AI 28, 'Man is the creative gaze of nature looking back on itself'). In the Literary Notebooks Schlegel speculates twice: "Ist die Kunst wie der Staat bloß Mittel?" (LN 87, 191, 'Is art, like the state, just a means?'), but it is a means whose operation necessarily never comes to an end. "Die Unvollendung der Poesie ist nothwendig. Ihre Vollendung = das Erscheinen des Messias, oder die stoische Verbrennung" (LN 2090, 'The non-completion of poetry is necessary. Its completion = the appearance of the Messiah, or the stoic burning'). But this permanent incompletion ensures the never-ending activity which is the total realization of mankind's cosmic function: "Hat die Fantasie den Sieg davongetragen über die Reflexion, so ist die Menschheit vollendet" ('When the imagination has achieved its victory over reflection, then humanity is complete'). The revolution is continuous and permanent, then, and, in a sense, specular to the continuum of deceptive fixity which it continues to traduce and raise in power towards the infinite.

This process, the kombinatorische Witz, the explosion of boundaries, the unlimited fusions, takes its fullest form in the Roman, the novel, as understood in its special meaning for Romanticism: "Alle Romane sind revoluzionär—nur ein Genie kann einen eigentlichen Roman schreiben" (LN 578, 'All novels are revolutionary—only a genius can write a genuine novel'). The eigentliche Roman, genuine novel, is really only very loosely connected with the unechter Roman, inauthentic novel, which here means the traditional narrative prose work as a special genre familiar to us under that name. Failure to give full weight to the difference obscures the real distance theoretical Romanticism has traversed in this area. It supersedes genre, as Fantasie supersedes Reflexion and all separate disciplines are drawn into the revolutionary/romantic essential activity of pursuing the lines of the mystical parabola into the infinite: "Alle Geisteswerke sollen romantisieren, dem Roman sich möglichst approximieren" (LN 583, 'All works of the spirit should follow the Romantic way, and approximate the novel as closely as possible'). This cancels the issue of genre, "denn Art läßt sich ohne Mitart nicht denken" (LN 583, 'for one genre cannot be thought of without another'). The task of romantisieren, like poetry as described in LN 2090 above, is a permanent process which is necessarily incomplete because it annihilates itself if it comes to a halt, identifying it once more with the model of progressive freedom: "Allgemeiner Grundsatz: Wenn alle Bestandteile des romantischen Gedichts verschmolzen sind, so hört es auf romantisch zu sein" (LN 837, 'General principle: when all the components of the Romantic poem are fused together, it ceases to be Romantic').

In this impulse, too, the meaning of the term "prose" is also reconstructed: "Was Prosa eigentlich sei, hat noch niemand gesagt.—Es giebt Poesie ohne Metrum (Meister) und metrische Prosa (Nathan).—Die Grundlage der Prosa ist dialektisch d.h. logisch politisch—dann grammatisch" (LN 584, 'What prose actually is no-one has as yet been able to say.—There is poetry without meter like Wilhelm Meister and metrical prose like Nathan the Wise.—The basis of prose is dialectical, i.e. logical and political—then grammatical'). Prose is the medium of universality here, expanded beyond any crude formal consideration. It becomes the written medium of the universal dialectic, the written equivalent of Messianic time or of a Jetztzeit in which all fragmented Geisteswerke are set in constellation. They appear there, however, in their ideal individuality, not obliterated in a collective generality, but absolutely revealed as themselves: "Roman überhaupt die Vereinigung zweier Absoluten, der absoluten Individualität und der absoluten Universalität" (LN 434, 'The novel is in general the uniting of two absolutes, absolute individuality and absolute universality').

Individuality and universality are complementary in that every poem and every work is an individual. Similarly, each discipline is an individual, and can only be understood as such: "Sinn für Poesie oder Philosophie hat nur der, für den sie ein

Individuum ist" (AF 415, 'A person only has an understanding of poetry or philosophy if each is for him an individual'). Thus, the Romantic novel is a "system of individuals." The individual as a concept is then the true expression of the unlimited, the infinite, for it combines, in the terms about which the whole of the Köln Lectures are constructed, das Unendliche der Einheit und das Unendliche der Fülle ('the infinity of unity and the infinity of plenitude'). Each individual implies a possibility of infinite variety (or infinite combinations), all of which are united in the system of its infinite singularity. The origin of this is its direct source in interiority, in a freely creative consciousness. The individuality of each science rests on an "ancestral" inner cognition, for "Die Deduktion eines Begriffes ist die Ahnenprobe seiner echten Abstammung von der intellektualen Anschauung seiner Wissenschaft. Denn jede Wissenschaft hat die ihrige" (AF 443, 'The deduction of a concept is its proof of nobility as a a genuine descendant from the intellectual cognition of its science. For each science has its own'). Both science and art concern themselves, in their capacity as "reflection of nature upon itself," with the historical or phenomenal, raising it to the higher power of the interior or unlimited. The autonomy of the intellektuale Anschauung, Schlegel's primary concept of an inner cognition or intellectual intuition, is the condition of that process. Individual consciousness, man or Ichheit, is therefore necessarily an open-ended "system of systems."

A political science would reflect the same essence. Its source could not, once again, be the additive idea of progress, nor yet the supply of what is lacking by a renewed conquest with renewed spoils. The chain of conquest and division is interrupted by raising the power of the political sphere, its Romantisieren, to cancel out this determined and restricted form of change. "Die Menschheit ist etwas ganz innerliches; hier gibt es eigentlich keine Fortschritte" (KA XVIII, p.259 #791, 'Humanity is something quite inward; here there is indeed no progress'). The interiorizing or making esoteric of a science of politics results in an ecumenical system of absolute individuals (each one itself a system of individuals) in which the fixity of hierarchical domination cannot have any meaning: "Das Leben des universellen Geistes ist eine ununterbrochene Kette innerer Revolutionen; aller Individuen, die ursprünglichen, ewigen nämlich, leben in ihm. Er ist echter Polytheist und trägt den ganzen Olymp in sich" (AF 451, 'The life of the universal spirit is an uninterrupted chain of inner revolutions; all individuals, that is the original, eternal ones, live in it. It is genuinely polytheistic and carries the whole of Olympus within itself').

A true politics is not excluded from Schlegel's view by the "flight from the world" envisaged in that commonplace conception of Romanticism. Its importance is, on the contrary, constantly reiterated, but always together with the primary idea that the central nature of consciousness is the teleology of absolute freedom, infinity. Politics is therefore a function of that principle: "Die Politik (als Kunst und Wissenschaft der Gemeinschaft aller Bildung) ist das für die Peripherie was Religion für das Centrum ist" (KA XVIII, p. 302 #1291, 'Politics, as the art and science of the community of all learning, is for the periphery what religion is for the center'). Though this sphere lies far from the centre, it is the correct form of activity in that context: "Politik ist Empirie in der höchsten Potenz" (p. 302 #1300, 'Politics is empirical knowledge raised to its highest power'), and it has its own source of _intellektuale Anschauung_ by which it may legitimate its descent: "Ohne musikalisches Gehör für das Leben und die Welt giebts keine wahre Politik" (#1290, 'Without a musical ear for life and the world, there is no true politics'). That inner "musical" dimension, which rests on an important body of speculation in Schlegel's work, is not a retreat from reality into subjectivity, but a perception shared with Benjamin that the oppression of thought is the obliteration of truth and the abuse of life.

The vulgarization of historical materialism into the mechanical operation of "laws of change," has no place here. Benjamin compares his thoughts, in _Thesis X_, to "The themes which monastic discipline assigned to friars for meditation . . . to turn them away from the world and its affairs." The time of writing (the _Theses_ were completed in the spring of 1940) was marked by a catastrophic failure of vulgar Marxism, and such a moment revealed that what had seemed clear, close at hand and inevitable, was only delusion and error. He declares, accordingly, that his own process of thought should negate the influence of a world of failed and faithless politicians:

> . . . these observations are intended to disentangle the political worldlings from the snares in which the traitors have entrapped them. Our consideration proceeds from the insight that the politicians' stubborn faith in progress, their confidence in their

"mass basis," and, finally, their servile integration in an
uncontrollable apparatus have been three aspects of the same
thing.   Its seeks to convey an idea of the high price our
accustomed thinking will have to pay for a conception of history
that avoids any complicity with the thinking to which these
politicians continue to adhere.

Writing and Scripture

A "musical" idea of truth is opposed to one that is in a conventional sense mimetic. Music is the mode of signification most nearly free of the constaints of outer appearance in reference. In a sense of the word distinct from common usage (and that of Schiller's essay on naive and sentimental poetry), Schlegel describes it as a "sentimental" art, explaining: "Was ist denn nun dieses Sentimentale? Das was uns anspricht, wo das Gefühl herrscht, und zwar nicht ein sinnliches, sondern das geistige" (KA II, p. 333, 'What is meant by this term sentimental? That which engages us where feeling reigns, yet not sensual feeling but rather spiritual'). This geistiges Gefühl, spiritual or intellectual feeling, is not an "emotion." It is not, that is to say, a non-reflexive response subjectively attached to an object or cicumstance and restricted by that limited scope. It is, rather, a "thought," and the thought of a piece of instrumental music (which does not involve itself in reference by an accompanying sung text) is a direct intuition, eine unmittelbare Anschauung. It should, accordingly, be allowed to take its place alongside philosophy as part of the objective realization of the Real, rather than being regarded as mere Sinnenkitzel, the limited indulgence of subjective feeling as in common sentimentality. He writes:

> Wer aber Sinn für die wunderbaren Affinitäten aller Künste und Wissenschaften hat, wird die Sache wenigstens nicht aus dem platten Gesichtspunkt der sogenannten Natürlichkeit betrachten, nach welcher die Musik nur die Sprache der Empfindung sein soll, und eine gewisse tendenz aller reinen Instrumentalmusik an sich unmöglich finden. Muß die reine Instrumentalmusik an sich nicht selbst einen Text erschaffen? Und wird das Thema nicht so

entwickelt, bestätigt, variiert und kontrastiert, wie der
Gegenstand der Meditation in einer philosophischen Ideenreihe?
(AF 444)
('A person who has some idea of the wonderful affinities of all
arts and sciences will not, at least, consider this question from
the dull viewpoint of so-called naturalness, according to which
music is supposed to be merely the language of emotion, and
consequently find a definite tendency in all pure instrumental
music inherently impossible. Does purely instrumental music not
have to create a text for itself out of its own resources? And is
the theme not developed, confirmed, varied and contrasted like
the topic of a meditation in a sequence of philosophical
speculations?')

This not only raises music to the level of philosophy, but reinterprets the
role of philosophy itself as an "arabesque" of ideas. Music shares in the
primal concept of Romantisieren, or mediation of genres and regional
disciplines in being "unter der Kunst was die Religion in der Welt" (LN
1416, 'within art what religion is in the world'). The musical nature of
philosophy and all arts is then re-iterated in LN 1417, which describes it
as the "höchste unter allen Künsten. Sie ist die allgemeinste. Jede Kunst
hat musikalische Prinzipien und wird vollendet selbst Musik. Dieß gilt
sogar von der Philosophie und also auch wohl von der Poesie, vielleicht
auch vom Leben" ('highest among all the arts. It is the most general.
Every art has musical principles and when perfected becomes music itself.
This is even true of philosophy and therefore also of poetry, perhaps even
of life'). The freedom from representational elements preserves it from the
dual tendency in other media, by which they may become corrupted,
diverted from the telos of absolute freedom, and become ensnared in
practical considerations and worldly purposes. For music, this pull is much
weaker, and Schlegel considered it to have been successfully resisted in
the music of his own time, which had "was die in ihr herrschende Kraft des
Menschen betrifft, ihrem Charakter im ganzen . . . treu geblieben" (KA II,
p. 333, 'remained on the whole true to its character so far as the primary

human power contained in it is concerned')—a confidence expressed so clearly for no other contemporary art form, and one which agrees with our own designation of the period as "classical."

It is a medium of pure relation "was . . . die Algebra in der Mathematik (ist)" (LN 1416, 'what algebra is in mathematics'), pure wit, and this condition is realized when other arts appear in their ideal state: "Die Zeichnung als ganz auf Proportionen beruhend, eine architektonische Musik" (LN 1403, 'Drawing as resting entirely on proportions, an architectonic music'). This is therefore also equivalent to terms he used to describe absolute or esoteric signification: "Allegorie ist Musik von architektonisirten Plasmen" (LN 1415, 'Allegory is the music of architecton-ically formed plasmas'). In consequence it must also contain an absolute time, and although this is not elaborated explicitly in Schlegel's early works, such an idea is developed in a very similar spirit in an essay by Gabriel Marcel entitled "Bergsonism and Music," where he considers the question of "pure duration" in that art. This is particularly interesting also, because he sees it as exhibiting close parallels with the "arabesques" of Proustian memory invoked by Benjamin.

The resource called upon in hearing music, Marcel argues, is "pure memory," understood as entirely heterogeneous with perception "that is, completely removed from the actualizing influence of the body."[15] This is elusive, he concedes, and he does not believe "that we could ever form an image of pure memory. We can only imagine it as a limit placed on, or more precisely on this side of, the representable" (p. 148). The past thus recalled "is not a particular section of a historical becoming" (p. 149), but part of the fundamental qualitative continuity in which a coherent consciousness is possible as active and self-sustaining against external impressions. "It is rather the inner depths of oneself" which the music retrieves for the present "like a prism through the anonymous and neutral, (optically neutral) Past that makes up the inner depths of each one of us, becomes decomposed, specific, and colored by personal nuances. A temporal prism . . . " (p. 148), and this " . . . builds me. It is formative" (p. 150).

The path to be struck from present awareness into this "unutilized past" (p. 151) is not opened by voluntary concentration, but by "the slackening off of an effort . . . a slackening off from above" (p. 150), which he associates with the Proustian mémoire involontaire. What Benjamin interprets as forgetting, turning day into night, is here evoked as that darkening of a room which allows a prism to project its light, its "miraculous power of putting an end to precisely that unavailability of ourselves" (p. 151), brought about by the daylight of the will.

For Benjamin, this process is caught in a deliberately imposed contradiction. Unlike Schlegel or Proust, he pitches the central consideration of this mystery at the very heart of the opposing imperium. There, in the struggles of the oppressed for material justice and power, on the battle lines of class and party, he conjures up his vision of a socialist redeemer. Even though the Theses are designed to lead the reader away from the hypnotic force, or blinding glare, of a world enthralled in progress, the very conception of the Messianic they contain denies access to the full gift of its alternate light. It is interesting to find an image invoking the effect of a prism in Benjamin's notes for the Theses also, underlining the connection between the two lines of argument: "Der historische Materialist, der der Struktur der Geschichte nachgeht, betreibt auf seine Weise eine Art von Spektralanalyse. Wie der Physiker Ultraviolett im Sonnenspektrum feststellt, so stellt er eine messianische Kraft in der Geschichte fest"[16] ('The historical materialist who investigates the structure of history practices in his own way a kind of spectral analysis. Just as the physicist demonstrates ultraviolet light in the spectrum of the sun, so he establishes the presence of a Messianic power in history').

But Benjamin goes on to stipulate that for unredeemed vision, before the false, or fallen, condition of history is brought to a halt, this remains "unavailable:" "Wer wissen wollte, in welcher Verfassung sich die 'erlöste Menschheit' befindet, . . . der stellt Fragen, auf die es keine Antwort gibt. Ebensogut könnte er sich danach erkundigen, welche Farbe die ultravioletten Strahlen haben" (ibid., 'Someone who wished to know in what condition a "redeemed mankind" existed . . . would be posing questions to which there is no answer. He might just as well ask what color ultraviolet rays are'). History only becomes available in its entirety on Judgement Day: "For this reason nothing historical can relate itself on its own account to anything Messianic." In contrast to the socialization of Messianic force in Schlegel, its universal dissemination among mankind as "the helpmeet of the gods," we find a powerful element of its paternal alienation in Benjamin. It is true that Schlegel does come to an equivalent view regarding revelation in the formulation: "Die Vorstellung eines Gegenstandes kann nur durch diesen selbst erregt werden—also die Gottheit nur durch die Gottheit (KA XIX, p. 57 #159, 'The idea of an object can only be elicited by itself—that of the Godhead therefore only by the Godhead'), but this comes only later, as he moves into the orbit of Catholic theology. The difference between their two positions can thus be simply put in these terms: For Romanticism the lower and higher aspects of the universe are mutually necessary as the poles between which man as an activity can appear, neither he nor his world being "fallen" in an absolute sense, and therefore there cannot be a redemption in a final sense either. For Messianic Marxism, the world of class history is fallen, is capable of redemption, but no force or knowledge which is fallen can effect the redemption by its own power, and "progressivity" does not breach the continuum of history.

Further mediation between these two outlooks cannot be pursued by considering each comparatively, as an absolutized, enclosed structure depicting history/the world and man's place in it, but rather genetically, or historically. These are not the creations of two rival demiurges, but historical products, limited and conditioned by the field in which they stake out their place and purpose. These texts reflect a particular stage in the development of textuality. The situation of each author determines that which each can see as possibilities of what can be achieved through writing, and how the world can be changed in response to the experience and the situation arrived at through their writing. Even though both write about politics and the world, the inevitable restrictions attendant on the specificity of the medium through whose means they represent these things deeply transform what they are able to see. What we read in their work clearly emerges for us as features in a landscape carved out by the influence of writing as such. The clarity of each one's consciousness of this is both important for our estimation of how clearly each understands the status of his own work, but also provides a fundamental criterion for measuring the differences between them.

In the additional, preparatory material for the Theses, Benjamin, noting that a true, or redeemed, universal history can only exist in the Messianic world, goes on: "Aber nicht als geschriebene, sondern als die festlich begangene. Dieses Fest ist gereinigt von aller Feier. Es kennt keine Festgesänge. Seine Sprache ist die befreite Prosa, die die Fesseln der Schrift gesprengt hat" (Ges. Schr. I iii, p. 1235, 'Yet not as something written, but rather as that which is celebrated. This celebration is purged of all ritual solemnity. It knows no festal songs'). The end of writing proclaimed here does not imply an end to reading, but rather the final availability of the "Book of Life," the book of all books, of all texts. "Die historische Methode ist eine philologische, der das Buch des Lebens zugrunde liegt. 'Was nie geschrieben wurde, lesen' heißt es bei Hofmannsthal. Der Leser, der hier zu denken ist, ist der wahre Historiker (p. 1238, 'The historical method is a philological procedure based on the Book of Life. "To read what was never written" is how Hoffmansthal puts it. The reader one imagines here is the true historian'). This is the real goal of the historian, fulfilled as universality in the Messianic redemption. Its language, like the language of Romanticism, is prose. Any text, Benjamin states, may be translated into it without loss. It differs from the Romantic conception, moreover, in not being a product of enthusiastic invention, or wit, but rather of Grace: "Seine Sprache ist die Idee der Prosa selbst, die von allen Menschen verstanden wird wie die Sprache der Vögel von Sonntagskindern" (p. 1239, 'Its language is the idea of prose itself, understood by all people as the language of birds is understood by children on Sunday').

Such language is equivalent to that which was lost at the Tower of Babel, whereas false universal history is described as a sort of Esperanto—a feeble human counterfeit of real universality. What attracts our interest here is the role of man as recipient of truth, not its creator. His creation, Esperanto, is false, as are the texts he writes, as are even the songs and rituals which are purged from the celebration of universal history. Schrift, writing, is the bondage which true textual language has thrown off. In Schlegel, we find the reverse. The goal is a liberated writing, not reading, for "Jede Prosa über das Höchste ist unverständlich" (KA XVIII, p. 254 #723, 'All prose on the highest theme is incomprehensible'). As established in his essay Über die Ünverständlichkeit ('On Incomprehensibility'), understanding is not the form in which the highest, the universal, manifests itself. Therefore, reading loses its significance once lower considerations fade: "Durch die Mythologie wird die Lektüre und der Buchhandel ein Ende nehmen. Das Lesen ist nah daran sich selbst zu vernichten" (KA XVIII, p. 257 #764, 'Through mythology reading and the book trade will come to an end. Reading is close to destroying itself').

The mythology introduced here is described in some detail in the Gespräch über die Poesie, and emerges as quite the opposite of a natural "Book of Life." Unlike the spontaneous growth by which that of ancient Greece came about, this new mythology "muß im Gegenteil aus der tiefsten Tiefe des Geistes herausgebildet werden; es muß das künstlichste aller Kunstwerke sein, denn es soll alle andern umfassen" (KA II, p. 312, 'must on the contrary be elaborated out of the most profound depths of the intellect; it must be the most artificial of all works of art, for it has to include all others'). The value of this construction is specifically noted as a condition of creation, as a center which permits the unconstrained writing of poetry, not the guarantor of universal comprehension, and is itself a vast poetic creation: "ein neues Bett und Gefäß für den alten ewigen Urquell der Poesie und selbst das unendliche Gedicht, welches die Keime aller andern Gedichte verhüllt" ('a new bed and vessel for the ancient and eternal wellspring of poetry and indeed the endless poem which contains the seeds of all other poems').

Mythology understood this way is not "discovered" truth, an impersonal entity proceeding from nature, history or any other transcendent agency, but something supremely human. At the same time, it differs from the traditional image in being infinitely elastic and ecumenical. It gathers up all mythologies, adding to them all imaginative speculations with a similar universal and systematic extension, and this includes not only philosophies, but also as the Gespräch stresses most emphatically, modern physics as well. The new mythology is, like these, a creative divination, and is their culmination: "Die Mythologie läßt sich nicht schließen, sondern nur durch eine Reihe von Monarchen hervorbringen. Doch muß sie als solche bald erscheinen durch einen Geist, der prophetisch ist wie es noch keiner war" (KA XVIII, p. 256 #751, 'This mythology cannot be concluded but only brought forth by a monarch. Indeed it must soon appear through a spirit who is prophetic as no other was before').

This "monarch" is, however, not a ruler: "Aber der soll nicht dirigiren wollen, sondern er soll eben Genius der Zeit, Repräsentant für diese Form der Kunst und Menschheit sein; sacrosanctus und Priester voll Majestät" (p. 255 #740, 'But he shall not wish to direct, but rather be simply the genius of the age, representative of this form of art and humanity; sacrosanct and a priest full of majesty'). He is not a Messiah in that he is part of mankind and part of the historical process which leads through the transformations of progressivity to the new mythology. Benjamin, by contrast, cannot accept the possibility of this form of continuity as an exit from historical oppression: "Der Messias bricht die Geschichte ab; der Messias tritt nicht am Ende einer Entwicklung auf" (Ges. Schr. I iii p. 1243, 'The Messiah breaks history off; the Messiah does not appear at the end of an evolution').

For Schlegel, nonetheless, it does represent an important revolutionary change—one which cancels the necessity for the monarch himself, and brings about a situation remarkable for its close correspondence to Benjamin's festlich begangene Universalgeschichte: "Die Mythologie kann nur ein Monarch stiften; der wird der letzte sein und dann wird Republik beginnen.— Cultus, wie man es nennt, wird ganz aufhören; bloß Mythologie und Feste und Priester" (KA XVIII, p. 256 #745, 'Only a monarch can found mythology; he will be the last and then a republic will begin. — Worship, as it is called, will come entirely to an end; just mythology and celebration and priests'). But here, without doubt, there will be Feier and Festgesänge.

In an image reminiscent once again of the symbol "⊂" used by Schlegel, and probably not fortuitously so, Kafka's work is described by Benjamin in a letter to Gershom Scholem as "an ellipse with foci that are far apart and are determined, on the one hand, by mystical experience (in particular, the experience of tradition) and on the other, by the experience of the modern big-city dweller" (Illuminations, p. 141). Yet the mystical, we notice, is here not an eternal transcendence, but, on the contrary, subject to decay: "Kafka's work presents a sickness of tradition" (p. 143). It no longer stands as wisdom, for "It is this consistency of truth which has been lost," (ibid.) and "Only the products of its decay remain" (p. 144). From the consideration of mankind's redemption, the only certainty in Kafka's situation is failure: "There is nothing more memorable that the fervor with which Kafka emphasized his failure" (p. 144). And the reason there was "no far-sightedness or 'prophetic vision,'" was that "Kafka listened to tradition, and he who listens hard does not see" (p. 143).

As Benjamin observes, the attention dedicated to decayed wisdom is misplaced, for that is "not meant for anyone's ears," it is "a kind of whispered intelligence dealing with matters discredited and obsolete" (p. 144). The corrective offered has a similar form, however. In the Theses, Benjamin writes of the effect a successful class struggle will have on the past: "As flowers turn toward the sun, by dint of a secret heliotropism the past strives to turn toward that sun which is rising in the sky of history" (Thesis IV). The ellipse is thus redrawn to enclose the image of the classless society, foreseen as the work of the Messiah, rather than the "discredited and obsolete" whisperings of tradition. The relationship is otherwise very similar in character, and the essential patience with which man awaits Grace in a traditional theology is repeated again. This still lurks as a shadow of misery in the Theologico-Political Fragment, where "The order of the profane should be erected on the idea of happiness" (Reflections, p. 312). The route of history/politics determined by that longing for happiness is one in which the worldly perishes: "For nature is Messianic by reason of its eternal and total passing away. To strive after such passing, even for those stages of man that are nature, is the task of world politics, whose method must be called nihilism" (p. 313). But is not such happiness all too close to Kafka's hope: "Thus, as Kafka puts it, there is an infinite amount of hope, but not for us. This statement really contains Kafka's hope; it is the source of his radiant serenity" (Illuminations, p. 144).

The idea of a sun, the source of all light, because it is an absolute of visibility, is also an absolute of legibility. Kafka's failed source of wisdom is not so much a deus absconditus as a disappearance of the sacred texts. If he could have looked instead of straining to hear, so Benjamin intimates, he would have found the light, which is undoubtedly a text. Because the reality of redemption for a materialist view of history must take worldly and thus political form, that text for Benjamin must be identified with the Book of Life. This must be distinguished clearly from the corrupted book of tradition, the Bible and the texts of Jewish canonical wisdom. There is, he suggests rather, the new sun to which the oppressed of history will turn at its revolutionary installation, but this is not separated from tradition by taking the form of tangible life itself. It is, paradoxically, also represented for Benjamin by the canonical tomes of Marxism. The concept of textuality in which reading takes precedence over writing, is precisely one modeled on Holy Writ. It elevates the authority of the Word as wisdom to which man can add nothing, and take nothing away, but only hope to perceive as the entirety of Truth. This is also the source of guilt, a debt which can never be repaid because the currency is not known to fallen man. He can no longer fulfill, nor live adequate to, the Law, because it is written in a language now lost to him.

In this case, reading concedes the nature of meaning to be prior, present, and transcendent. The world as text is the sphere of a Messianic Logos which is only partially and uncertainly legible to a historical effort at deciphering it— even though Benjamin attaches great importance to that fragmentary realization towards which it is necessary to strive. To a degree which would later change, but which was most complete in the period which produced Lucinde, Schlegel reversed this structure of textuality. In place of a theology of the Logos, he affirms the religion of poetry. The Truth has no priority over the text, for in both writing and reading, the emphasis is on production of something new and independent. In Schlegel's view, literature does not build up its language around the idea of reproduction, or conformity to prior meaning from which the text derives its authority. It need not be "comprehensible," which is to say, make itself transparent as a window on something else.

The Messianic modality of truth is outside history, and not expressible within the modality of historical acts. Romantic poetry, by contrast, is, in Hamann's phrase, die unverlernbare Muttersprache der Menschheit, the inalienable mothertongue of mankind. Its light is not solar, but universally disseminated—republican, not monarchical. This position is still sustained in the allegorical Theorie der Natur section of the Köln lectures, where Schlegel states: "Das Licht ist das geistigste aller Elemente, ist Geist überhaupt, ordnender Geist, bildender Verstand" (KA XII, p. 440, 'Light is the most spiritual of all elements, is spirit altogether, ordering spirit, formative understanding), but maintains that its source is not the sun. That merely belongs with the planets on the lower plane of Beharrlichkeit, and not even then as their progenitor: "Man hat sich im Gegenteil die Sonne als eine Hervorbringung der anderen Planeten zu denken, die im Brennpunkte des Zusammenwirkens zu ihrem gemeinsamen entsteht" (p. 424, 'One should on the contrary think of the sun as being brought forth by the other planets, arising at the focus of their combined effect as their common center').

This cosmic republicanism is reflected, furthermore, in a republicanism of texts as well. It is a deliberate antidote to the dominion of Holy Writ. One finds, for example the following observation in the Athenäum Fragments: "Man hat von manchem Monarchen gesagt: er würde ein sehr liebenswürdiger Privatmann gewesen sein, nur zum Könige habe er nicht getaugt. Verhält es sich mit der Bibel ebenso? Ist sie bloß ein liebenswürdiges Privatbuch, das nur nicht Bibel sein sollte? (AF #12). The Bible was of great concern to both Schlegel and Novalis, but from the aspect of writing, not of reading. Schlegel wrote to Novalis in October of 1798 that "Was mich betrifft, so ist das Ziel meiner literarischen Projekte eine neue Bibel zu schreiben,"[17] to which the recipient responded that he had, by a coincidence which intrigued them both, come upon a startlingly similar line of thought in his own work, and was engaged in "eine Kritik des Bibelprojekts—ein Versuch einer Universalmethode des Biblisierens—die Einleitung zu einer echten Enzyklopädistik" (Preitz, p. 132, 'a critique of the bible project—an attempt at a universal method of bible-writing—the introduction to a real theory of the encyclopaedia'). And, in agreement with such speculation, Schlegel concludes in his philosophical notebooks: "Es muß unendlich viele Bibeln geben können" (KA XVIII, p. 236 #516, 'It must be possible for there to be an infinite number of bibles').

It is said that there is nothing new under the sun, and this may very well be true. Only let us, like Schlegel, take this literally enough to consider that Lucinde, hovering "ex-centrically" between the rising and setting of two suns in intellectual history, and depending on light from neither, might well present a new, unfamiliar face. Whereas Walter Benjamin's Marxism applies his dialectical construction to combine and counterbalance two tendencies out of history, the authority of an otherworldly Messianic theology and the Enlightenment concern with material, worldly justice and justification, Schlegel achieves a mysterious indifference to both. It is by this step that he can project a new light, a mythological formula through whose power an entirely new kind of writing could come about for the very first time. Thus the word of Schlegel's intention to write his novel and the announcement of his plan to compose a new Bible in the letter to Novalis come together in a way that neither the theological nor the rationalistic focal elements of Marxism could permit.

If Lucinde was conceived in an impulse to eclipse the traditional centralizing ideology of fiction as uninhibited as the concern to revolutionize the traditional status of the Bible, then it is not surprising that it falls so far from what one expects of a novel. Learning how to read it involves constructing an appropriate sense of how far one will permit oneself to be transformed in the role of reader. At no point does it offer the secure singularity of an unambiguous narrative line unfolding before us. The reader does not have the firm ground of a continuing path beneath his or her feet.

The sensibility behind this fiction has dispensed with the unity of a determinate agent at work in a determinate world. There is no narrative illusion because there is no narrative world, no literary mimicry of the way experience constitutes itself in the unreflective dogmatisms of a "real" world. Schlegel refuses to share in the enthralling conformities by which one is seduced into illusion. To be lulled into mistaking recognition of the familiar patterns which determine experience, for discovery of the truth, is to him only a humiliation for the naive and unphilosophical. It is for this reason that he does not even need to retreat into the domain of fictive events to find material which will conform to the typical weave of a generalized and common experience so that its imagery will be open to the illusion of recognition. The erratic fragments of his own particular life could, scandalous though it seemed to the contemporary public, serve as the basis of this uncompromising representation.

As perspective melts into perspective, as parabasis weaves into parabasis, and the chinese box of texts within texts and narrative recollections and voices within those extends, reading expands into a dimension of freedom beyond the traditional limitations of unitary form in aesthetics, or the coherence of singular existence in the traditional subject. The reader enters the pattern of a new structure of experience in this idiosyncratic work. The question I will pursue in the subsequent chapters of this book is whether there is a significance beyond idiosyncrasy possible here, and whether it is possible to extend the novel pattern it develops into the larger domain of experience in life, society and politics.

NOTES

[1] KA XVIII, p. 156 #397. 'Fire must be invisibly present everywhere there is earth—that is the meaning of the central fire. Fire is the esoteric, earth the exoteric.'

[2] Fragmente aus dem Nachlasse eines jungen Physikers, Hrsg. Arthur Henkel (Heidelberg: Verlag Lambert Schneider, 1969), p. 37, #56. 'Plants and animals move around man, the way planets and moons move around the sun. Everything lives only through and for man, he is the central sun of the organism on the earth.'

[3] Illuminationen, ausg. Siegfried Unseld (Frankfurt am Main: Suhrkamp, 1980), p. 252. Fourth of the "Theses on the Philosophy of History" in Illuminations, p. 255. 'As flowers turn towards the sun, by dint of a secret heliotropism the past strives to turn toward that sun which is rising in the sky of history.' Hereafter quotations from this material are cited by thesis number.

[4] Friedrich Schlegel, Literary Notebooks, ed. Hans Eichner, (Toronto: University of Toronto Press, 1957), p. 106, note 973. Hereafter quotations from this source are indicated as LN followed by note number.

[5] KA V, p. xlviii.

[6] KA I, p. xxix.

[7] Ludwig Tieck und die Brüder Schlegel: Briefe, Hrsg. Edgar Lohner (München: Winkler, 1972), p. 191.

[8] Aus Schellings Leben. In Briefen, Hrsg. G. L. Plitt (Leipzig: 1869), quoted by Hans Eichner LN p. 264.

[9] See Ernst Behler's authoritative "Friedrich Schlegel und Hegel," Hegel-Studien 2 (1963), p. 203.

[10] Søren Kirkegaard, The Concept of Irony, Trans. Lee M. Capel (Bloomington & London: Indiana University Press, 1968), p. 305.

[11] Friedrich Schlegel, Seine prosaischen Jugendschriften, Hrsg. J. Minor (Wien: Konegen, 1906), Bd. I, p. 124.

[12] Letters of R. M. Rilke, Ed. Jane Bannard Greene and M. D. Herter Norton (New York: Norton 1969), Vol. 2, p. 374.

[13] KA II, p, 154. Henceforward, the three series of fragments from this volume will be noted as LF (Lyceums-Fragmente), AF (Athenäums-Fragmente), and AI (Ideen).

[14] Walter Benjamin, "Theologico-Political Fragment" in Reflections: Essays, Aphorisms, Autobiographical Writings, Ed. Peter Demetz, Trans. Edmund Jephcott (New York: Harcourt Brace Jovanovich, 1978), p. 312. References to this edition hereafter indicated as Reflections.

[15] "Bergsonism and Music" Trans. C. K. Scott Moncrieff in Reflections on Art, Ed. Susanne K. Langer (Baltimore: The Johns Hopkins Press, 1958), p. 148.

[16] Gesammelte Schriften, Hrsg. Rolf Tiedemann u. Hermann Schweppenhäuser (Frankfurt a. M.: Suhrkamp, 1974), Bd. I iii, p. 1232. Quotations from this source henceforth indicated as Ges. Schr. I iii.

[17] Friedrich Schlegel und Novalis, Biographie einer Romantikerfreundschaft in ihren Briefen, Hrsg. Max Preitz (Darmstadt: Hermann Gentner, 1957), p. 139. This edition hereafter indicated as Preitz.

CHAPTER II

THE COMING OF THE MESSIAH OR THE STOIC BURNING—

THE NEGATED TEXT IN WALTER BENJAMIN AND FRIEDRICH SCHLEGEL

> Aber es Gibt eine Art zu zerstören, welche gerade der Ausfluß jener
> mächtigen Sehnsucht nach Heiligung und Errettung ist, . . . Alles Dasein,
> welches verneint werden kann, verdient es auch verneint zu werden; und
> wahrhaftig sein heißt: an ein Dasein zu glauben, welches überhaupt nicht
> verneint werden könnte und welches selber wahr und ohne Lüge ist.

Friedrich Nietzsche, <u>Schopenhauer als Erzieher</u>[1]

Messianic Reading

The book on German Romanticism which Walter Benjamin originally wrote as
his doctoral dissertation, <u>Der Begriff der Kunstkritik in der deutschen
Frühromantik</u> ('The Concept of Art Criticism in Early German
Romanticism'), is a text which stands in several histories. In it we can
read the early development of Benjamin's own critical procedure and the
origin of his special perspective on the phenomena of modernity in
literature. In it, too, one can find much revealed about evolving views on
Romanticism, and the prevailing positions established at the time of writing
(1917-19). Perhaps the most striking change to have affected the book's

significance, however, is that which has occurred in its avowed subject matter—in the corpus of Friedrich Schlegel's writing itself. To a quite unusual degree with a figure of such stature, the picture which it has been possible to construct of Friedrich Schlegel's thinking has been subject to profound revision as new materials from his hand have been discovered and belatedly made public.

It is ironic indeed that this work of Benjamin's should have become so widely influential in recent years, because it represents an attempt to overcome gaps in Schlegel's oeuvre which no longer exist. There has been very little recognition of this, and no systematic investigation. A most notable example of the work's newly disseminated influence is to found in L'Absolu littéraire by Philippe Lacoue-Labarthe and Jean-Luc Nancy (Paris: Seuil, 1979), who acknowledge it at the beginning of their study of Jena Romanticism as one of the two critical texts on which they have depended. It is thus promoted to the status of an authority of the first order. Since L'Absolu littéraire is an important document of the new interest current theoretical concerns are devoting to German Romanticism, and has been a particularly effective focus of the renewed attention paid to Benjamin's work, it is singled out here for special mention. The argument elaborated in this critique, however, applies equally to virtually all contemporary references to Der Begriff der Kunstkritik.

I do not take issue with the interpretation of Benjamin's writing as such, but with the entirely erroneous status which it has now acquired as an authoritative commentary on Friedrich Schlegel and Jena Romanticism. As historical entities, these two must be considered separate from what Benjamin represents under those terms in his book. The textual sources on which that study was based are only a part of the corpus produced by Schlegel during the period in question, and, as we can read now, a rather misleading selection at that. In this chapter I will attempt to expose the effect produced by Benjamin's very individual critical approach and this peculiarly restricted selection of materials in generating a picture of its subject matter, and show how far it deviates from what can be argued with historical force today.

Regarding L'Absolu littéraire, as with the source on which it depends, I take the position that it is not necessarily without significance because of the error it has repeated, but only that it is deprived thereby of its force as a historical account. The success with which it endures that loss depends on factors which are perhaps not yet entirely clear. Certainly, Benjamin's work does survive in a new role, for it continues to exist as a document of those histories which produced it. Indeed, it is a superior instrument of measurement to detect the character of Benjamin's method, and the perspective he constructed on the past, now that his image of it is not obscured by correspondence with ours. His errors are more evidently his own than a viewpoint we might have shared with him in the conviction of accuracy.

Having completed the main body of Der Begriff der Kunstkritik in der deutschen Frühromantik in the version he submitted as his doctoral dissertation, Benjamin observed in a letter: "Was sie sein sollte ist sie geworden: ein Hinweis auf die durchaus in der Literatur unbekannte wahre Natur der Romantik"[2] ('It has turned out the way it was intended to: an indication of the true nature of Romanticism which has been completely unrecognized in the literature'). The work itself takes a clear stand here, and is able to bracket the ideas of Novalis and Friedrich Schlegel during the Jena and Athenäum period together with developments traditionally regarded as quite opposed to Romanticism: "Wollte man die Kunsttheorie eines so bewußten Meisters wie Flaubert, die der Parnassiens oder diejenige des Georgeschen Kreises auf ihre Grundsätze bringen, man würde die hier dargelegten unter ihnen finden" (Schriften II, p. 511, 'If one were to reduce the art theory of such a conscious master as Flaubert, that of the Parnassians or the Stefan George Circle, to their fundamental principles, one would discover those that are set out here among them'). He finds the principles he has identified on which this judgment is based quite sufficient to overturn a then common perception of that period and the term by which it is known, for "sie sind dem Geist dieser Epoche so sehr eigen, daß Kircher mit Recht erklären konnte 'Diese Romantiker wollten gerade das "Romantische" von sich abhalten—wie man es damals und heute versteht'" ('they are so much a part of the spirit of this epoch that Kircher could declare quite correctly "These Romantics wanted nothing to do with the 'Romantic'—the way it was understood then and is still today"').

The letter quoted above goes on to qualify the achievement of his study, which is:

> auch nur mittelbar . . . weil ich an das Zentrum der Romantik, den Messianismus—ich habe nur die Kunstanschauung behandelt—

ebenso wenig wie an irgend etwas anderes, das mir höchst gegenwärtig ist, herangehen dürfte ohne mir die Möglichkeit der verlangten komplizierten und konventionellen wissenschaftlichen Haltung, die ich von der echten unterscheide, abzuschneiden. Nur: Daß man diesen Sachverhalt von innen heraus ihr entnehmen könne, möchte ich in dieser Arbeit erreicht haben.

('only achieved indirectly . . . because I could not approach the centerpoint of Romanticism, Messianism—I have only covered the view of art—any more than I could deal with all the other things that were most important to me, without cutting off the possibility of keeping to the complicated and conventional manner expected of one, which I myself would separate from the genuine style of analysis.')

This is extraordinarily important because it not only gives a clear indication that the issue of Messianism is indeed the real, if hidden, core of the work, but also makes it quite explicit that even though Benjamin was constrained to manage and modify his procedure so as not to separate himself from the conventional scholarly method, this is described as distinct from that appropriate to his real concerns as the false to the true. To make good on the task he sets his reader, that is, to hear the Messianic sense whispered along with the doctoral pronouncements, requires more than an ear attuned most finely to the former. It requires in addition a precise discrimination of what is only there as camouflage, to permit the hidden contraband to pass the customs-house guarding the realm of that false knowledge, so the Messianic transmission might penetrate to those ready to receive it.

The problem thus has two halves which are both complex in quite different ways—the Messianic reading intended by, and the academic performance required of Benjamin. Both these have to be resolved in relation to their subject-matter at the same time as they are distinguished from one another, and although none of these issues can be settled in isolation, none of them may be considered answered until the tight weave that binds them is grasped as made up of a profoundly different warp and woof.

The standing accorded Friedrich Schlegel's writing in Der Begriff der Kunstkritik is itself an example of the method he referred to as the "true" one in the letter to Schoen quoted above. In the introductory section he states: "Als die Romantische Theorie der Kunstkritik wird im folgenden diejenige Friedrich Schlegels dargestellt. Das Recht, diese theorie als die romantische zu bezeichnen, beruht auf ihrem repräsentativen Charakter" (Schriften II, p. 423, 'Friedrich Schlegel's theory of art criticism will be taken as the Romantic one for this discussion. The right to designate this theory as that of Romanticism depends on its representative character'). The vague and apparently innocuous idea of a representative view then undergoes an expansion whose implications are far greater than the subtlety of the change suggests. He introduces the conception of a "school" of Jena Romanticism: "Nicht daß alle Frühromantiker sich mit ihr einverstanden erklärt oder auch nur von ihr Notiz genommen hätten: Friedrich Schlegel ist auch seinen Freunden oft unverständlich geblieben. Aber seine Anschauung vom Wesen der Kunstkritik ist das Wort der Schule darüber" ('Not that all the early Romantics had expressed their acceptance or even taken any notice of it: Friedrich Schlegel was often incomprehensible even to his friends. But his view on the essential nature of art criticism is the position of the school on that matter').

Relations between the members of the Jenakreis certainly present a convoluted question, combining profound sympathies and remarkable collaboration or Symphilosophie with the equally profound differences, incomprehension and indifference which Benjamin acknowledges. The notion, however, of a school in the sense that might seem to be applied here, that is, of a unity sufficiently defined internally for Schlegel to stand as its mouthpiece, must be regarded as having no more than a chimerical existence when condidered against conventional historical criteria. But of course the issue of school versus circle, group or movement could easily be an extraneous terminological quibble, were it not for the way in which Benjamin constructs Schlegel's views, and here I refer in particular to his method of drawing on a source not from the latter's hand in order to complete gaps in the written material available. The instance of this which is initially most striking is his use of Novalis to supply the missing epistemological basis that he insists is implicit in Schlegel's early Romantic writings, and plays an indispensable part in the thesis of Der Begriff der Kunstkritik.

The procedure undertaken with Novalis' remarks on epistemology is in reality an intriguingly close precursor to the technique of "quoting out of context" Benjamin would later embrace, with the difference that an apparent context is still presented here in order to disguise the break with conventional method. Two factors give me encouragement to maintain this position—first the letters expressing Benjamin's intent, and secondly the fact that a vast number of those missing writings from Schlegel's oeuvre whose absence generated both the necessity and opportunity for Benjamin's own special construction, have since been discovered and may be summoned in evidence. We now have positive means of identifying and criticizing all the tactical manoeuvers he uses to arrive at his conclusions. The new documentary witness exposes the deviation between his "true" and the conventional "false" method, permitting it to be made accessible to a kind of scrutiny not possible in its own time or for many years after its first appearance.

He justifies his use of Novalis as a completion or complement to Schlegel's work by the intimacy of their friendship and the closeness of their literary association, arguing that "diese enge Gemeinschaft macht die Untersuchung der wechselseitigen Einflüsse größtenteils unmöglich, für die vorliegende Fragestellung ist sie vollends entbehrlich" (Schriften II, p. 414, 'this close association makes an inquiry into the reciprocal influence for the most part impossible, and for the present discussion it is completely dispensable'). This did not express itself in collaboration on the specific topic of art and criticism to which Benjamin addresses himself, as he has to concede: "Das Problem selbst hat Novalis weniger interessiert" ('This problem itself interested Novalis less'), but he goes on to insist on a dovetailing of the two for which he had inadequate textual support: ". . . aber die erkenntnistheoretischen Voraussetzungen, auf Grund deren Schlegel es behandelte, teilte er mit ihm, und mit ihm vertrat er die Konsequenzen dieser Theorie für die Kunst" ('. . . but he shared the epistemological presuppositions on the basis of which Schlegel treated it, and like him he held to the consequences of this theory in art'). We may set aside the second assertion since the "consequences" of the theory are a major step beyond what we are considering now. They require substantial interpretation in their own right, though as I have already noted, Novalis' and Schlegel's practice as writers by no means indicates an identity of approach. Benjamin's first point, however, clearly involves a distinct and damaging measure of cirularity, for here the common epistemological basis is to substantiate that unity of views which is itself then to permit the use of Novalis' utterances on the question to overcome Schlegel's silence. That is, Benjamin must in fact presuppose the exact form of their relationship in order to work out the principle he posits as shared between them.

Some sense of what is meant by "school" begins to emerge as a result of this. Benjamin writes: "Die Heranziehung der Schriften des Novalis zu denen Schlegels rechtfertigt sich durch die völlige Einhelligkeit beider hinsichtlich der Prämissen und der Folgerungen aus der Theorie der Kunstkritik" (p. 423f, 'Consulting Novalis' writing with reference to Schlegel's is justified by their perfect unanimity regarding the premises of a theory of art criticism, and the deductions made from it'), and then goes further: "In Form einer eigentümlichen Erkenntnismystik und einer bedeutenden Theorie der Prosa hat er beide manchmal schärfer und aufschlußreicher formuliert als sein Freund" ('In the form of a very particular mystical view of perception and an important theory of prose, he sometimes gave sharper and richer expression to both than his friend'). The interchangeability of the two figures is now brought to the point where whichever provides the most suitable statement in elaborating the posited common body of thought may be introduced indifferently. They are fused into one.

Now it is of course true that there is considerable parity between these two, and they offer many references to the harmony they perceived in their thinking, both in the character of their ideas, and in their method of working. Nonetheless, given the nature of those ideas and of that method of working, the inexorable bridge of logic which would tie in Novalis' thoughts in one area with Schlegel's in another, could not be conventional in nature. Indeed, as the close scrutiny we pursue will confirm, there is for Walter Benjamin a further element at work, a hidden nexus whose existence is not purely textual, but must rather be classified as esoteric or mystical. The method or principle here demands to be made explicit, for it depends directly on the distinction betweeen the conventional and the genuine form of knowledge announced in his letter. I will express it this way: in the former reasoning, where a man remained silent, he did not speak; by the latter, where two associate themselves with a single truth, it may, on any question, speak through one as through the other.

The nature of the terrain, that is the oblique, aphoristic mode of expression used by the early Romantics, and the fluidity of their focus, was to Benjamin's advantage because it helped him avoid the tactically difficult open break with the standard method. More advantageous, as alluded to above, was the situation regarding available textual evidence. The relative poverty of this basis had left the picture vague and uncertain in the first instance, and in the second, all too susceptible to that simplistic and still tenacious notion of Romanticism as an ecstatic body of subjective inspirations without a binding structure. But by the same token, nevertheless, the assumption that these materials invoke only the indeterminate illuminations that apparently star the Romantic firmament, is also itself vulnerable because of the inconclusive state of the evidence. A vigorously inventive style of interpretation could be applied with some freedom in working on those fragments in order to challenge that view. An analysis that could begin to restore a real intelligence and substance to its topic would necessarily enjoy a powerful attractiveness. The appeal of such a project clearly would justify a certain inevitable and apparently well-calculated risk in spanning the empty spaces in its foundation.

His motivation in opposing the generally held view was undoubtedly rooted in an astonishingly forceful and impressive intuition which is to be acknowledged. It points along a far more fecund and honorable avenue of questioning than that which it resists. As we retrace and expose his tracks in the light of new information, it is impossible not to concede that he has prepared the way for a clarification of this difficult territory which emerges step by step as we correct his misprisions.

The principal new materials to which I shall refer are the Jena Vorlesungen of 1800-01 (die Transcendentalphilosophie) rediscovered by J. Körner and published in 1935, the Literary Notebooks 1796-1803 made available by Hans Eichner in 1957, and the Philosophische Lehrjahre 1796-1803 edited by Ernst Behler and published in 1963.

Schlegel and Novalis

The difference which Benjamin observed between Schlegel and Novalis in earlier letters, written while he was still preparing for the work, is interesting because it suggests lines of distinction which are not brought out or developed later. First, he declares that Schlegel's voice has more than representative status: "Ich lese viel in Friedrich Schlegel und Novalis. Bei dem ersten wird mir immer deutlicher wie er von allen Romantikern wohl der einzige ist . . . der den Geist dieser Schule ohne konstitutionelle Schwäche und Trübung entfaltet hat. Er ist dichterisch rein, gesund und träge"[3] ('I have been reading a lot by Friedrich Schlegel and Novalis. With the former it is becoming ever clearer to me that he is the only one . . . who developed the spirit of this school without constitutional weakness or opacity. He is poetically pure, healthy and solid'). Novalis is not only separated from him by a different focus of interest, but by qualitative shortcomings: "Im tiefsten Innern des Novalis aber, wie des Brentano, wohnt ein Krankheitskeim. Ich hoffe genau zu sagen worin eigentlich die Krankheit des Novalis liegt" ('In the most inner aspect of Novalis, as with Brentano, there is a kernel of sickness. I hope to say where precisely this sickness of Novalis lies'). A letter written to the same recipient one month later expands most intriguingly on the theme of Schlegel's special characteristics, but adds, a little frustratingly: "Von dem 'Krankheitskeim' des Novalis ein anderes Mal. Ich denke noch darüber nach" (Briefe I, p. 138, 'On the "kernel of sickness" in Novalis another time. I am still thinking it through'). Unfortunately, there seems to be no further reference to this, and it does not appear in the argument of Der Begriff der Kunstkritik. Nevertheless, the evidence we do have permits some possibly fruitful speculation on the dual question of what he had in mind here, and why it was subsequently dropped from his expressed concerns.

The second letter describes the essential atmosphere at the core of Romanticism as a kind of central fire and states: "Friedrich Schlegel hat in dem überirdischen Feuer dieser Atmosphäre länger als ein anderer geatmet, länger vor allen Dingen als Novalis, der aus seinem im tiefen Sinne praktischen oder besser: pragmatischen Ingenium das zu verwirklichen suchte, was Schlegel nezessitierte" ('Friedrich Schlegel breathed longer than anyone else in the celestial fire of this atmosphere, longer above all than Novalis, who, having a mind that was in a profound sense practical, or rather pragmatic, attempted to realize what Schlegel made necessary').

This image suggests something like the reverse of the myth of Daedalus and Icarus. It is the more practical Novalis whose sober or pragmatic quality left him incapable of withstanding the full force of Romantic illumination and who perishes in the blaze of "überirdischen Feuer" ('celestial fire'). Schlegel, more daring, and unfettered by the pull of lesser thoughts, can soar to it and hover there unharmed. The source of Schlegel's superior power here may be equated with a certain added freedom, even heedlessness, leaving it to others to make earth-bound sense of that fire which, in the momentary flare of _Witz_, he brings before their eyes. At the same time, he is "dichterisch rein, gesund und träge," that is, sober and precise in his flight.

When examining the central thesis of Benjamin's dissertation, the soberness of art, it should be born clearly in mind that there are thus two forms of soberness in Romanticism invoked in this correspondence, even though they become conflated in the later text. One is born of strength in Schlegel, the other born of weakness in Novalis. The former, evidently, is the more important, and by far the more difficult both to demonstrate, and even to express. It is this which he associates with Hölderlin's term "heilignüchtern" ('hallowed-sober') and which is crucial in grasping the true nature of Romanticism, for it is a mystical soberness which appears to the eyes of the profane as intoxication. And it is this dual character of intoxication and soberness which constitutes the rich complexity of both Benjamin and Romanticism, and the extraordinary constellation that they generate together. It is here that one should look to understand the notion of Romantic Messianism to which Benjamin refers, and, no less perhaps, to comprehend his own Messianic view of historical materialism in later years.

The letter offers some quite specific ideas to confirm this interpretation, for in it he writes: "Das Zentrum der Frühromantik ist: Religion und Geschichte. Ihre unendliche Schönheit . . . daß sie . . . im eigenen _Denken_ und Leben die höhere Sphäre zu produzieren suchten in der die beiden koinzidieren mußten" ('The centerpoint of early Romanticism is religion and history. Its eternal beauty . . . that it . . . tried to generate in its own thinking and living that higher sphere where both would have to coincide'). The mutual interpenetration of religion and history is certainly the sphere of Messianism. And it would be hard to deny that the cosmic telos of Schlegel's Köln Lectures shows an approach to something in just this sense. Yet what is significant is that Benjamin rejects that phase of Schlegel's work, to which he had access in the Windischmann edition, as being wholly colored by Catholicism.

Similarly, in the letter quoted above, he goes on to praise his early Romanticism for the distance it took in its relation to Christianity: "Es ergab sich nicht 'die Religion' aber die Atmosphäre, in der alles was ohne sie und was angeblich sie war vebrannte, zu Asche zerfiel. Wie auch ein solcher stiller Zerfall des Christentums Friedrich Schlegel vor Augen stand . . . weil seine Moral nicht Romantisch: das heißt . . . weil letzten Endes unhistorisch erschien" ('What emerged here was not "religion" as such, but the atmosphere in which everything which was without it or falsely supposed to be it, fell into ashes. In the same way a silent crumbling away of Christianity was evident to Schlegel . . . because ultimately its morality did not seem Romantic: that is . . . because ultimately it seemed unhistorical'). If the particular Messianic union of religion and history Benjamin regards as its true manifestation is not adequately represented by Christianity, then the Christian element in the spirit of Novalis' _Hymnen an die Nacht_, _Geistliche Lieder_, and _Die Christenheit oder Europa_, all demonstrate a failure of the historical moment which could be equivalent to a _Krankheitskeim_, and this would also find support in the example of Brentano whose name is similarly linked to it.

Benjamin concedes that the position he describes here is not to be found in Schlegel's words, but is his own construction. That being so, his meaning cannot be reconstructed from any examination of Schlegel alone, but rather through Benjamin's own line of questioning in his dissertion. The crux of that, the soberness of art, echoing Kircher in redefining the term Romantiker itself, may be regarded as a surrogate for the issue of Messianism because both carry the significant factor of a determining order within an esoteric or mystical mode. That is, if he can establish that the apparently unbounded activity of artistic creation in early Romanticism, which is pre-eminently mystical in nature, has an ordering principle at its heart, and responds only to the sober recognition of this central form, then the presence and influence of a Messianic order will be half-way towards demonstration. The other half is evidently much more difficult, for what distinguishes the Messiah from any other mystically-conceived entity is that he must have the power to penetrate and transform the exoteric or earthly realm—he must have a historical role, either to end history, or to begin it anew in redeemed form.

A Messianic presence is capable of a final entry and realization in the world so that the esoteric and the exoteric are knit up into one. The difficulty we encounter in accepting this for Schlegel's early Romanticism is that while history is assimilated to the divinatory knowledge of religion, as in the Athenäum Fragment no. 80: "Der Historiker ist ein rückwaärts gekehrter Prophet" ('The historian is a prophet facing backwards' —a proposition to which Benjamin returns two decades later when he quotes it in notes pertaining to the Theses on the Philosophy of History), the reciprocal movement in which mystical knowledge becomes determinate and visible in the natural or historical spheres, implied by the Messianic component of such knowledge, cannot be found anywhere. Quite the reverse, in fact—except perhaps in the separate dispensation of the Köln Lectures of 1804-05, or the subsequent phase of Catholic zealotry.

A problem of my own method must be made quite plain here, for there is no doubt that to consider two esoteric philosophical outlooks and to give an acount of the configuration they produce together without this also being esoteric, involves questions of representation which cannot be dismissed lightly. The esoteric is that which necessarily cannot be presented in explicit and visible (or public) form, and to impose exoteric criteria of meaning on such esoteric utterances is simply to pass them by. We may not demand that the content of Schlegel's mystical formulations be made subject to rationalist scrutiny and judgment, any more than we can ask of Benjamin who or where the Messiah is, and on that basis alone decide whether these are "real" or "irreal" in character. Accordingly, I must operate within a quite specifically restricted framework.

The standard of commonplace critical judgment is based on the notion that knowledge properly so-called is homogeneous—all that is or can be known must of necessity pass the same test of truth or reality, and this test itself be available as part of that knowledge. The esoteric principle accepts that there is knowledge which is quite discontinuous with the "ordinary" or "natural" kind understood in familiar discourse. To deal effectively with both Schlegel and Benjamin, it is necessary that we respect this idea, or nothing in either will reward our examination of them. Furthermore, all that can be rendered fully explicit in our first clarification will necessarily be in the mode of exclusion or division. That is, the most binding criterion of comparison between Benjamin's Messianism and Schlegel's Romantic esotericism is not in their content per se, but rather in the modality of that which they separate from the commonplace continuum of the world. It has to be measured by comparing the ways in which they set up a separate sphere for the parts thus articulated, and the way the beginning of that sphere establishes a boundary and a limit for the ordinary domain. The character of that limitation imposed on conventional knowledge is all that is fully visible from and available to the exoteric perspective. That is, and must be, the object of our present investigation.

Determination of a stable point or structure defining the break in homogeneity is required for Benjamin's first task, which is to rescue his topic from the bland chaos of a crude subjectivity or vulgar idealism, and set it up as a thoroughgoing philosophical mysticism (or idealism). This opens the way for that second task which he could not pursue directly, the identification of a Messianic center as the determination of the heterogeneous structure. The implicit argument for Romantic Messianism, then, depends on the explicit one in support of the soberness of art, which in turn has to be carried forward by the conflation of Novalis' lower soberness with Schlegel's truer one. Even though he may have continued to nurture the same reservations about Novalis' "Konstitutionelle

Schwäche," the use of his more available resources in demonstrating the true Romantic "atmosphere" or center could be justified by the ideal that "he tried to realize what Schlegel made necessary." There is stilll some claim, in other words, that it is a legitimate representation or reflection of the central truth, even though it is a less perfect one. And since full expression of the real truth could not be approached ("because I could not approach the centerpoint of Romanticism, Messianism . . . any more than I could deal with all the other things that were most important to me . . .") the distinction might indeed be "completely dispensable"——provided that this short-circuit still maintains contact with its apparent object.

Nevertheless, the attendant distortion can be gauged by the way in which the concept of soberness has been moved into the commonplace traditional pattern: "Das Prosaische, in dem die Reflexion als Prinzip der Kunst sich zuhöchst ausprägt, ist ja im Sprachgebrauch geradezu eine metaphorische Bezeichnung des Nüchternen. Als ein denkendes und besonnenes Verhalten ist die Reflexion das Gegenteil der Ekstase, der μανια des Platon" (Schriften II, p. 508, 'The prosaic, in which reflection manifests itself to the highest degree as a principle of art, is even, in normal usage, a metaphorical term for the sober. As a thinking and collected attitude reflection is the opposite of ecstasy, the μανια of Plato'). The two terms pressed into service as synonyms for soberness here only heighten the problem. The concept of prose cannot, in Schlegel, be identified with the prosaic, and where Reflexion approaches the implication of reflectiveness in the familiar usage, he explicitly reduces it to secondary status—though neither of these points could be determined unambiguously from the texts available to Benjamin. Even for Novalis, however, the concept of Reflexion, which Benjamin discusses superbly as the basis of his interpretation of Romantic epistemology in relation to Fichte's idealism, does not lend itself to that idea of soberness without some continuing tension.

As noted above, Benjamin states in Der Begriff der Kunstkritik that Novalis had formulated the theory of prose better than his friend, observing further for example: "Auch in Schlegels Theorie des Romans steht der Gedanke der Prosa . . . nicht klar im Mittelpunkt. Er hat ihn mit der Lehre von der Poetisierung des Stoffes kompliziert" (p. 507, 'Even in Schlegel's theory of the novel the idea of prose . . . does not stand clearly in the middle. He complicated it with the doctrine of a poeticization of content'). One may assume Benjamin is not being disingenuous here, for the importance of prose in early German Romanticism is a significant point which he is right to emphasize, and a clear position was necessary. Yet it is unfortunate that he had to choose in the way he did, for the rediscovered material shows us that the direction Schlegel takes away from Novalis' simpler positions is precisely towards a more authentic, and far more sophisticated, mystical concept consistent with the line of inquiry begun in Benjamin's letters— that is, substantiating the special force unique to Schlegel's vision. One would judge that Benjamin has either failed to penetrate a perceived difference in Schlegel and substituted the less developed version, or he has genuinely failed to perceive what can now be fully documented. In either case, it is a loss which can indeed be made good. The chief source here is the Literary Notebooks, which include many important entries on prose, the most trenchant being in the series of nos. 585-610. Since this issue has been discussed already in Chapter One, I will not pursue it here.

The idea of Reflexion and the theory of the Reflexionsmedium are more complex questions, however, because the dialectical structure Benjamin introduces through the language of Fichte, and bears the mark of his own awareness of Hegel, is such an elaborately devised position. To give it the extended analysis it demands in explication would be a very cumbersome procedure for present purposes. I therefore want to restrict myself to demonstrating that the concept of Reflexion does not have such a high priority in Schlegel's thinking as Benjamin assumes. It is now quite evident that Schlegel does not place Reflexion in the predominant role Benjamin's argument would demand, but makes it distinctly secondary to produktive Fantasie ('productive imagination'). In the important relation to Fichte, it can be regarded as a resolute transferal of significance to and expansion of the original Setzen or absolute thesis, wherein the Ich, the ego, posits itself by a pure act— absolutely primitive, without antecedent or derivation—and away from the subsequent positings of Nicht-Ich in the reflexive succession that generates the concept of world.

Fichte's own emphasis, minimizing that element which he considers can only be proposed apodictically, makes it possible to begin the philosophical articulation of his system with reflection, which then determines its orderly construction. This is the form of orderliness with which Benjamin resists the image of Romanticism as chaotic subjectivity or intoxication. Schlegel, however, in bringing Poesie to the fore, and asserting the primary role of art and the productive imagination, reverses the basis of that position. He is here much more radical an idealist than Fichte, for even the minimal exterior fixed point of an unthematizable Setzen is for him too much of a restriction on speculative freedom in constructing the universe. This, as indeed any systematic form, is opposed to Schlegel's conception of religion as freedom, which negates any fixed quality in such a construction: "Das Universum zu neutralisieren ist wohl das Wesen der Religion" (KA XVIII, p. 71 #516, 'Neutralizing the universe is the essence of religion'). Consequently, he expresses a conviction that reflection is empty and inadequate to the true task to which philosophy should contribute: "Alles Setzen ist practisch und also ein Constituiren oder ein Produciren. Das bloße zum Objekt machen des Subjekts, also Reflexion, ist durchaus nicht productiv" (KA XVIII, p. 408 #1059, 'All positing is practical and therefore a constituting or production. The mere making of the subject into an object, reflection, is entirely non-productive').

Reflection implies the priority of an involuntary and imposed presence as the content of consciousness when it is emphasized in systematic form. Only imaginative productivity, as the active phase of consciousness, can overcome that passive moment. Reflection is associated with the lower and commonplace mode of human thought which art/religion is to negate: "Die eigentliche Form unseres Denkens ist Reflexion; das entgegengesetzte ist das objektive Denken—produktive Fantasie. Also ist die Kunst nicht menschlich sondern göttlich' (p. 179 #643, 'The actual form of our thinking is reflection; the opposite is objective thinking— productive imagination. Therefore art is not human but divine'). Thus the activity of religion is to neutralize reflection in favor of art.

This brings us to a precise point at which to identify the erroneous imposition of Novalis' thinking on Schlegel, where Benjamin writes: "Die Reflexionsakt transzendiert die jeweilige geistige Stufe, um auf die höhere überzugehen. Daher sagt Novalis mit Beziehung auf den Reflexionsakt in der Selbstdurchdringung: 'Jene Stelle außer der Welt ist gegeben, und Archimedes kann nun sein Versprechen erfüllen'" (Schriften II, p. 499, 'The act of reflection transcends the particular spiritual level in order to ascend to that above it. Therefore Novalis says, referring to the act of reflection in self-permeation: "That place outside the world is provided, and Archimedes can now fulfill his promise"'). Archimedes' mystical lever and fulcrum by which he could move the world are no less characteristic an image in Schlegel's work, which enables us to use it as an exact indication of the order of dignity ascribed to reflection: "Das Hypomochlion der Poesie ist die Fantasie, das der Philosophie die Reflexion" (KA XVII, p. 391 #844, 'The hypomochlion of poetry is the imagination, that of philosophy is reflection').

The term Philosophie is used in various ways by Schlegel, but there can be no doubt that wheresoever it is made separate and distinct from art or poetry, (which is not always) it stands below them: "Künstler sind Menschen in der höheren Potenz; nur durch sie eine Hierarchie möglich" (p. 403 #987). The concept of such a hierarchy, a level of consciousness superior to the thinking of commonplace human life—which we have already seen includes reflection—functions in a way which is similarly expressed in the sense of the "place to stand" Archimedes required: "Zur Selbsterkenntnis fehlte es bisher an einem festen Puncte außer uns: Dieser wird durch die Hierarchie gegeben" (p. 406 #1031, 'For perception of oneself there was until now no fixed point outside ourselves: That is now provided by hierarchy'). The conclusion "Es giebt nichts Reelles als die Hierarchie" (p. 403 #996, 'There is nothing real but hierarchy') thus renders the priority of Fantasie quite explicit.

It follows also that this religious function of artistic productivity should be a major contradiction of the Messianic order which Benjamin attempts to ground in Reflexion. Indeed it can be shown that there is an immediate contradiction of the Messianic idea necessitated by Schlegel's position here.[4] The never-ending progressivity of imaginative production precludes any image of redemption in finality or completion. It offers, moreover, the central motif for what I set out to argue here, for he writes: "Die Unvollendung der Poesie ist nothwendig. Ihre Vollendung = das Erscheinen des Messias, order die Stoische Verbrennung. Hat die Fantasie den Sieg davongetragen über die Reflexion, so ist die Menschheit vollendet" (LN 2090. 'The non-perfection of poetry is necessary. Its perfection = the coming of the Messiah or the stoic burning. When imagination has achieved its victory over reflection, then humanity will have been perfected').

Our first concern in these forms of opposition to naive conceptions remains with the term nüchtern itself. The only occurence which Benjamin can utilize is in a letter from Novalis to Caroline Schlegel (Friedrich's sister-in-law). He quotes: "Ich fange an das Nüchterne aber echt Fortschreitende, Weiterbringende zu lieben" (Schriften II, p. 511, 'I am beginning to love that which is sober but genuinely progressive and furthering'). The word appears, in fact, twice in that letter, for towards the end he apologizes for the brevity of the accompanying letter to Friedrich (which contains no reference to soberness at all), explaining he is busy with his mining responsibilities "und . . . mit so vielen nüchternen Studien geplagt bin"[5] ('and . . . am plagued by so many sober studies').

What is more striking about this letter is Novalis' expansion of thoughts on his "mercantilischer Plan" and "der oeconomische Geist" ('mercantile plan' & 'economic spirit'), which he had already broached in an earlier letter written to Friedrich Schlegel (dated 10th December 1798, KS IV, p. 267-70). At this time, Schlegel himself is using such terminology in entirely commonplace ways, for he has been trying for some weeks to persuade Novalis to lend him 200 Talers. Later (March 1799) probably after reading what we know as number 1059 of the Allgemeines Brouillon fragments (KS III, p. 261), Schlegel responds with interest, asking him to develop the idea in an article for their journal, the Athenäum. Subsequently, it makes an occasional appearance as a weakly developed concept in some of the formulations in Schlegel's notebooks.

The wider context from which Benjamin drew his quotation reads: "Tiecks Fantasieen hab ich gelesen—So viel Schönes darinn ist, so könnte doch weniger darinn seyn. Der Sinn is oft auf Unkosten der Worte menagiert. Ich fange an das Nüchterne, aber ächt Fortschreitende, Weiterbringende zu lieben—indeß sind die Fantasieen immer fantastisch genug und vielleicht wollen dies nur seyn" (KS IV, p. 275, 'I have read Tieck's fantasies—There are so many beautiful things there, they could even do with a little less. The meaning is often managed at the cost of the words. I am beginning to love that which is sober but truly progressive and furthering---on the other hand the fantasies are always fantastic enough and perhaps need only to be so'). The mercantile or economic spirit is represented here specifically in the word menagieren, and in broader terms one cannot only see the pragmatic side of Novalis in this, but also a particular aspect of it which further divided the two men—the issue of communicability. He shows his concern with well-managed expression in some friendly criticism he wrote Schlegel the previous year:

> Deine Recension von Niethammers Journal hat den gewöhnlichen
> Fehler Deiner Schriften—sie reizt, ohne zu befriedigen—sie
> bricht da ab, wo wir nun gerade aufs Beste gefaßt sind—

Andeutungen—Versprechungen ohne Zahl—Kurz man kehrt von
der Lesung zurück, wie vom Anhören einer schönen Musik, die
viel in uns erregt zu haben scheint, und am Ende ohne etwas
Bleibendes zu hinterlassen—verschwindet. Augen haben Deine
Schriften genug—helle, seelenvolle, keimende Stellen—aber gib
uns auch endlich, wenn Du anders nicht ganz Künstler werden
willst—wo nicht etwas Brauchbares, doch etwas Ganzes, wo man
auch kein Glied mehr supplieren muß. (KS IV, p. 226)
('Your review of Niethammer's Journal has the usual flaws of your
writing—it stimulates without satisfying—it breaks off where we
expect the best part—indications—innumerable promises—In
short, one comes away from reading it like having heard some
beautiful music which seems to have evoked much in us, and then,
without leaving anything lasting behind—vanishes. Your writing
has eyes enough—bright, soulful, living places—but once and for
all, give us, even though you refuse to be an artist in any other
sense—if not something usable, then at least something complete,
where one does not have to supply the missing part oneself.')

Just how far Novalis fails to grasp Schlegel's intention in such
comments can be illustrated by recalling Athenäum Fragment no. 444, which
contrasts solidly with the view of music above: "Muß die reine
Instrumentalmusik sich nicht selbst einen Text erschaffen? und wird das
Thema in ihr nicht so entwickelt, bestätigt, variiert und kontrastiert, wie
der Gegenstand der Meditation in einer philosophischen Ideenreihe?" (KA
II, p. 254, 'Does a purely instrumental music not have to create a text for
itself? and is the theme in it not developed, confirmed, varied and
constrasted like the topic of a meditation in a series of philosphical
speculations?'). The idea of text, the idea of meaning, are quite different
here, and so also is the character of meditative thoughtfulness or
"soberness" which apprehends them.

Despite Benjamin's declaration that their 'close association makes the
inquiry into their mutual influence for the most part impossible; for the
present discussion it is entirely dispensable,' this crucial element reveals

itself as inextricably tied to just that aspect on which they can be most deeply separated. As we look more closely at those points on which the idea rests and construct a more solidly based picture of Schlegel's epistemology and his own mystical idealism, it should not be surprising that these positions fall outside the area defined by Novalis. In equal measure, it can be shown that they contrast sharply with the epistemological basis of the Köln Lectures also (or Windischmannsche Vorlesungen, as Benjamin refers to them).

Notwithstanding the unequivocal dislike expressed for this work, which is seen as revealing Schlegel's future dark descent into the service of Metternich and Catholic reaction, (he writes: "Oberwunden scheinen ihm seine ehemaligen Aussprüche über Humanität, Ethik und Kunst" p. 425, 'his former statements on humanity, ethics and art all seems to have been left behind'), Benjamin insists that it both confirms the validity of his judgement on the equivalency of Novalis' and Schlegel's views, and offers a separate source to make up the missing systematic account of the early years, because epistemology is the single issue on which no substantial alteration has taken place: "Aber die Erkenntnistheoretische Einstellung der vergangenen Jahre tritt hier zum ersten Male deutlich, wenn auch modifiziert, in Erscheinung" ('but the epistemological position of the past years appears here, albeit modified, for the first time'). From the Jena Lectures discovered by Körner, we know this is not correct, and the literary and philosophical notebooks further show that it was precisely in the area of epistemology that the principle change can be identified. The other material can be traced back in large degree to the earlier years in those notes, refuting Benjamin's contention that "Die Hauptmasse der Gedanken in diesen Vorlesungen ist neu . . ." ('The main body of the thoughts in these lectures is new . . .'), since the major modifications and developments actually follow in the wake of this primary factor.

Therefore I want to provide a case for the idea that despite the correct intuition on Benjamin's part that Schlegel, in his early Romanticism, was not an intoxicated subjectivist as in the naive and widespread view, the essential order and seriousness of his thinking may not be reduced to a kind of soberness which is set in simple contrast to it.

Instead, I want to assert that, although the task itself must be deferred, a full understanding of Friedrich Schlegel should be looked for elsewhere— outside the pervasive and stubborn rationalist opposition of soberness and intoxication. Nor may this soberness be assimilated to the Messianic view of an essence that will overcome the profane, i. e. an absolute with the power to reabsorb the fallen realm and bring closure to the Romantic mode of history.

A Foundation for Freedom

In justification of his method of substitution, Benjamin writes:

> Seine Theorie der Kunst, geschweige ihrer Kritik, ist auf das ent-
> schiedenste auf erkenntnistheoretischen Voraussetzungen fundiert,
> ohne deren Kenntnis sie unverständlich bleibt. Dem steht
> gegenüber, daß Friedrich Schlegel vor und um 1800, als er seine
> Arbeiten im "Athenäum," welche die Hauptquelle dieser Abhand-
> lung bilden, veröffentlichte, kein philosophisches System nieder-
> gelegt hat, in dem allein man eine bündige Erkenntnistheoretische
> Auseinandersetzung erwarten könnte (p. 424).

> ('His theory of art, to say nothing of its criticism, is most
> decidedly based on epistemological preconceptions, without an
> understanding of which it remains incomprehensible. At the same
> time, Friedrich Schlegel had not yet set out any philosphical
> system at the time up to and around 1800, when he published
> most of his pieces for the "Athenäum," which make up the primary
> source for this discussion, and in that system alone could one
> expect to find a concise treatment of epistemology.')

Following his appoinment at the University of Jena in June 1800,
however, Schlegel delivered a series of lectures on the subject of the
Transcendentalphilosophie which lasted from October 27th 1800 until March
24th, 1801. A handwritten text taken down at the time by a student
rewarded an exhaustive search by J. Körner in 1927, and was published
eight years later in an edition by him entitled Neue philosophische
Schriften. This document reveals a Herculean effort, though one not always

triumphant over obscurities, to establish an idealism in which the productive imagination is given the fullest and most unrestrained responsibility for the Real. No principle is set higher, and the singularity of a systematic truth with restrictive power is permitted no place in philosophy, which is "das Palatium der Erfindung" (KA XII, p. 95, 'the palace of invention'). He goes on to state in the boldest terms what the consequences of this position are: "Es gibt keine absolute Wahrheit—dies spornet den Geist an, und treibt ihn zur Thätigkeit. Alle Wahrheit ist relative; dem Satz ist beygeordnet: es giebt eigentlich gar keinen Irrthum" ('There is no absolute truth—this spurs the spirit on, and stirs it to activity. All truth is relative; from that it follows: there is actually no error'). The basis of this is the conviction that the division between thought and things is illusion. Schlegel opposes his idealism here to what he terms Dogmatismus, where theory and the empirical are distiguished. Thinking is therefore not subordinate to the Real: "Nach unserem System ist Wahreit das Reelle, in so fern es mit Bewußtseyn und Kraft gedacht wird" ('In our system truth is the Real, so far as it is thought with consciousness and energy').

Nor need thought itself be constrained in its production of unlimited reality:

> An den combinatorischen Geist, der zu substituieren ist der Erfindung, schließt sich an die Methode Experimentieren. . . . Die Sphäre des combinatorischen Geistes ist durchaus unbestimmt. Aber es muß eine Methode geben, nach welcher dabey verfahren wird. Diese Methode wird experimentieren seyn. Wer nach dieser Methode verfährt, der darf sich die kühnsten Versuche erlauben. Er wird gewiß auf Realität stoßen.
>
> Wie das Denken als Experimentiren zu behandeln sey, hieße den combinatorischen Geist bestimmen: wir haben das nicht erst nötig, unsere ganze Art zu philosophiren war schon so (p. 102).
>
> ('To the combining spirit, which one may substitute for invention, the method of experimentation is joined. . . . The sphere of the combining spirit is completely undetermined. But there must be a method according to which one may proceed. This method is experimentation. Anyone who proceeds by this

metnod may permit himself the boldest experiments. He will certainly hit on reality.

To say how thinking is to be handled as experimentation would be to determine the combining spirit: that we do not need to do, our entire way of philosophizing shows that.')

And from this absence of a singular fundament of truth, it follows quite consequentially that there should also be repercussions on communication, the realm where meanings coincide as understanding:

Ein absolutes Verstehen wird geleugnet in der Philosophie, die eine absolute Wahrheit leugnet. Der Idealist, da nur das Gleiche das Gleiche versteht, muß behutsam seyn, wenn er sich mitteilen will. Er muß sehen, ob diejenigen, denen er sich mitteilen will, denselben Begriff haben, wie er. Erkennen sie beyde die Realität, so wollen sie dasselbe, sey auch der Unterschied in den Worten noch so groß. Dieser wird sich auch bescheiden, den andern nie ganz verstehen zu wollen. Es ist unmöglich, daß sie einander absolut verstehen (p. 192-3).

('An absolute comprehension is denied in philosophy which denies an absolute truth. The idealist must be wary if he desires to communicate his ideas, for like only understands like. He must see whether those with whom he wishes to communicate have the same concept as he. If they both perceive reality, then they want the same thing, however great the difference in their words might be. The other will also accept the limitation of never wanting to understand him completely. It is impossible that they should understand one another absolutely.')

The new factor in the Köln Lectures departing from this position is a higher order of consciousness transcending and comprising individual subjectivity and manifesting itself in the latter as revelation. This superordinated transcendent presence constrains freedom and autonomy in the productive imagination, and generates a ground for the authority of revealed truth---a stark contrast with the ideas of textuality and meaning indicated here. It also led toward that rabid Catholic zealotry and political agitation to the dark side of Metternich which Benjamin rightly does not wish to associate with soberness.

And yet the logic of Christian authority suggested by Novalis' Die Christenheit oder Europa ('Christianity or Europe') can be seen to ensnare the strain of thinking in the mercantile or economic spirit, and by extension the whole line of reasoning along which Benjamin has decided to advance his thesis. That is, the orderliness of Novalis' epistemology, insofar as it is associated with the "soberness" of the mercantile spirit, is also implicated in the establishment of factors opposed to Schlegel's uniquely open outlook in the Athenäum period, no less than those trends Benjamin castigates in the Köln Lectures. The primary account of the mercantilischer Geist, given in Fragment no. 1059, shows that it corresponds with the Köln era movement toward an over-arching principle which transcends purely human capacities. It, too, is an absolute basis by virtue of which man may meet with man in the realm of thought and speech under the transcendental guarantee of an absolute truth. In order to raise and distinguish it from the common worldly bond of trade, Novalis must first set it apart from the material and human, that is historical, phenomena which go by that name: "Der historische Handelsgeist---der sklavisch sich nach den gegebenen Bedürfnissen—nach den Umständen der Zeit und des Ortes richtet---ist nur ein Bastard des ächten schaffenden Handelsgeists" (KS III, p. 464 #1059, 'The historical spirit of trade— which slavishly follows on given needs—which is determined by circumstances of time and place—is only a bastard of the the real creative spirit of trade'), but the two forms of economy are parallel in their establishing and elaborating a community, a garment of relationship which envelops the world as one body. In its special character, this idea posits a spirit which is universal and a-historical, but which subtends all history, determining historical achievements by drawing them forward toward a perfection formulated as its own perfect expression: "Der Handelsgeist ist der Geist der Welt. Er ist der großartige Geist schlechthin. Er setzt alles in Bewegung und verbindet alles. Er weckt Länder und Städte— Nationen und Kunstwerke. ER ist der Geist der Kultur—der Vervollkommnung des Menschengeschlechts" ('The spirit of trade is the spirit of the world. It is the grand spirit itself. It sets everything in motion and unites everything. It awakens countries and cities—nations and works of art. IT is the spirit of culture—the perfection of the human race').

The Messianism of this spirit, therefore, is also clear. But first and foremost it is set up as a factor which allows for the mediation of meanings between person and person only by its superordinated status above any activity of human kind. Thus, it is an element conspicuous by its absence in the Transcendentalphilosophie, where humanity itself is responsible for creation of the human world.

Nevertheless, there does exist an equivalent to this idea in Schlegel's work, but it is separate from metaphysics, and separate from epistemology. This is the concept of a new mythology. Benjamin does not deal directly or in depth with the motif in Begriff der Kunstkritik, but his use of certain quotations from Schlegel's Rede über die Mythologie ('A Talk on Mythology') invites us to reserve that area as one from which the essence of his procedure may also be drawn into view. Immediately after his citation from Novalis' letter to Caroline (from which he derives his term Nüchternheit), he goes on to write: "Auch hierfür gibt Friedrich Schlegel die extremste Formulierung: 'Das ist der eigentliche Punkt, daß wir uns wegen des Höchsten nicht so ganz allein auf unser Gemüt verlassen'"[6] ('Here too, Friedrich Schlegel gives the most extreme formulation: "That is the real point, that on account of the highest we do not rely quite so entirely on our temperament"'). While this may not sound exactly "extreme," it is still a sharp qualification of the vulgar notion of Romanticism. The context from which it is taken, however, is entirely consonant with the Transcendentalphilosophie inasmuch as das Höchste is not to be differentiated in principle from the freedom of the productive imagination. Mythology is conceived here as a kind of mediation of all such productions in a form which assists and supports individual creative efforts. Where it differs—profoundly- —from Novalis' concept, is in its historicity.

It is evident that the mercantilischer Geist is an absolute which precedes human consciouness, or at least any of its historical acts. Not so with this new mythology. What Schlegel calls for in the Rede über die Mythologie is very much the deliberate work of man—far more so than the spontaneous or unconscious growth of the older phenomenon of mythology, such as that of Greek antiquity in its own time: "Die neue Mythologie muß im Gegenteil aus der tiefsten Tiefe des Geistes herausgebildet werden; es muß das künstlichste aller Kunstwerke sein" (KA II, p.

312, "The new mythology must, on the contrary, be built up from the deepest foundation of the spirit; it must be the most artificial of all works of art'). As a human product, it can only be understood to the extent that the process of its production can be grasped with it. Because it is an expression in human terms of the human situation in the world—"Und was ist jede Mythologie anders als ein hieroglyphischer Ausdruck der umgebenden Natur in dieser Verklärung von Fantasie und Liebe" (p. 318, 'And what is this mythology if not a hieroglyphic expression of the nature surrounding it, transfigured by imagination and love')—it can be grasped or understood by another human consciousness only as an _act_ of representation. It is not a revelation vouchsafed by grace, nor a transparent transmission of any kind. There is never any direct presence of an absolute nature itself implied for such works. The world conceived as being _behind_ or anterior to its transfiguration in those representations is as always inaccessible and irrelevant to man, a sphere, as it were, of silence rather than another language, but out of which the magical process of creative genius renders the human tongue of mythology—the hieroglyphs in which form alone nature is perceptible.

The conditions under which the energy of that genius becomes active and purposeful are also a confirmation of the quality and essence of the delineation it effects. Where the community of culture, nation, work of art in Novalis is produced by the _oekonomischer Geist,_ the magic of creation is dependent in Schlegel on the priority of the community itself: "_Allein_ kann niemand die _Magie_ üben, wohl aber in Gemeinschaft können es die Menschen" (KA XVIII, p. 369 #579, 'No-one can practice magic _alone,_ but in a community people can do it'). It must be acknowledged that there is a measure of circularity here, too, for it appears that such association itself is not possible without some form of mythology as "mütterlicher Boden" ('maternal soil'). To be sure, the contemporary circumstance of poetry composed "gleichsam von vorn an aus nichts" ('as it were from a beginning in nothing') must be seen as a relative condition, concordant with the _Rede_'s description of its own times as falling into an old age to which the new center would bring rejuvenation, but there is a problem here to which Schlegel is not insensitive. It does leave the beginning of history trapped in the darkness of a contradiction.

The seemingly permanent state of transition in Schlegel's thought is rooted in precisely such loci, and here it is possible to identify a major factor in the development of his first systematic concept of revelation. The question of the beginning (and therefore the end) of history is taken up in two notes dated in 1799, the tension between which indicates the unfolding philosophic process that brought him to accept revelation in the later positions. But, by the same token, it demonstrates equally that this conclusion had not yet been arrived at, nor is it obviously inevitable at this stage that it shoud be. In the first case, he writes: "Anfang und Ende der Historie wird erst Mythologie fassen, mir verborgen bleiben. Nichts ist göttlicher als seine Gränzen zu kennen" (KA XIII, p. 257 #759, 'The beginning and end of history will only be grasped by mythology, but remain hidden to me. Nothing is more divine than to know one's limitations'), and then against this he protests: "Soll vielleicht der Anfang und das Ende der Menschheit ewig verhüllt bleiben? Das ist ein Ungedanke" (p. 361 #486, 'Should then perhaps the beginning and the end of humanity stay hidden for ever? That is a monstrous thought'). Nevertheless, he is still able to insist that "Alle Magie ist immanent d.h. der Mensch ist nur menschlich . . ." (p. 389 #825, 'All magic is immanent, i.e. man is only human').

Schlegel specifies in the passage immediately preceding where Benjamin cites that "extreme" formulation of the Romantic position: "Einen großen Vorzug hat die Mythologie. Was sonst das Bewußtsein ewig flieht, ist hier dennoch sinnlich geistig zu schauen, und festgehalten, wie die Seele in dem umgebenden Leibe, durch den sie unserem Auge schimmert, zu unserem Ohre spricht" (KA II, p. 318, 'Mythology offers a great advantage. What otherwise always escapes consciousness is visible to the senses and spirit here, held fast like the soul in the surrounding body through which it shines out for our eyes and speaks for our ears'). We should note, however, that even the simile of soul and body must be understood as indicating more (or perhaps less) than the conventional sense of an imperfect expression, or even an alienation, where this is a full relationship between two entities— particularly with the overtone of a work of God which could permit a Messianic perfectibility. Without doubt the "soul" here is not separable as an existent entity, for whereas the magic of creation proceeds on a positive basis in the context of a community, and therefore of other works, other creations, it is prosecuted "von vorn an aus nichts" ('from a beginning in nothing') in that degree to which the general basis of "mythology" is lacking. That which precedes, the essence to be made existent in the hieroglyphics of human creation, is a nothingness, a pure absence.

This necessary absence of a determining foundation to the new mythology makes its contents representations of a very particular kind. The distance between them and what is represented remains absolute and undiminished no matter how they might strive to capture and render visible an essence of "Truth." The representation thus does not reveal the nature of a separate Being, but only the result of an imaginative creation. Signification is then not given in the correspondence of that result to prior Being, but in what it reveals of its own production: "In der Mittheilung soll enthalten seyn, nicht immer eine Darstellung der Resultate, sondern der Art und Weise, wie sie entstanden ist. Die Darstellung soll also genetisch seyn. Die wahre Methode der Darstellung ist demnach genetisch, oder historisch" (KA XII, p. 102, 'Communication should not contain a representation of the results, but rather of the way in which it came about. The representation should be genetic. The true method of representation is thus genetic or historical'). Naturally, this transmutes the metal of all writings, whose status is no longer set according to their measure of "Truth." The hierarchy of authority dependent on that distinction between true and false gives way to the quite different order and hierarchy of poetic freedom "da die Wahrheit unendlich sey: daß der menschliche Geist vom Irrthum ausgehen muß" (p. 103, 'since it is an infinite truth that the human spirit must set out from a beginning in error').

This functions as the dialectical neutralization of what Schlegel terms "dogmatic" views---those claiming to represent the determinate nature of the universe. But in demonstrating they are necessarily deceived in the desire to make that claim, he does not reject or dismiss them. On the contrary. In place of the competitive struggle to assert truth, the old philosophers should all accept equality of status in the universal republic of poetry. Thus he cites Spinoza as having been driven from the house of philosophy as Saturn was forced from his throne by new gods, but he should "entkleide sich vom kriegerischen Schmuck des Systems, und teile dann die Wohnung im Tempel der neuen Poesie mit Homer und Dante . . ." (KA II, p. 317, 'put off the warlike accoutrements of the system and share a dwelling in the temple of new poetry with Homer and Dante . . .')

A Romantic Theory of Reflection

Benjamin's disposition toward the Romantic transmutation of tradition is far from positive. In the June 1917 letter to Gerhard Scholem, he criticizes its intemperate, promiscuous character: "Denn freilich ist die Romantik die letzte Bewegung, die noch einmal die Tradition hinüberrettete. Ihr in dieser Zeit und Sphäre verfrühter Versuch galt der unsinnig orgiastischen Eröffnung aller geheimen Quellen der Tradition, die unentwegt in die ganze Menschheit überströmen sollte" (Briefe I p. 138, 'For Romanticism is the last movement to take up and preserve the whole of tradition again. Its efforts, premature in that time and sphere, were committed to the unthinking and orgiastic opening of all the secret wellsprings of tradition, which were supposed to pour without hindrance into the whole of humanity'). Yet it can be argued that this perspective contains a double error, for not only does it seem to present an inadequate picture of what Schlegel is doing in his work at this stage, but it also overlooks a foundation present in the approach to tradition by which the concept of soberness may be grounded in a far more powerful and effective relationship with the textual material than that achieved in Der Begriff der Kunstkritik. The idea expressed in this passage that traditional sources are simply unleashed in an overwhelming, indiscriminate flood, misses the essential point in Schlegel's New Mythology, which is the dialectical relationship with all that it absorbs.

The indiscriminate envelopment of all contents, whether in physics, metaphysics, mythologies, or poetry, is not unentwegt, but mediated by their negation. The price of entry into New Mythology for any body of ideas is the sum total of all its authority as truth, or all the transcendental presence to which it may have laid claim in its prior state. The relationship between the religion whose essential function is to "neutralize the universe," and that of Schlegel's conception of mythology, which is to neutralize doctrine, is quite explicit in the notebooks' apodictic formula "Mythologie: theoretischer Philosophie = Religion: praktischer Philosophie" (KA XVIII p. 382 #742, 'Mythology is to theoretical philosophy what religion is to practical philosophy'). The multiplicity of neutralized contents as characteristic of mythology follows from this, just as the unity of the world to be aufgehoben by religion: "Der Hebel ist Symbol der praktischen Philosophie, das Prisma der theoretischen Philosophie" (p. 406 #1027, 'The lever is a symbol of practical philosophy, the prism that of theoretical philosophy'); or, put in terms of that "dogmatism" which, in particular, Romantic Idealism itself absorbs and negates: "Religion ist die nüchterne Form der Mystik; Mythologie die poetische" (p. 346 #302 'Religion is the sober form of mysticism; mythology the poetic'). That is, both religion and (original) mythology are transformed by the same counter-dogmatic moment of Schlegel's Romantic thought. Romantic religion is "Religion der Religion" ('religion of religion'), and New Mythology "Mythologie der Mythologie," in precisely the same sense that Schlegel describes Romantic poetry as "Poesie der Poesie."

Where Benjamin applies the word verfrüht, premature, to this effort, he makes us wonder about the point in time and conditions under which the recovery of past forms would satisfy him as legitimately and meaningfully accomplished. If such a question should induce us to speculate about this with regard to Schlegel's own development and his own evaluation of the problem, it inevitably returns us to the issue of revelation. The later studies of the history of culture and literature, especially the extraordinarily encyclopaedic Vienna lectures of 1812, are drawn up in a systematic framework of Catholic Christianity. Such an organizing core marks out the presence of tradition as quite a different modality from its earlier configuration. Yet we find the first stirring of that change whenever Schlegel is exercized by the absence of a transcendent center, and among the uncertain glances toward revelation which occur as early as 1799, we note one that is especially striking (and the emphasis is his own): "Die intellektuale Anschauung ist gleichsam das KATHOLISCHE Phänomen" (KA XVIII, p. 406 #1025, 'Intellectual cognition is really the CATHOLIC phenomenon'). Schlegel's feeling here for a theological basis of content and truth as the ground of human thought, invention and experience, once again appears as an unconscious vector in the direction away from the early Romantic thinking, falling in with the later opening to Catholicism.

Benjamin's letter continues: "In einem Sinne . . . sucht die Romantik das an der Religion zu leisten was Kant an den theoretischen Gegenständen tat: ihre Form aufzuzeigen. Aber gibt es eine Form der Religion??' (Briefe I, p. 138, 'In one sense . . . Romanticism tries to achieve with religion what Kant did for theoretical objects: to demonstrate their form. But is there a form in religion??).[7] His answer to this question, and the constructed point of contact in his discussion of the concept of criticism with the larger one of Messianism, are assembled in Begriff der Kunstkritik with skill and ingenuity. Nevertheless, the conclusion is not consistent with the totality of Schlegel's early writings touching this matter. Benjamin devises the principle of Reflexion as the fulfillment of the missing ground; it is put forward as the Medium in which the unending movement of progressive Universalpoesie takes place, and as such a priori and necessary (the Kantian aspect in the letter's formulation of the problem should be recalled here), providing a dimension of stability and even purpose to this change.

There Benjamin takes his stand: "Die Unendlichkeit der Progression darf also den Blick von der Bestimmtheit ihrer Aufgabe nicht ablenken, and wenn schon in dieser Bestimmtheit nicht eigentlich Schranken liegen, so könnte doch die Formulierung, daß es für 'diese werdende Poesie . . . keine Schranken des Fortschritts, der Weiterentwicklung . . . gibt,' irreführen") Schriften II, p. 497, 'The infinity of progression should not distract one from the determinate nature of its task, and even though limitations are not actually contained in this determinacy, it is also true that the formulation that "there are no limits to the progress, the continued development . . . of this evolving poetry," could be misleading'). The corrective for this misleading idea has been prepared for, with characteristic tactical vigor, as the absolute of a continuum of forms which it is the task of poetry to fulfill. The erroneous formula he quotes (from Ricarda Huch's Blütezeit der Romantik, Leipzig 1901, p. 112) has failed to emphasize what is most essential: "Denn sie legt den Ton nicht auf das Wesentliche. Wesentlich ist vielmehr, daß die Aufgabe der progressiven Universalpoesie in einem Medium der Formen als dessen fortschreitend genauere Durchwaltung und Ordnung auf das Bestimmteste gegeben ist" ('For this does not stress the essential factor. What is essential is that the task of progressive universal poetry is laid down most distinctly as the achievment of an increasingly precise orderliness in a medium of forms').

He follows this with a quotation from Athenäum Fragment no. 256: " . . . die Schönheit . . . ist . . . nicht bloß der leere Gedanke von etwas, was hervorgebracht werden soll, . . . sondern auch ein Faktum, nämlich ein ewiges transzendentales." What attracts our interest here is what has been left out, for the complete text reads:

> Der Grundirrtum der sophistischen Ästhetik ist der, die Schönhiet bloß für einen gegebenen Gegenstand, für ein psychologisches Phänomen zu halten. Sie ist freilich nich bloß der leere Gedanke von etwas was hervorgebracht werden soll, sondern zugleich die Sache selbst, eine der ursprünglichen Handlungsweisen des menschlichen Geistes; nicht bloß eine notwendige Fiktion, sondern auch ein Faktum, nämlich ein ewiges transzendentales (KA II, p. 209).
>
> ('The basic error in the aesthetics of sophists is in taking beauty merely for a given object, a psychological phenomenon. Certainly it is not just the empty thought of something which has to be brought forth, but at the same time it is also the thing itself, one of the primitive modes of action in the human spirit; not just a necessary fiction, but a fact, indeed an eternal and transcendental one.')

Benjamin's tactical elisions are clearly intended to isolate the idea of a fact as something determinate and permanent to support the argument of the Reflexionsmedium as a fixed ordering element in the Romantic conception of art. There is no reason to believe, however, that Schlegel has at this point abandoned the entire enterprise evidenced in the <u>Transcendentalphilosophie</u> or the notebooks. Beauty as a thought which is "zugleich die Sache selbst" ('at the same time the thing itself') reveals exactly the structure which would confirm Schlegel's view of representation as established in those sources. The nature of a "fact" must stand subject to appropriate interpretation in this spirit.

A fact in the commonplace sense would only imply a position of sophistry or "dogmatism," a false limitation of freedom by the claim that a particular representation might resist the validity or reality of others on the basis of a privileged correspondence to transcendent Being. Schlegel's usage is that of "mystical terminology," which obeys a different principle. No expression may oppress the religious reality of freedom, but must rather manifest it. The "fact" of beauty may not, therefore, be any more restrictive than the criterion of truth in its non-dogmatic or poetic version. Instead of that, the progressive universality of the fact of beauty or truth corresponds to the transcendental form of religion—that form which Benjamin queries in his letter of June 1916. This form itself is wholly one of becoming and not of being, and consequently is not specifically restricted in the ways that it might manifest itself.

Since it is not determinate and predictable in fixed terms it is expressed by productions of the imagination whose fluidity is best grasped by a cognitive process resembling divinations or religious prophecies. These, as history, are the manifested record of that form, which is why the historian is "a prophet facing backwards," and why, in the sequence "Zur Grundlage der Kunstlehre" ('On the Foundations of the Theory of Art') Schlegel notes: "Alle Lösungen der Antithesen und Antinomien dieser Grundlage können überhaupt nur historisch sein" (LN 188, 'All solutions to the antitheses and antinomes in this foundation can only ever be historical').

The situation built up here supports neither the ". . . Fortschreiten ins Leere . . . ein vages Immer-besser-Dichten . . ." (<u>Schriften</u> II, p. 497, 'Progress into the void . . . a vague always-writing-better . . .') which Benjamin attacks, nor the presence of ". . .das Absolutum, der Inbegriff der unendlichen, erfüllten Reflexion" ('the absolute, the quintessence of infinite, fulfilled reflection') which he proposes as a Messianic transparency and completion of the poetic medium. There is a task, if not a _telos_, in Schlegel's aesthetics, consciously and vigorously represented, but it is identified with the historical productions of the subject, rather than his Messianic clarification. In the Jena lectures, Schlegel states: "Schönheit mit Bewußtsein und Realität gedacht, ist Wahrheit. Also ist Wahrheit und Schönheit eins; alle Trennungen sind nur relativ" (KA XII, p. 95, 'Beauty thought with consciousness and reality, is truth. Therefore truth and beauty are one; all divisions are merely relative'), for the "fact" is that without any pre-ordaining principle both beauty and truth will be manifest in acts of a transcendent capacity of mind which, in freedom, is necessarily coincident with itself. These two are brought together in fulfillment of a task which is simultaneously the activity of representation and that condition of imaginative production which guards against the contraband of any content as a restrictive demand—"Daß jeder GEDACHTE GEDANKE wahr sey, ist gut um die Täuschung der Wahrheit zu vernichten" (KA XVII p. 407 #1041, 'That every THOUGHT THOUGHT is true, is good for destroying the illusion of truth').

Criticism by Fire

History is situated in the subject in the same form as Romantic poetry, "Poesie der Poesie;" it is "Geschichte der Geschichte" ('history of history'). But Benjamin must impose a call to order here, a sacred objectivity of purpose as fulfillment of an ideal entity he perceives "als Kontinuum der Formen, als ein Medium, dessen Versinnlichung durch das Chaos als dem Schauplatz ordnender Durchwaltung schon bei Novalis begegnet ist" (Schriften II, p. 497, 'as a continuum of forms, as a medium whose embodiment through chaos is already met with in Novalis as the explicit site where the rule of order is established'). It is the desire to locate such a point of soberness which, paradoxically, compels him to strike out across spaces which no bridge of evidence may span, as with the citation of Novalis in demonstration of Schlegel's thought. The force of that same desire is at work where he brings forward a relationship to which he attaches colossal significance, even though he concedes it must remain a correspondence of spirit rather than a connection describable in philological terms, between the Romantics and Hölderlin's "heilignüchtern" poetry. It is in the name of das Heilignüchterne that he supports the Messianic claim made for the Reflexionsmedium in the soberness imputed to Schlegel.

But if that presence is chimerical in nature, it is nonetheless far more than simply a failure of reading. On the contrary, given the circumstances, it was a rather successful, albeit perilously balanced, achievement. The primary effort to change the general picture of subjective and intemperate formlessness in Romantic thinking certainly reveals a much more accurate insight into the process of progression than the obstinate prejudice Benjamin resists. Even if the developing trajectory of that thought was not determined by the Reflexionsmedium, it was a sober course—as Friedrich Schlegel makes clear in his choice of the parabola as a symbol. The path of this unlimited progression is a smooth and elegant curve, which Schlegel describes as "stretching away in clear constancy and regularity" (see Chapter One, p. 36). Even such startling errors as his drawing on the Romantic idea of prose for a supporting link in the thesis of the soberness of art would not have been open to emendation until access was gained to the Literary Notebooks. Only then was it demonstrable that the notion of the "prosaic" was no more expressive of sobriety than it was likely the author of Lucinde would have acknowledged Flaubert's Madame Bovary as a legitimate novel. Some of these were absent texts, and some essential features in the total philosophical fabric of Schlegel's Athenäum Period. The motivation that dictated they should be filled, and the methodology followed in the resolution of that task, must now be brought into the critical field of action.

As early as 1916, Benjamin gives a trenchant account of a conviction regarding the theory of criticism which is unquestionably significant for his work on Romanticism. Indeed, the letter in which it occurs reads almost as if it were the original program which was realized in Der Begriff der Kunstkritik. He speaks here of "das Licht Hölderlins" ('Hölderlin's light') in exactly the same sense as he does in the later work, where he writes: "Wie bei Frühromantikern gelegentlich das Licht als Symbol des Reflexionsmediums, der unendlichen Besinnung auftritt, so sagt auch Hölderlin: 'Wo bist Du Nachdenkliches, das immer muß zur Seite gehn,/ zu Zeiten, wo bist Du, Licht?'" (Schriften II, p. 508, 'Just as with the early Romantics light sometimes symbolizes reflection as a medium, and an infinite thoughtfulness, so Hölderlin also says: "Where are you, pensive ways, that always must step to one side,/ in these times, where are you, light?"')

The letter states that true criticism is not a matter of the distinctions which constitute or differentiate particular entities and outward forms, nor the points at which language represents any such distinctions, which is already far from the light, but something prior to language and contained in it as an origin: "Die Sprache beruht allein im positiven, ganz in der Sache die innigste Einheit mit dem Leben anstrebt; den Schein der Kritik, des κριων , des Unterscheidens von Gut und Schlecht nicht aufrecht hält; sondern alles Kritische nach innen, die Krisis in das Herz der Sprache verlegt" (Briefe I, p. 131, 'Language is vested solely in the positive, entirely in the thing which strives for the most intimate unity with life. It does not sustain the appearance of criticism, κριων, the separation of good from bad, but rather directs all critical work inward and sets up criticism in the heart of language'). Criticism, as he notes elsewhere of its image in Romanticism, is a mystical concept. For him, moreover, it involves the question of inner truth, a core of meaning which transcends its representation in language—to be laid bare as objectively real and present in a way we proposed could not be found in the early Romanticism of Friedrich Schlegel. The integrity of the text is therefore demoted. The intuition of light takes precedence in finding the freight of meaning over consideration of the hull of language: "Dies zu leisten ist Sache der äußersten Peripherie des Lichtkreises um jedes Menschen Haupt, nicht der Sprache" (ibid., 'Achieving this is a matter for the outermost periphery of the illuminated circle about each person's head, not of language').

This opens the text up to a vulnerability of profound significance, for just as Benjamin argues for the role of criticism as the realization of the text, its salvation in its own truth, he authorizes its destruction as outer form: "Die wahre Kritik geht nicht wider ihren Gegenstand: Sie ist wie ein chemischer Stoff der einen andern nur in dem Sinne angreift, daß er ihn zerlegend dessen innre Natur enthüllt, nicht ihn zerstört" (p. 132, 'True criticism does not oppose its object: It is like a chemical substance which only attacks another in the sense that by decomposing it, it reveals the other's inner nature rather than destroying it'). Thus, the actual practice of criticism as a worldly judgement of value is an alienation from its true function. Vested in the aspect of language as communication, it bears a burden of external "meaning" which is involved in the corruption and falsity of the fallen world. It knows only how to offer measures of "value" along a dimension which is spurious from the start.

It has become divided from its true role where it has submitted to the alienation of the body from the soul of fallen man. Only by abandoning the alienated dimension and returning to the heart of language can it fulfill its real task. That task, like that of the translator, is to recall an absolute mode of language, the divine correspondence of naming in the Adamic tongue described in Benjamin's Über die Sprache des Menschen. The inviolable nature of the soul in this hierarchy of the true and false has therefore left the body without any claim to defense or mercy. It may, indeed must, be sacrificed in a critical auto-da-fé, for the light of criticism is also fire. Its task is to divide the false from the authentic on the pyre of destruction: "Da erscheint dann die besondere kritische Magie daß das nachgemachte Ding mit dem Licht in Berührung kommt; es zerfällt. Das Echte bleibt: es ist Asche" ('The special critical magic is manifested when a counterfeit thing comes into contact with the light. It crumbles away. The genuine remains: it is ash').

The relationship derived from traditional Judaeo-Christian theology of the body and the soul both allies him with the Messianic principle of violence and destruction, the burning of bodies and of texts in pursuit of final truth, and sets him apart from Schlegel. In completing the context of that "most extreme formulation" Benjamin offers to support his thesis of a Romantic soberness of art, I also quoted the way Schlegel used the image of body and soul in justifying his New Mythology: "Was sonst das Bewußtsein ewig flieht ist hier dennoch sinnlich geistig zu schauen, und festgehalten wie die Seele in dem umgebenden Leibe, durch den sie in unser Auge schimmert, zu unserem Ohre spricht" ('What otherwise always escapes consciousness is visible to our senses and spirit here, held fast like the soul in the surrounding body through which it shines out for our eyes and speaks for our ears'). That which corresponds to the soul cannot be separated, for it does not exist in a separate state, it is a nothingness which eternally eludes consciousness.

Benjamin's criticism is like the conventional allegorical figure of justice, who must be blind. She may not look at the outer forms, the visible aspect of the deeds she weighs, for it is the inner essence of motive, desire and intent which must be sifted from the extraneous matter. But in the esoteric Gnostic tradition there is another version. Because the occult teachings of this ancient, pre-Christian lore hold, like the Transcendentalphilosophie, that the division between matter and spirit, body and soul, is itself illusion, esoteric justice possessing this wisdom needs no blindfold. And in like spirit, the Gnostic Christians of ancient times did not hold there was any value in martyrdom, and were immune to the lure of immolation at the hands of Roman persecutors.

The image of destruction of the spurious by fire is carried over into the letter of June 1917, with its lengthy discussions of Romanticism and the style of interpretation Benjamin feels is appropriate to it. Here, he attempts to identify this line with the thought of Schlegel himself, and then concedes: "Diese Worte finden sich bei ihm nicht, sie sind Interpretationen: aber die Romantik muß man (verständig) interpretieren" (Briefe I, p. 138, 'These words do not come from him. They are interpretations: but Romanticism must, judiciously, be interpreted').

Already at work on the project which was to be his dissertation, he writes: "Von einer Zusammenstellung Friedrich Schlegelscher Fragmente nach ihren systematischen Grundgedanken gehe ich aus; es ist eine Arbeit, an die ich schon lange dachte" (p. 137, 'I am starting out from a collection of Friedrich Schlegel's fragments put together according to their systematic foundation; it is a task I have been thinking about for a long time'). But it is the thoughts in that "systematic foundation" which can only be made out by a blinded eye, revealed in the pre-emptive flash of Messianic light. He also acknowledges that this manner of proceeding is conditioned directly by an absence of textual basis: "Sie ist natürlich rein interpretierend und welcher objektive Wert in ihr liegt bleibt abzuwarten. Auch sind die Grenzen für diese Arbeit durch die beschränkte Anzahl der wirklich auf das System hin zu interpretierenden Fragmente eng gesteckt" ('This is of course purely interpretive, and what objective validity it has remains to be seen. Also there are narrow limits to this project set by the restricted number of fragments which can really be interpreted as referring to the system').

He must depend on intuitions, gamble on hitting the correct formula of interpretation by blind judgement—and be guided by the absolute commitment that such a systematic core as he will construct must exist. With such a conviction to .cut his path across all evidence, present and absent, it was inevitable he should arrive at the conclusion he did, which was his starting point, the conviction itself. But that gamble on the missing texts is also an expression of an absence in the wider context in which Benjamin thought and wrote. This is the decay of tradition which he later described in his essays on Kafka and Leskov, or the letter to Gerhard Scholem of June 12th, 1938 (Briefe II, p. 756-64), the disappearance of wisdom, the advent of "progress." This was a kind of second Fall, separating mankind from the eternal aura of "epic" truth that was known when, as Lukács wrote in Die Theorie des Romans, the fire that burned in mens' souls was of the same substance as the fire of the stars. The longing for redemption in this condition may make it impossible to believe that there is no quarter from which that order of intercession might come. And the intensity of that longing and that gambler's conviction is the source of an equally intense rage and violence. All the false forms which hide the true essence, which hold it in chains and corrupt its workings, must be burned in the holy fire of criticism.

But early Romanticism was a unique moment in history, perched on the merest knife-edge of perhaps no more than five years, which saw the "epic" side of tradition as lost, yet not quite so lost that it could not be replaced by human agency alone. Therefore, where Benjamin's dialectic is a negation of inadequate forms to permit the appearance of a deeper (true) content, Schlegel negates that remote content access to which he regards as a false desire and illusory claim, in order to recover the nearer prize of a multiplicity of forms. These are human creations, human acts and therefore legitimately susceptible to our energies, whereas the Messianic side of history, so Benjamin specified in the Theologico-Political Fragment,[8] is independent of the sphere of human intentions. One can see this difference in an "objective" central meaning reflected even in the "Harmonie" of Novalis' fragments Benjamin reports, in the June 1917 letter, he is constructing to complement the work done with those of Schlegel. The very notion of Harmonie itself, though a profoundly Romantic concept, is also subject to Schlegel's desire to unburden manifest of their latent element of transcendent content. It cannot, as is most conclusively intended in Benjamin's project, imply an underlying absolute and fixed unifying presence, for the notebooks plainly state: "Die Harmonie ist die Seele des Wissens; aber ihr müßt sie nicht objectiviren und ein System der Wissenschaft fodern' (KA XVIII, p. 408, 'Harmony is the soul of knowledge, but one must not objectify it and demand a system of knowledge').

The light of Benjaminian criticism is of a singular nature, proceeding ultimately from the centrality of an absolute illumination. Restoration of this sun is the telos of the critic's labor. Schlegel fears such a construction of truth, because it entails a division between a primary and secondary being which is inevitably ranged against mankind—the world, experience, and productions of men and women. If that which is absent is contrued as higher and fuller being, rather than simply nothing, then what is seen and felt is indefensible dross, the fallen state. His revolution is directed against the idea of any such division, against all images of the one true light.

By eclipsing the final source of truth as "illusion," he rescues all theories, all creations and imaginings from the shadow of illusion. The alternative to that revolution looks bleak to him: "Kann es aber nicht auch vielleicht mit der Menschengeschichte ein recht elendes Ende nehmen sollen, halb tragisch, halb komisch, so daß nichts daraus wird, und diejenigen Recht hätten, die das Reich

Gottes schlechthin nur jenseits suchen?" (KA XVIII, p. 192 #789, 'Could it not be that human history will come to miserable end, half tragic, half comic, so that nothing comes of it, and those people prove to be right who only seek the Kingdom of Heaven in a world beyond?') On the same page of his notes he characterizes the positive form of human destiny, the successful revolution: "Die letzte Revolution der Welt wird eine unendliche Geburth, wo alle Sonnen sich in Licht verwandeln. Wenn alle Sonnen sterben, dann ist die Erlösung vollendet" (p. 192 #785, 'The last revolution on earth will be an unending birth, where all suns are transformed into light. When all suns die, then the redemption will be complete').

To cast one's lot in with an absent redeemer is a gambler's choice; it is also a choice of desperation. The gambler's position exhibits the ultimate stage of disaffection, for he does not want what he risks losing. The stake he lays against any odds is rejected as worthless, and the reward is not in the same visible currency as winnings, but in winning itself—the invisible sign carried in victory that fate has been mastered. Messianism, whether political or theological, is the symptom of a position from which no escape may be effected. It is a recognition that the Antichrist is in possession of the world, and one's life's strength is inadequate to oust him. The Messianic gambler, therefore, bets his life on the invisible, that it will be better, that it could not be worse. He no longer finds any reason to hold back as he plays out that single hand.

Here Nietzsche and Benjamin come together, both unable to justify anything that exists before the wheel under which everything is destroyed and replaced by such restitution as fate may produce, or as it must produce. For Schlegel, in those brief years, the hour of redemption had already struck in a unique guise. The world's life was not to be transformed by the entry of an alien presence from beyond, but by the penetration of a philosophy which could cut off such points of ingress, and eliminate the depredations of that transcendental thief—"dogmatic illusion." The magical power to do that was manifest in the Jena years. The circle was unbroken, the spirits strong, the clay of the triumphal vessel of Romantic poetry firmly grasped in the makers' hands.

But then the vessel was broken . . .

NOTES

[1] Friedrich Nietzsche, _Werke_, Hrsg. Giorgio Colli und Mazzino Montinori (Berlin: De Gruyter, 1972) Bd. III 1, p.368. ('But there is a kind of destruction which is actually an expression of that great longing for sanctification and redemption, . . . All existence which can be denied also deserves to be denied. True being means believing in an existence which cannot be denied and which is true and free of falsehood.')

[2] Walter Benjamin, _Briefe_, Hrsg. Gershom Scholem und Theodor W. Adorno, 2 Bde. (Franfurt am Main: Suhrkamp, 1966), Bd. I, p. 208.

[3] _Briefe_ I, p.135, addressed to his close friend Gerhard (later Gershom) Scholem.

[4] Although Benjamin does not cite it, Athenäum Fragment 222, discussed in Chapter I, p. 50, is perhaps the only reference which he might have used to establish the presence of a Messianic idea in Schlegel's theory of art and art criticism. Nevertheless, taken in the context of the religious project at large, the apparent Messianic goal referred to is without doubt a sort of limiting idea, the trajectory approaching it asymtotic. Being, in Schlegel's word, _elastisch_, it corresponds to the universal compass of the New Mythology, and is therefore an ironic desire whose effect, reducing all else to _Nebensache_, is to neutralize the error of other modes of finality in line with the general definition of religion in KA XVIII, p. 71 #516. It cannot be convincingly argued to imply a realizable finality itself.

[5] Novalis, Schriften, Hrsg. Paul Kluckhohn und Richard Samuel, 4 Bde. (Stuttgart: Kohlhammer, 1975), IV, p. 276. This edition henceforward cited as KS.

[6] Schriften II, p. 511. This occurs in the section of Gespräch über die Poesie entitled "Rede über die Mythologie" ('A Talk on Mythology'). The edition giving Benjamin access to this material, and other important texts, including most of the fragments, was Friedrich Schlegels Jugendschriften, Hrsg. Jakob Minor, 2 Bde. (Wien: Konegen, 1906). That quotation is from p. 361, Bd II. In the Kritische Friedrich-Schlegel-Ausgabe it is in KA II, p. 318.

[7] Kant does in fact receive rather significant mention in Begriff der Kunstkritik, but the letters indicate that this work was in fact something of a substitute for a study of Kant which he had to postpone because of the difficulties involved. Suggestions of this occur in Briefe I, p. 137, 150, 158-9, 161, 165, 174, 176, and 180, where he writes: "Die Aufgabe wäre, Kants Ästhetik als wesentliche Voraussetzung der romantischen Kunstkritik in diesem Sinn zu erweisen" ('The task would be to show Kant's aesthetics as the essential premise of Romantic art criticism in this sense').

[8] Reflections, p. 312. There is some uncertainty as to the date of this item. It may have been written as late as 1938, but in any case recalls thinking of the period in which the dissertation was written, referring to Ernst Bloch's Geist der Utopie, a book Benjamin read in December 1919 (Briefe I, p. 217), and whose author he had met in Bern in 1918 (ibid., p. 218).

CHAPTER III

BETWEEN INTOXICATION AND SOBERNESS

Nur ein Teil der Kunst kann gelehrt werden, der Künstler braucht sie
ganz. Wer sie halb kennt, ist immer irre und redet viel . . .

Goethe, Wilhelm Meisters Lehrjahre[1]

The Cynic

During those electrifying years he spent in Jena, Friedrich Schlegel
was known among those closest to him as a "hypermystischer,
hypermoderner Hyperzyniker"[2]—a hypermystical, hypermodern hypercynic. The
designation is apt indeed, for it conveys that uninhibited espousal of tendencies
which he pursued with contradictory consistency to their diverse extremes in their
various directions. The resultant picture cannot be expected, of course, to form a
stabilized unity, but neither is this to be interpreted as a lack. Where the image of
a simple and unchanging reality is regarded as an unwarranted prejudice, as it
unequivocally was by Schlegel, it is conventional orderliness which is the lack. The
lines of investigation he follows are accordingly not set to converge within the
established range of a finite compass, but to lead on through an infinite array of
possibilities. This is the principle of "modernity" itself which he begins to propound
very early, even before the inception of his Romantic period proper. It is
elaborated in his Ueber das Studium der griechischen Poesie and Die Griechen und
die Römer, where the contrast between the endliche Realität of the ancients is
distinguished from the unendliche Realität of the contemporary age (see Minor I, p.
82).

The early notebooks also develop this idea, but begin to give it a philosophical rather than purely historical slant, for the focus and singularity of viewpoint in the poetry of antiquity is there discussed as misleading, and a failure of the understanding. The simple polarity of subjective and objective as it had been applied with such assurance in characterizing the art of antiquity as "classical" is deftly undermined, and with it the implicit order of value: "In Rücksicht auf die Poeten scheinen die alten Gedichte nur objectiv und sind höchst subjectiv. Die modernen sollen subjectiv scheinen, und objectiv sein . . ." (LN 991, 'With regard to the poets, the ancient poems appear purely objective and are most subjective. The modern should appear subjective and be objective'). This follows because the appearance of "objectivity" in the uncritical sense of adherence and adequacy to an independent, external world posits a singularity and uniformity for the scheme of things which is itself pure invention. It is therefore (in Schlegel's conception) less in harmony with the necessary contradictions and fluid variety of the real, than a form which reflects those characteristics (although this may not be so easily achieved, since he adds "das kann man nur von sehr wenigen sagen"—'that can only be said of a very few'). The terms are therefore reversed for "modern" conditions as Schlegel sees them. The apparently conflicting positions of the cynic and the mystic may be read within the "modern" form of objectivity as complementary phases of the polyform real, and therefore brought together in that common function. He argues in the philosophical notebooks that mysticism is, in fact, far more susceptible to accomodation with the infinite form of the objective because, unlike the other two tendencies of "dogmatism" Schlegel criticizes— eclecticism (or empiricism), and scepticism—it is that which is least embedded in the false version of objectivity through being, precisely, the most "unworldly." Thus, the very fact that mysticism eschews "worldly" criteria of validity is both its claim to strength in the new cast of objectivity, and the locus of its connection with cynicism. It is quite wrong, therefore, to regard the lack of "rational" support in the phenomenal sphere for the mystic's claims as a failing, since it reflects commitment to an absolute which is fully separate from the illusory fixity of rationalist or empiricist criteria:

Die Mystiker sind Meister in der Urwissenschaft des Absoluten. Daß die Beschäftigung mit dem Absoluten sie ganz absorbiert und

sie in der Welt durchaus unfähig macht und ungeschickt ist sehr
begreiflich. Sehr unkritisch ists ihre Denkart desfalls bloß
pathologisch erklären zu wollen (KA XVIII p. 7 #39).
('Mystics are masters in the fundamental knowledge of the
absolute. It is altogether understandable that their concern with
the absolute absorbs them completely and makes them quite inept
and incapable in the world. It is thus very uncritical to seek
only a pathological explanation for their way of thinking.')

Refusal of the world in this way is not to be regarded as a spirit of
unconstrained credulity, since the empiricist or eclectic shows much
greater credulity where he accepts as final the evidence of his senses. To
be sure, mystics are "dogmatic" in positing singular views of their own, but
in rejecting the illusory simplicity and solidity of the world, they display
methodological stringency and rigor rather than incapacity: "Sie sind also
nicht aus Unvermögen ungeschickt, sondern aus Vermögen" (ibid., 'They are
therefore not inept from a lack of ability, but from a plenitude of ability').

The "modern" objectivity of an infinite reality is necessarily opposed
to the partiality of a finite one, which is exclusive and sets itself against
alternatives. The false objectivity rooted in "dogmatism" can only subsist
in the positing of one view over any other. It must ascribe truth to itself
alone, in the assertion of a finite or closed unity in place of that open or
infinite unity which is the nature of a multifarious and unlimited reality.
This is alien to the way Schlegel conceives the role of philosophy:

Das Wesen der Philosophie ist die Allheit des Wissens zu suchen.
Darin liegt schon die Verneinung alles willkührlichen Setzens (was
dem Wissen entgegensetzt) und alle Widersprüche (was der Einheit
und also der Allheit entgegensteht). (p. 13 #101)
('The essence of philosophy is to seek the universality of
knowledge. This includes the negation of all arbitrary positing,
which is the opposite of knowledge, and all contradictions, which
are opposed to unity and thus to universality.')

Here mysticism, of course, falls into the same error as the other two directions: "Also sind Skeptizismus, Empirismus, Mystizismus nur philosophierende Unphilosophie" ('Therefore scepticism, empiricism and Mysticism are just philosophizing nonphilosophy'). Nonetheless, the character of the error in the case of the mystic is less pernicious than both of the others for "er erzeugt seinen Widerspruch; jene lassen sich denselben geben—das ist Widerspruch in der dritten Potenz—es ist ein positiver Widerspruch. Der Empiriker baut auf die Leere, auf negative Widersprüche" (KA XVIII p. 5 #13, 'he creates his own contradiction; the others accept theirs from elsewhere---that is a contradiction to the third power---it is a positive contradiction'). The principles on which any of the "dogmatic" systems are based must be arbitrary, and therefore in Schlegel's view contradictory to the aim of the system: "Es muß sich a priori zeigen lassen daß man nichts willkührlich setzen kann, als das Widersprechende" (p. 13 #96, 'It should be possible to show a priori that one can can posit nothing arbitrarily except the element of contradiction'). That element in mysticism, however, is exposed, singular and visible: "Der Mystiker setzt nur einen Widerspruch, freiwillig zugebend daß es ein solcher sei . . ." (p. 4 #9, 'The mystic sets up only one contradiction, freely conceding that it is such . . .') Consequently, Schlegel notes in both fragments that this outlook is, compared to the others, "mäßig" or "nüchtern"—moderate or sober.

The argument here is reminiscent of the Athenäum Fragment 288, attributed to Novalis: "Wir sind dem Aufwachen nah, wenn wir träumen daß wir träumen" ('We are close to awakening when we dream that we are dreaming'). Recognition of ourselves as suffering confinement within a state to which there is a complementary alternative implies a real chance of becoming aware of and going forward into that exterior condition. The philosophical alternative to the unphilosophical "Rasereien," or frenzies, of which mysticism is the least noxious version, is expressed by various terms at different points in Schlegel's writings of this period. The context from which the cited notes were drawn (Zur Wissenschaftslehre, 1796) contrasts them to "Kritik," and, insofar as such dogmatisms are Unphilosophie, to the term Philosophie itself. Other expressions developed later, but which clearly belong in the same family, are absolute Polemik, Parekbase, Ironie, Religion, Urbanität, Liberalität, Freiheit and Cynismus. All valorize the liberating aspect of conscious contradiction, because the exoteric conflict leads one to the understanding of an esoteric, or infinite, harmony (in the 'universality of knowledge'), whereas an exoteric or finite consistency is impossible, and doomed to error.

The cynic is described, for example, as "der sokratische Heilige im Kampf gegen den Staat und Familienbande" (p. 203 #78, 'the Socratic saint struggling against the state and the bonds of family'), for the detachment he displays will disrupt even the dogmatic hold these fundamental concepts have over thought and understanding. Moreover, this determination is expanded to cover the procedure by which he accomplishes the task: "Wenn der Sokratiker tätig wird, so wird er Autor" ('When the follower of Socrates becomes active, he becomes an author'). This does not simply mean author in the sense of Schriftsteller, or writer, but as indicated in Lyceum Fragment 68, Urheber—initiator or innovator. That is, the way to set oneself free of a particular image or construct of the universe is to relativize it by creating another independently to set beside it. This is the only and essential way to accomplish the task of overcoming dogmatism: "Nur der Autor ist wahrer Priester und Taktiker und Oekonom nämlich Geistiger" (p. 203 #79, "Only the author is a true priest and tactician and economist, that is, man of the spirit').

This, as already noted, is also the pattern of New Mythology, and in that sign the character and role of the text is defended against the status accorded it by all the phases of dogmatism:

> Alle drei haben ihre eigene Sprache und doch protestieren alle drei . . . gegen die Terminologie. . . . Der Mystiker haßt nicht nur den Buchstaben, sondern auch den Begriff. Apologie des Buchstabens, der als einziges ächtes Vehikel der Mittheilung sehr ehrwürdig ist (p. 6 #15).
>
> ('All three have their own language and yet all three protest . . .against terminology. . . .The mystic not only hates the letter, but the concept as well. Apologia for the letter, which, as the only genuine vehicle for communication is highly honorable.')

Dogmatism in all forms is wary of language because words can never aspire to the full integrity of that Being whose presence it proclaims, nor express this Being adequately. Thus, although each terminological strategy conflicts with the other, they are all held at a protective distance from one another by a mutual incommensurability rooted in that inadequacy of the medium. It is therefore necessary, in order to set up the communication between system and system by which dogmatic privilege can be canceled, that language itself not be compartmentalized in each region by the inadequate function of reference. Overcoming dogmatism depends on negating this factor which blunts the sharp edge of their polemical weapons and brings up their critical sallies short, so that they are not able to fulfill their efforts at mutual disruption.

This is why Schlegel defends language and the letter, even though he is not in any way more inclined to ascribe an unphilosophical referential authority to it than the doctrines he describes. This also explains the purpose at work in the particular theory of terminology developed in the Jena Lectures:

> Ferner verbinden wir diskursiv und intuitiv, so erhalten wir die Terminologie. Es ist hier die Aufgabe, das Diskursive sichtbar zu machen. (Man hat sich aber hier unter Terminologie nicht das zu denken, was man gewöhnlich darunter versteht. Es bezeichnet hier den Ausdruck solcher Begriffe, die gleichsam einen Widerspruch enthalten. Z.B. Intellektuale Anschauung, transcendentaler Standpunkt, objective Willkühr pp.) (KA XII p. 19)
>
> ('Furthermore if we combine the discursive and intuitive, then we arrive at terminology. Our task here is to render the discursive visible. Yet one should not understand terminology here to signify what is usually meant by that word. Here it indicates the expression of those concepts which as it were contain a contradiction. For example intellectual intuition, transcendental standpoint, objective arbitrariness and so on.')

The division expressed by the symbol ⊂, the notion of paradox as exoteric expression of an esoteric connection, replaces the dogmatic division between substance and representation. There is, for Schlegel, literally nothing prior to representation because the absolute is nothingness, rather than presence. Even the division between Vorstellung and Darstellung, which results from the necessary limitation of language as communication, is not, therefore, significant here as a diminution of truth, since even if they became perfectly correlated, there would still be no closer approximation to an absolute substance as truth. The honorable function of writing as the vehicle of communication is not in communicating something, but in revealing the contradictory nature of the being of that thing. All linguistic constructs are commensurable because language, the visibility of the discursive, is always equidistant from the absent absolute, as are all phenomena of all kinds.

Intellektuale Anschauung, which Schlegel is also able to define as "das Bewußtseyn der prästabilisirten Harmonie" (KA XVIII p. 364 #519, 'consciousness of the prestabilized harmony'), is the understanding that all appearances are not Being, nor reflections of Being, but projections of non-Being, and therefore it is in that esoteric dimension that they correspond. The text, and all readings of it, cannot be secondary re-presentations of a prior presence, since all productions have equal status before the absence of the invisible absolute, which all express with equal versimilitude.

Language and textuality are clearly changed very radically by this view from that in dogmatism, both with regard to the penetrability and impenetrability of meanings. Even though the medium of the text can, conventionally, never wholly coincide with the signified Being, it is transparent enough, if it can be permitted to claim any real status at all in dogmatism, to make its reference discernible. This is called "understanding" the text. Schlegel writes: "Man muß sehr viel Verstand haben, um manches nicht zu verstehen" (p. 114 #1022, 'One must have a great deal of understanding in order not to understand some things'). One could say this is precisely the point achieved by the "hypermystischer Hyperzyniker," for he has penetrated by mystical intuition to the insight that there is no core as such which can be signified in that way: "Der

Schwerpunkt des Universums liegt im leeren Raum d.h. nirgends" (p. 419 #1192, 'The center of gravity of the universe lies in empty space, i.e. nowhere'). To "grasp" the center as meaning in the dogmatic sense is to fall into "Raserei"—madness. The fully developed reading passes that by; it is, so to speak, "not inept from a lack of ability, but from a plenitude of ability," for "Es gibt ein positives und ein negatives Nichtverstehen" (p. 129 #89, 'There is a positive and a negative non-understanding'). Thus the Schlegelian reader will typically "misunderstand" metaphysics as myth, and scientific theory as metaphor or analogy.

A text or reading, like any production, is consequently both subject to that limitation on its exoteric meaning, and at the same time gains in the individual autonomy of all phenomena as esoteric symbols or allegories of that absolute which cannot appear. This contrasts very noticeably with a view common in the Western tradition and generally considered closely identifiable with Romanticism, that the truth of poetry lies ultimately in the experience of the poet. There is a vision or inspiration which comes into being in his consciousness, and the reader has understood or realized the literary creation derived from it as he is able to recuperate that—as the real "content." Since, for Schlegel, the primary vision of genius is the "intellektuale Anschauung," intellectual intuition or inner cognition, of nothingness, the correctly read text should lead beyond experience to that esoteric focus apart from all phenomena, inner and outer, and the necessary correspondence is coincidence at that point. Therefore its function of "Mitteilung" is not dependent on understanding the "dogmatic" aspect of its content or import, including the supposed Romantic emphasis on the inner aspect of life as subjective experience, or its projection into the natural universe. This is highlighted in a comment by Schlegel which, once more, reminds us to be wary of assuming simple generalities of that kind about the term "Romanticism:" "Meine Hauptideen über die Natur sind mythologisch---die romantische Vergötterung des Lebens davon verschieden" (KA XVIII p. 290 #1131, 'My main ideas on nature are mythological—the Romantic deification of life is different from that').

Astrology and the Occult

The distinction to be drawn between Schlegel's concept of textuality and those which stand in opposition to it thus inevitably divides his work from the image of Romanticism which has arisen in the traditional framework. And this, as we have seen, has already been foreshadowed in Walter Benjamin's thesis of the soberness of art in early German Romanticism, and with the quotation from Kircher to the effect that "These Romantics wanted nothing to do with the 'Romantic.'"

The traditional picture of Romanticism is constructed at one end of such axes of contrast as subjective-objective, personal-general, irrational-rational, emotional-real and so on. All these cover slightly different ground, but they run essentially parallel to one another. They also run parallel to the opposition romantic-classical. This is certainly not part of Schlegel's understanding, for in most cases he uses the term klassisch, clearly separable from the historical designation die Antike or die Alten, to signify that which has fulfilled its individual character. He notes, for example: "Nur wer classisch gelebt hat verdient eine Biographie" (LN 665, 'Only a person who has lived classically deserves a biography'). Romantic poetry, as a historically new departure with its own character, can also be "classical" in that sense without resembling antiquity in any way: "Die Alten können künftig einmahl in dem Classischen selbst übertroffen werden" (LN 111, 'In the future the ancients may even be excelled in the classical quality of their work').

Although the axis sober-intoxicated as normally understood also echoes and reinforces all the other polarities which seem to situate romanticism—whether as a historical period or as a recurrent mode or tendency—it, too, is equally inapplicable to Schlegel. The unilinear logic here compels Benjamin, in Der Begriff der Kunstkritik in der deutschen Frühromantik, because it sets Schlegel apart from the ecstatic or somnambulistic proclivity of some romanticism, to associate him with "die Kunsttheorie eines so bewußten Meisters wie Flaubert, die der Parnassiens oder diejenige des Georgeschen Kreises . . ." (Schriften II, p. 511, 'the art-theory of such a conscious master as Flaubert, or that of the Parnassiens or of the Stefan George Circle . . .'), but this is completely unhelpful. It leads to no insights on him at all, for such patterns of opposition are based on a system of principles from which Schlegel has quite evidently and elaborately taken his distance.

Fortunately, in his later writing on Surrealism, and elsewhere too, Benjamin develops his views on the concept of intoxication to a point where the whole issue may be considered more deeply. Unlike the question of romanticism and classicism which, unless pursued as a relatively simple matter of historical categorization, tends to resolve itself into other issues, the opposition of intoxication and soberness persists and expands when it is lifted from its basis in common assumptions, and takes on extremely complex features. The nature of what is involved here is not restricted to questions concerning Romanticism, of course, but the contrast between Schlegel's thinking and the frequent association made linking romanticism and intoxication offers a useful point at which to apply a critique. This becomes especially interesting when that critique is applied, like Benjamin's, within a Marxist framework which gives absolute priority to considerations of concrete social change and material justice.

The simple, commonplace sense of the term "romantic" is called on in the essay on the Surrealists, when Benjamin castigates them for the "pernicious romantic prejudices" that "the aesthetic of the painter, the poet en état de surprise . . . is enmeshed in,"[3] and describes their fascination with the black arts of occultism and satanism as "a romantic dummy" (Reflections, p. 187). He is quick to perceive that the turning away from standard forms of bourgeois reality which this represents still functions within the bourgeois orbit because it does not, in fact, efface the particular boundary between the irreal and real which it transgresses. On the contrary, it depends on that artificial and ideologically constructed division.

The surprise, the shock, the excitement and novelty of transgressing the boundary between order and its opposite depend on an upending of the system which may not only be without any practical effect on it, but need not in itself change or threaten it philosophically. This "romanticism," as the intoxicated counterpart of sobriety's everyday responsiblity toward what is "real," chooses for itself a separate region within the territory laid out and charted by bourgeois dogmatism. That rationalist structure itself is drawn upon for its prior separation from the "irreal," which defines and creates the alternative realm. The source and significance of the boundary itself is not grasped as anything other than "natural"; thus the movement unwittingly deprives itself of a chance to make a far more radical penetration of the reigning conditions which it purports to oppose. Unlike Schlegel's progressive Romanticism, it remains at a standstill. The very separation by which it constitutes itself, maintains a status of incommensurability in which both sides are unable to make any advance in their conflict with each other. As with the "Unphilosophien" criticized by Schlegel, "Wechselerzeugung," mutual production (see KA XVIII p. 3 #1), going hand in hand, goes nowhere.

In this paralysis, Benjamin brings a dialectical solution essentially similar to Schlegel's New Mythology, for it promises to break down the isolation which holds each side in its unfruitful state, and allow them to react on one another. The Surrealist enthusiasm for the illumination of intoxication, whether in the form of drug-induced visions, or the occult divinations of automatic writing, seances or other portents, is a retreat into spiritual ecstasy from which a point of egress is not easily found. In this respect it is a precise counterpart of the bourgeois rationalism from which it divides itself, since for its part, the world of the "everyday," of "soberness," with its ideology of empirical evidence and causality, is built into an equally hermetic system by which the workings and effects of its own prejudices are supressed within that enclosure, and nothing may penetrate and disturb its harmonious circle. Benjamin protests that:

> Any serious exploration of occult, surrealistic, phantasmagorical gifts and phenomena presupposes a dialectical entwinement to which a romantic turn of mind is impervious. For histrionic or fanatical stress on the mysterious side of the mysterious takes us no further; we penetrate the mystery only to the extent that we recognize it in the everyday world, by virtue of a dialectical optic that perceives the everyday as impenetrable, the impenetrable as everyday (Reflections, p. 189-90).

The "dialectic of intoxication" which he goes on to describe, cancels both those elements as autonomous worlds, the bourgeois ideological order and its opposite, occult illumination, as well. To the extent that this mutual disruption clears away a polarity of opposed errors, it is consistent with Schlegel's "cynicism." But inasmuch as Benjamin regards this clearing process as making way for a material and political objectivity which he calls "profane illumination," the parallel ceases to be anything like so direct. This objectivity is rooted in the world as a finite sphere of social praxis, which does not correspond at all with the "infinite reality" of the productive imagination, or that objectivity in Schlegel's modernity which takes the form or appearance of subjectivity.

The contrast with Surrealism is, nonetheless, very much sharper. Here one can hold to a definite and complete distinction in which no rapprochement with New Mythology is possible at all. The realm which appears to the Surrealist in the illumination of intoxication or in the ecstatic revelations of occult experiences is a quite particular discovered aspect of Being, and not, as it would be interpreted by Schlegel, an invented allegory of non-Being. Thus, André Breton writes in the opening pages of the first Surrealist Manifesto: "It was, apparently, by pure chance that a part of our mental world which we pretended not to be concerned with any longer---and in my opinion by far the most important part—has been brought back to light."[4] Breton gives higher, or truer, status to the domain of this part of the mental world, not to any inventive imagination which produced it. It is discovered, after all, by chance, he says, not by an imaginative or productive act. Schlegel, on the other hand, moves in the opposite direction, for in abandoning the metaphysics of Being (or presence), he is brought to recognise that all knowledge is "occult" by one and the same principle. There is an inherent equality in the humanness of its origin. It is always "divinatorisch," "Allegorie," or derived "as it were from nothingness" as a matter of epistemological necessity.

The difference between his concept of the occult and that of the Surrealists is therefore essentially that separating dogmatic from critical mysticism (or "mystical cynicism"). When Schlegel writes about Magie or Astrologie, which of course figure prominently in his work, there is a radical contrast between his usage and the vulgar versions adhered to by Surrealism. Indeed, there is no difficulty in reconciling that aspect of Romanticism with Benjamin's acute dislike of such "spiritualist" involvements, as when he asks: "Who would not wish to see these adoptive children of the revolution most rigorously severed from all the goings-on in the conventicles of down-at-heel dowagers, retired majors and emigré profiteers?" (Reflections, p. 180). This seedy company is sunk in Raserei, and has nothing to do with Schlegel's Romantic Bildung.

Though Schlegel writes: "Die Astrologie ist erhaben über alle Methoden" (KA XVIII p. 355 #414, 'Astrology rises above all other methods'), this may not be interpreted in any crude or popular sense. There is no question here of a meaning in the configuration of the heavens which indicates something in the mode of information. The skies are not read by some fixed rule of grammar in which a presence to which the visible forms are bound may be brought forth. Quite the reverse, in fact, for all configurations are symbolic or allegorical of the intellektuale Anschauung of nothingness, and those of the heavenly bodies no less so. The correspondences by which they are interpreted are pure analogy, and thus exemplary for their absence of content in the (false) "objective" sense which would imply, and be implied by, the singularity and unitary cohesiveness of a system. The empirical observation of the heavens, or any constellation of phenomena, offers the basis for analogic connections which may be constructed between them, but these are not discovered truth which systematically militates against contradiction:

> Außer der Empirie ist das Geschäft des Physikers Analogie, die nur
> wo großer Vorrath von Empirie ist, fruchtbar sein kann. Hier ist
> Synthese für Dynamik und Astrologie. Sie muß nur Analogie
> bleiben, nicht System werden wollen (p. 168 #527).
> ('Apart from the area of empirical observation, the business of the
> physicist is analogy, which can only be fruitful where there is a
> great supply of empirical information. Here we have the synthesis
> of dynamics and astrology. But it must remain analogy, not strive
> to become a system.')

The dynamic productions of the astrological method belong to that infinite reality which is erhaben, or sublimated, above the limitations implied by a separate, fixed world as presence. Neither interpreted phenomena, nor the textual representations in which they are gathered up, need have the grammatical or systematic consistency of correspondence to a finite sphere which must appear through them. The modern condition has left that behind.

> Die Ansicht der Menschheit aus dem Standpunkt des Universums oder Natur nicht mehr philosophisch und poetisch, sondern magisch und astrologisch. Magie ist mystische Grammatik, Astrologie ist mystische Physik (p. 253 #719).
> ('The view of humanity from the standpoint of the universe or nature is no longer philosophical and poetic, but magical and astrological. Magic is mystical grammar, astrology is mystical physics.')

And this is clearly a critical mysticism which does not discover a second world, but cancels the illusion of any such presence. The revelation or illumination of Schlegel's mysticism and his occult forms is not that of a hidden world, but the nothingness which any "world" will hide: "In der Mystik erscheint die Welt als Nichts, in der Mythologie als Spiel oder Poesie" (p. 359 #467, 'In mysticism the world appears as nothingness, in mythology as play or poetry'). Therefore, when he writes "Symbole sind Zeichen, Räpresentanten der Elemente die nie an sich darstellbar sind" (p. 420 #1197, 'Symbols are signs, representatives of elements which may never be protrayed in themselves'), this does not refer to obscured Being, but still to non-Being. The forms of astrology, of the method of analogy, constellation and combinations, are not indications of a truth, but only of themselves as pure constructs, and the nothingness of which they are ultimately representations.

Since neither meanings, nor phenomena in any modality, are the parousia of transendent Being, there is no reason why Schlegel should follow the Surrealists in seeking out "wise women" to read the true import of signs. It is quite certain, when we read in Nadja about Madame Sacco's warning to Max Ernst on which clairvoyant basis he decides not to draw the girl, that this is "romanticism" of a quite different order. The superstitious behavior which so disgusts Benjamin in a Surrealism which pursues the vulgar notion of a second reality among seers, or clings to it in spiritual transports, has no connection with Schlegel at all. He would discard all aspects of visionary rapture which adhere to the undialectical conception of intoxication, plainly regarding it as no less void than does Benjamin. Neither man's view concedes anything to the idea that intoxication carries revolutionary power purely in itself, that its potential may be realized solely by the transposition of consciousness to this newly-discovered antipodal continent.

The profound difference between him and Schlegel lies in what Benjamin envisages beyond its dialectical transformation, or the end to which he would employ the potential which such rapture does possess for producing revolutionary change. Benjamin's concept of "profane illumination" contains an idea of grammaticality, of reading phenomena in the social and material sphere, which is much more closed and specific than Schlegel's mysticism. The dingy aspects of existence among Breton and his cohorts are signs to be read as indications of something quite precise and concrete about the world, and released into political life as the disruptive consciousness of what is unequivocally true about it. Sadly, Benjamin still finds the Surrealists largely unequal to this chance—so long as they are caught in the quagmire of that fundamental error concerning the power of the occult. The grievous delusion which has brought them into the conventicles of the lost and helpless seekers after illumination, is the weakness in their movement which, lacking an unequivocal political discipline and purposefulness, taints and cripples their conception of intoxication, and delivers up to impotence the emphatic freedom of which they are determined to be exponents.

Nevertheless, while he sees little good in this tendency in itself, the forces which bring the poet into such insalubrious company do figure as part of a larger picture of marginalization and alienation out of which the real dialectical moment may spring—a medium of social and political realities which make the hostile withdrawal and resentment implicit in emphasizing the "irrational" far more insidious and far more dangerous to established conditions. The original character

138

of Surrealism is "contemplative." It withdraws from the political factor on which the bourgeois claim to legitimacy depends. Its revolt, where it manifests itself with any direct impact at all, is mainly in the direction of "crime," an offense against that order, but one which does not carry the threat of an alternate political legitimacy to dethrone it. (For example, at the end of Nadja, André Breton calls for murders of asylum doctors by mental patients.) Yet, at the same time, the radical image of freedom which is nurtured by their ecstatic transports does contain the possibility of becoming active. There is the chance that it may reach into the political foundations of bourgeois ideology, causing them to crumble until the structure still in command over the practice of Surrealism will also sag and collapse.

From the Surrealist side, intoxication is an objective movement away from the false, deceptive restriction of the bourgeois Real which has calumniated the realm characterized by rapture and reached in dreams as inferior and void. It is not the loss and retreat by which "intoxication" is defined in bourgeois terms, but gain and advance by rejection of those chains binding thought to a lop-sided conventional view. Benjamin perceives the dual thrust of such raptures as their redeeming feature. There is potential here not only for an immediate gratification in momentary experience, but an extension through the latter of negative toxicity affecting the broader bourgeois reality in which it is contained. That is, Surrealist intoxication is also a poisoning. Its power may do more than please and delight the artist who indulges in it. There is a corollary effect also for those areas in his existence in which he continues to depend on and profit by his relationship with the first reality, his identity as a bourgeois class-member. Partaking in such trances is not without its influence on that basis which both sustains him, and keeps him from completing his emancipation. "In the world's structure," Benjamin declares,

> dream loosens individuality like a bad tooth. This loosening of the self by intoxication is, at the same time, precisely the fruitful, living experience that allowed these people to step outside the domain of intoxication (p. 179).

From this point of view, that is, the disruption introduced by the unreal, by dabbling in what is in itself empty, flows back through the barrier thus breached and reveals a much more important complementary emptiness in the ideological reality from which the movement took its departure. This influence, weakening the solid stone holding up the everyday world, was realized insofar as "the threshold between the waking and sleeping was worn away in everyone as by the steps of multitudinous images flooding back and forth . . ." (p. 178).

Benjamin hopes, and believes he can already perceive as an incipient development, that this should produce a positive political response in the intelligentsia. The world emerges as fraught with irrationalities and monstrosities from this erosion of the cultural bounds whose integrity had hitherto preserved its form as the necessary and natural state of material existence. Those who are in a position to receive this revelation should be mobilized toward social transformation in much the same manner as the proletariat, to which that lesson is taught through the direct impact of social conditions themselves.

But "This profane illumination did not always find the Surrealists equal to it, or to themselves, and the very writings that proclaim it most powerfully, Aragon's incomparable Paysan de Paris and Breton's Nadja, show very disturbing signs of deficiency" (p. 179). These authors continue to seek intimations of "truth" in their second reality, and persist in obeying its fascination, while letting the messages concerning the profane world, which they turn up on those same wanderings through the shabby side of Paris, go unnoticed and unread. To reach this necessary effect of insight into the first reality, Surrealism must exchange the spurious comfort and optimism of that second truth for an equal and opposite pessimism about the world whose emptiness initially propelled it into the search for freedom and veracity in that other emptiness.

Despite his own hopeful evaluation of the potential of the movement, and the overt signs of its increasing sympathy towards Communism—part, of course, of a general tide among bourgeois intellectuals during that period— Benjamin is under no illusion regarding the scope of what it still had to learn and unlearn. Its internal politics, which led to the attack on Breton Benjamin was able to observe at close quarters in Paris shortly after the essay was written (see Briefe II, p. 507), and which are described in the Second Manifesto of Surrealism, give vivid confirmation of this. The "romantic" vices of individual arbitrariness had not been surpassed. The continued addiction to "that most terrible drug—ourselves— which we take in solitude" (Reflections, p. 190), combined with a narcissistic weakness in many who had to be reminded by Breton that "The approval of the public is to be avoided like the plague" (Manifestoes, p. 177), still mark Surrealism as a limb in the intricate and varied elaboration of bourgeois literature.

Whether or not the "dialectic of intoxication" is to be successfully set in motion, Benjamin's essay is quite explicit about the goal to which it is to be brought, and in which it will find its only redemption. But in the finality of that goal, Benjamin opposes himself to the metaphysical and epistemological positions represented by Schlegel. The materialist "world of universal and integral actualities" (Reflections, p. 192) which emerges with the negation of bourgeois ideology, appears to be an uncompromising version of "metaphysics of presence." Indeed, it also bears an unmistakable relationship to a prelapsarian condition of singular and unmediated Truth, and it would be easy to read it simply as an essentially Messianic restoration of the plenitude of manifest Being. It is proposed here, nevertheless, to resist this clear-cut conclusion and return to the question later in the light of additional factors which cannot be left out.

The concrete immediacy of reality which emerges in the condition of materialist redemption is indicated by the significance of the role of "image" which is to replace "metaphor" in the making of meanings. That change is correlative also with the displacement of contemplation by action, and the intellectual predominance of the bourgeoisie by contact with the masses (p. 191). The way to bring the bourgeois artist to this point is a matter "of deploying him, even at the expense of his artisitic activity, at important points in this sphere of imagery" (p. 191), for "That image sphere to which profane illumination initiates us" is the condition in which "reality (has) transcended itself to the extent demanded by the Communist Manifesto" (p. 192).

The question which imposes itself here in relation to Schlegel is whether this is a static picture of reality, in which the dialectical tension between Surrealistic ecstasy and established rationalism has simply resolved itself and come to rest, or whether, like the "permanente Parekbase" (KA XVIII p. 85 #668, 'permanent parabasis') of Romantic irony, there is the continued possibility of renewed division and progression. The patterns identified by Schlegel may be expressed for the purpose of contrast as the dialectic at a standstill in dogmatism, opposed to that in eternal movement of New Mythology or Transcendentalphilosophie. Does the materialist dialectic simply return to the dogmatic condition when contradictory ideologies of class domination have been brushed aside, or is this only a misconception? And what is at stake in deciding on that issue?

Intoxication and Ideology

Benjamin observes that "The dialectics of intoxication are indeed curious" (Reflections, p. 181), for his investigation of the rapturous transports in Surrealism seems to confirm a suspicion which undermines the plenitude of all convictions about the world and experience. He asks: "Is not perhaps all ecstasy in one world humiliating sobriety in that complementary to it?" This question immediately brings the issue from the margins where illumination figures as an exceptional and extraordinary moment, and sets it at the center, at the point where solidity and familiarity seem to guarantee the naturalness and dependability of established truths. Considered dialectically in this way, any such center is only the site from which a dream sees itself alone, and cannot envisage any point beyond itself, any perspective in which it is not the absolute expression of what is. From the dialectical position, the dream discovers it is a dream, which means it has already formed an implicit sense of the further possibility of awakening, though this can still only be in the terms given by the dream itself. That conception of intoxication operates on the axis of a boundary relative to which there is no fixed objective standpoint, and the two-sidedness of its phenomena leave both intoxication and soberness as double systems, each with a positive and negative aspect which will naturally obscure one another.

From the perspective of bourgeois rationalism, both modes of illumination—profane and sacral—are intoxications. The irruption of an unmediated material reality or "universal and integral actuality" into consciousness, no less than a dream-world of images from the subconscious or the occult, contains that negative connotation of irrationality—of lost critical distance, retreat into an unverifiable conviction whose distortions leave one unable to deal with the exigencies of life. At the same time, each takes itself to be an "intoxication" in the positive sense of an unconstrained realization of the Real, a joyful liberation and release from bourgeois restriction. Meanwhile, the soberness of the latter is conversely a deluded, though self-satisfied, intoxication in the purely negative sense. That is, as that same inability to perceive a reality which is here suppressed beneath the heavy carpet of political and material privilege. The word intoxication itself is thus completely embedded in the ideological context from which it is spoken.

We can also expand Benjamin's dialectic to say that what is a humiliating intoxication in one world, is also a proud soberness in that complementary to it. Any viewpoint which attempts to bring itself to a halt in relation to its alternatives, will perceive itself to be as dependable and in command as the materialist sphere "where nearness looks with its own eyes" (Reflections, p. 192). Each of the three outlooks we have discussed as "intoxication" regards itself as "sober" inasmuch as it displays the correct focus on "truth" and "the world." And yet, for Schlegel, all three, like all conceptions of a fixed truth or world as Being, are Raserei—intoxication in its negative slant. From this perspective, the idea of intoxication cannot be purged of its character as poisoning. To be enraptured, enthralled, is a loss of freedom, but is not experienced as such. Only from the outside of the magic circle do those inside appear enslaved. To themselves they are in the most liberated paradise.

In Lyceum Fragment 37, the longest and most closely argued in the series, Schlegel takes up a position which might surprise anyone with a naive understanding of his Romanticism, but one which reflects informatively on this issue. He writes:

> Um über einen Gegenstand gut schreiben zu können, muß man sich nicht mehr für ihn interessieren; der Gedanke, den man mit Besonnenheit ausdrücken soll, muß schon gänzlich vorbei sein, einen nicht mehr eigentlich beschäftigen. So lange der Künstler erfindet und begeistert ist, befindet er sich . . . in einem illiberalen Zustand (KA II, p. 151).
> ('In order to write well about something, one should not be interested in it any more; the thought which one would express with sobriety must be completely past and no longer occupy one.

So long as the artist is inventing and filled with enthusiasm, he is
. . . in an illiberal state.')

That is, as long as one is fascinated, one's freedom is suspended, and the object itself dictates the form of reality it will possess. This is also the form of reality which characterizes the notion of "World," which Schlegel does not regard as possessed of a positive function in any philosophical understanding.[5] In his literary notebooks he observes: "Welt ist Verwicklung der kleinlichen Verhältnisse, Furcht, Schwäche, Krankheit, Vernunft, Unvernunft alles zusammen" (LN 2178, 'World means the confusion of petty relations, fear, weakness, sickness, reason and unreason all together'), adding, in both the senses of pertaining to commonality, and of petty meanness: "Welt=Gemeinheit." He also notes the curious duality on which its power rests, in terms similar to those we found applicable to the image of intoxication: "Sonderbar, daß diese Gemeinheit eben da Statt findet, wo sonst das Paradies war" ('Strange that this meanness occurs precisely where at other times there was paradise').

And what marks this paradisal World as such is not that it is just a pleasant place, but that the illusory presence it imposes will hold out the hope of an expression that is fully adequate to it.[6] An image of fixed Being can delude the writer who is under its spell into dreaming that, as with the old Adamic language in which things corresponded essentially with their names, he might create a representation of it in full: "Er wird dann alles sagen wollen; welches eine falsche Tendenz junger Genies, oder ein richtiges Vorurteil alter Stümper ist" (KA II p. 151, 'He will then want to say everything, which is a false tendency of young geniuses or a real prejudice of old bunglers').

This might appear to be how Walter Benjamin envisages the condition of a revolutionary artistic representation fired by "profane illumination." He describes this at the close of his essay on Surrealism as a sphere of images where "nearness looks with its own eyes" at "the world of universal and integral actualities." Even though his dialectic of intoxication has reincorporated what he calls "the constructive, dictatorial side" (Reflections, p. 189) of revolution and revolutionary discipline, and shifts the ground of this imagery towards a more radical and purposeful expression of materialist political contents, Benjamin still seems willing to accept a view of art which does not really depart significantly from the epistemology of Surrealism. The vision of revolutionary language and text seems here to fall back towards an all too close resemblance to the sur-reality captured from the occult depths by a poetic language where "sound and image, image and sound interpenetrated with automatic precision and such felicity that no chink was left for the penny-in-the-slot called 'meaning'" (p. 178-9).

But what is it that Schlegel finds wrong with this triumphant and ecstatic immediacy?

> Dadurch verkennt er den Wert und die Würde der Selbst-
> beschränkung, die doch für den Künstler wie für den Menschen das
> Erste und Letzte, das Notwendigste und Höchste ist. Das
> Notwendigste: denn überall, wo man sich nicht selbst beschränkt,
> beschränkt einen die Welt; wodurch man ein Knecht wird (KA II p.
> 151).
>
> ('Because of this he mistakes the value and dignity of self-
> constraint, which for the artist and for any person is the
> beginning and end of everything, the most necessary and the
> highest. It is the most necessary because everywhere that one
> does not constrain oneself, the world will constrain one; this
> reduces one to a vassal.')

Benjamin insists the world of universal and integral actualities is the realm of action rather than contemplation. Here conventional artistic production is interrupted in favor of a more direct and concrete establishing of what is real. The condition of self-limitation by the artist through the separate discipline of practice in an autonomous domain of art seems therefore to be suspended too. The imagery appears to be that which is imposed by the truth of material relations in a concrete world of social and economic activity. In fact this new domain and role of art in "the long-sought image sphere" (Reflections, p. 192) is specifically announced as a reversal of the dominion of metaphor, and of "poetic politics" of which he writes: "We have tried that beverage. Anything, rather than that!" (p. 190). The metaphor is the vehicle of the world as it is imagined, not as it really appears in its raw, gritty materiality.

The equivalent for Schlegel to that positive soberness which maintains its freedom from fascination by a singular, and therefore false, realm is Besonnenheit, but this is not the illumination from without by an external sun, the light of the "world" which reveals itself in the immediacy of truth. On the contrary, it is the negating power of intellektuale Anschauung, the interior projection of ironic wit, the contradictory illumination of a hypermystical, hypermodern, hypercynic. Such a core of contradiction, however, persists for Benjamin too, quite differently situated, it is true, but nonetheless of vital importance in understanding all that may be learned from bringing these two together. The revolutionary condition to which Benjamin looks is "the sphere, in a word, in which political materialism and physical nature share the inner man, the psyche, the individual, or whatever else we wish to throw to them, with dialectical justice, so that no limb remains unrent" (p. 192). The division and tension between those antitheses ensures that the production of meaning must continue, and not come to a halt in a final grasp of material presence resembling the absolute correspondences of paradise. The contradiction between them does not resolve itself and come to a standstill, "For it must in the end be admitted: metaphysical materialism . . . cannot lead without rupture to anthropological materialism. There is a residue" (p. 192).

The generation of structures of expression and interpretation continues to be necessitated by the demands of that "residue." The sphere of political materialism and physical nature remains one of a dialectic in movement, at no point being able to dispense with forms of synthesis or mediation---that is, representation: "Nevertheless—indeed, precisely after such dialectical annihilation—this will still be a sphere of images . . ." but because action has now precedence over contemplation, the dialectic expresses itself pre-eminently in forms intimately involved with praxis. It will be a "sphere of images and, more concretely, of bodies." The situation between Benjamin and Schlegel is thus more complicated than that which holds between Schlegel and the "dogmatic" romanticism of the Surrealists. Insofar as Benjamin holds himself back from the more explicit Messianism of later years, a more instructive relationship can be worked out between his work and Schlegel's thinking of the Jena period—before he, too, in converting to Catholicism, changed his view to a form of Messianism, albeit of a different stamp.

The positions here cannot be assimilated one to the other, but Benjamin may now evade Schlegel's most powerful critique, the account of dogmatism, and instead confront Schlegel's weakest flank, the opposition between theory and praxis.

Theory and Praxis

Schlegel compares words to money: "Vielleicht sind wir auf der Erde nur zu Gold und Worten verdammt" (LN 1944, 'Perhaps we are condemned on earth to words and gold'), because like anything limited to exchange-value only, they are both nothing in themselves. The cynic knows that wealth (see AF 35) and words may be brought together under the sign of that parabola indicating the symbolic or allegorical nature of all phenomena. To him, any aspect of the world, whether waking or in dream, whether perceived in soberness or in intoxication, is always error. And these errors are canceled by bringing them together so that they mutually contradict and annihilate one another: "Die Wahrheit entsteht, wenn entgegengesetzte Irrthümer sich neutralisieren" (KA II p. 93, 'The truth arises when opposing errors neutralize one another').

This, once again, is the basis of New Mythology, which does not divide the possibilities of representation into those which lie within its perimeter, and are therefore true, and the false realm beyond. All such boundaries are always provisional and constantly negated axes of privilege. Their authority or exclusivity is repeatedly superseded by progression of constant revolution as new representations are added. This changed and changing state of myth, freed from the task of delineating a sphere of truth, is thus separated from that concept of world which is "allerdings eine nothwendige Bedingung aller immanenten (i.e. aller nicht mythischen) Poesie" (LN 2178, 'however, a necessary condition or all immanent, i.e. all non-mythical, poetry'). It is, therefore, completely contrary to the usual signification of myth, which is a system of knowledge that encloses itself in such a way as to refuse the test of falsification by reference to alternatives. It is quite clear that the oppositions sober-intoxicated or illumined-benighted are similarly patterns of privilege in which people may enclose themselves hermetically on one side of an absolute division, and therefore "mythic" in the old sense.

If Benjamin maintains the epistemological concept of world, as he appears to, he cannot avoid returning to the assertion of privilege (truth). This contains the philosophical problems of old myth, and as "arbitrary positing," resembles what Schlegel would call "philosophizing non-philosophy" (see KA XVIII p. 13 #101). On the other hand, if Schlegel steadfastly refuses that recognition of any permanent boundary, but only right of unhindered passage across an endlessly expanding juxtaposition of alternatives, this has difficulties of its own. The human interest in justice is separated here from the philosophical concern to avoid "prejudice." The practical, concrete and material issues of politics, social equity and just conditions in economic life require focused and resistant forms of representation. In the imperfect historical world they have to struggle hard against hostility and oblivion. Without a position of privilege, the concept of justice has no power, and in the absence of such power, how can its reality come into existence? This is no light matter, and must be taken up again later.

Now, one could suggest that, even if Benjamin does not attempt in his essay to resurrect an Edenic condition of meaning as the immediate result of a successfully achieved social revolution, and the dialectic remains alive there, his "dialectic of intoxication" does come to a halt. Profane illumination of the image sphere is, it would appear, a positive synthesis which then stands as the mode in which "world" or "truth" continue to unfold. When he argues that:

> The most passionate investigation of telepathic phenomena, for example, will not teach us half as much about reading (which is an eminently telepathic process), as the profane illumination of reading about telepathic phenomena. And the most passionate investigation of the hashish trance will not teach us half as much about thinking (which is eminently narcotic), as the profane illumination of thinking about the hashish trance (Reflections, p. 190).[7]

he touches on a central thesis. It is not enough, he implies, for Surrealism simply to assert the privilege of ecstatic modes of knowledge. It must become "profane." If it is to produce that "dialectical optic" by which the confidence of rational knowledge is shaken by being exposed as no less rhapsodic and no less deluded than a drug-induced rapture, Surrealism must cut into itself. When transformed to this function, Surrealism is deprived of its most valued original claim, for it does not regard its revelations as delusion. In fact, it was certainly not willing to surrender its autonomy in this regard, or allow its own peculiar avenues of insight to be made subordinate in the interest of solidarity with the political movements with which it made common cause; Breton, for example, continued to insist on the autonomy of surrealistic sources of truth in the Second Manifesto:

> . . . to be sure, Surrealism, which as we have seen deliberately opted for the Marxist doctrine in the realm of social problems, has no intention of minimizing Freudian doctrine as it applies to the evaluation of ideas: on the contrary, Surrealism believes Freudian criticism to be the first and only one with a really solid basis (Manifestoes, p. 159-60).

Bourgeois soberness and Surrealist intoxication are each presented as delusions, but it is evident that profane illumination, as the relativization and clarification of both, is the form of truth—even though its "content," its images, are part of an active productive process which we need not expect to see reduced to single and final adequacy. The epistemological basis of that form is not visibly secured; it represents a closure of a kind which is expressly not permitted to enter New Mythology. A further examination of the latter may project the issue into unexpected relief.

The Transcendentalphilosophie leaves it quite explicit that the empirical takes no precedence over the theoretical (see KA XII p. 98, p. 102). On the contrary, there can be no special authority allowed it since both are co-equals in an undivided reality. The assault on privilege also provokes observations which raise the standing of dreams or intoxication, but they are, in like manner, not granted that pre-eminence otherwise held by the empirical which occurs in the Surrealist model. They are raised, rather, in order to relativize both. It would be easy to misread the note: "Von den Bewußtseynsformen ist die Trunkenheit die vorzüglichste—als Rückkehr in das elementare Bewußtseyn" (LN 1316, 'Among the forms of consciousness drunkenness is supreme---as the return to elementary consciousness'), to indicate a close parallel with Surrealism, or at least with that common notion of romanticism as retreat into a subjective dream world. Further examination, nevertheless, reveals a much more subtle and complex picture. The dialectical interpenetration for which Benjamin calls, and to which he claims "a romantic turn of mind is impervious," is significantly in evidence here.

"Warum finden die Menschen nur ihre Träume so bedeutend, wie sie eigentlich alles finden sollten?" (KA XVIII p. 150 #323, 'Why do people find only their dreams so significant in the way they should find significance in everything?') Schlegel wonders, but not to propose a world of integral actuality which may emerge when the ideology in which the distinction subsists is swept away: "Sie werden es dann gewahr, daß sie sich ewig fremd sind" ('Then they will become aware that they are eternally foreign to themselves'). All constructions are just as divinatory as dreams are, and so not even the empirical experience of the present has privilege as better founded than any other. On the contrary: "Das persönliche Bewußtsein, der Geist, ist nur da, um die Gegenwart zu vernichten" (p. 190 #763, 'Personal consciousness, mind, is only there in order to eliminate the present'), for empirical time is itself without authority: "Kein Augenblick des Lebens ist der Vergangenheit oder Zukunft näher wie die andere. In Rücksicht auf das Ganze ist das Leben Einheit—nur ist hie und da die Beziehung einleuchtender, wie die Bedeutsamkeit der Träume" (p. 132-3 #127, 'No moment of life is closer than another to the past or the future. With regard to the whole, life is a unity---except that here and there the connection is more evident'). Accordingly, the distinction between a supposedly reliable experience of the present and an unreliable perception, perhaps by "second sight," of the future, is disallowed:

> Man wundert sich immer mißtrauisch wenn man zu wissen scheint: das und das wird so sein. Und doch ist es grade ebenso wunderbar, daß wir wissen können: das und das ist so; was niemandem auffällt, weil es immer geschieht (AF 218).

('We always react with surprise and suspicion when someone appears to know that such and such will happen this particular way. Yet it is quite as marvelous that we can know that such and such a thing is so, which never strikes us as remarkable because it happens all the time.')

The real significance of the dream lies in the fact that it is open to the experience of waking, which transforms it from an apparent "present" to a clearly extra-temporal mode of being; that is, non-Being. Thus, it is the model of all mythological thinking in Schlegel's sense because the permanent parabasis which constitutes the latter's irony is closely analogous to the relationship of waking to the dream, except that the movement is a bilateral one, without priority: "Das Schlafen und Träumen ist ein Zurücksinken in den Schoß der Erde. Das Denken ist ein Erzeugniß des Lichts, der Luft des Mittags. Alle Poesie also Morgenröthe und Abendröthe" (KA XVIII p. 179 #635, 'Sleeping and dreaming is a sinking back into the womb of the earth. Thinking is a product of the light, of the noonday air. All poetry therefore is the red sky of morning and evening'). Thus, when he writes: "Waches Träumen ist der höchste Zustand, . . . seelig genannt" (p. 147 #289, 'Waking dreaming is the highest state, . . . called blessed'), it is the interpenetration of the two conditions which is important. Each aspect signals the limitation of the other. But, we should stress once again, this mutual cancellation is not a dialectical moment ideologically, leading to a passage to a new sphere, but has only ontological significance, leading simply to the continued moment of enlightened suspension by which Being itself is canceled out.

Failure to recognize this necessary mixed position is described in Lyceum Fragment 92:

Auch der Geist kann, wie das Tier, nur in einer aus Lebensluft und Azote gemischten Atomsphäre atmen. Dies nicht ertragen und begreifen zu können ist das Wesen der Torheit; es schlechthin nicht zu wollen, der Anfang der Narrheit.

('Mind or spirit can, like an animal, only breathe in an
atmosphere of oxygen mixed with nitrogen. Not to be able to
accept and grasp this is the essence of stupidity; simply not to
want it, the beginning of foolishness.')

The two branches of misconception he distinguishes here, foolishness and
stupidity, are clarified in other notes: "Der Dumme denkt was er sieht, der
Narr sieht was er denkt" (KA XVIII p. 188 #749, 'The stupid man thinks
what he sees, the fool sees what he thinks'). These two, one can say,
correspond generally to the negative aspects of rationalistic bourgeois
soberness and Surrealistic intoxication or "romanticism" respectively. The
former ascribes reality only to the visible present, to the empirical,
material and exterior; the latter takes the reverse position of vesting
Being in thought, in the idea, in the interior or "subjective" realm. In
order to keep the charge of Dummheit from covering the sphere of
universal and integral actuality also, it is necessary to interpose arguments
of considerable sophisticaton. One cannot simply say that Benjamin's image
sphere differs from Schlegel's concept of world because it does not project
material Being into thought contemplatively—that it does not look, but acts—
since Schlegel also identifies the power over Dummheit of that which it sees, with
the dominion of praxis. To answer the challenge, we will have to both expose the
weakness in Schlegel's evaluation of praxis, and also blind the vision "with which
nearness looks with its own eyes." The latter formula has an unwelcome Messianic
tone. Perhaps, if it is replaced with a historical perspective that will explicitly
distinguish revolutionary from non-revolutionary praxis in its determination of what
is seen, the human purpose of revolution will be better served.

Precisely because the error of Dummheit is so widespread and secure as the
normal or "commonsense" outlook ("Dummheit ist der Grundcharakter des
menschlichen Bewußtseins" (p. 191 #777, 'Stupidity is the fundamental character of
human consciousness'), it is far more dangerous in Schlegel's view than its
counterpart. There is no general observation (in his judgement) of "irrationality"
interrupting and canceling "rationality," of dream relativizing the waking state the
way waking negates the dream. Therefore this is the mode of awareness to which
disruptive attention must be directed: "Die Aufgabe ist, dieses in Raserei zu

verwandeln. Die Welt zu überwinden ist die höchste Aufgabe—durch Wollust, Kunst, Zorn" ('The task is to transform this into madness. The supreme task is to overcome the world—by sensual lust, art, anger'). The appearance of the world is unequivocally aligned with a loss of judgement. It is a deceptive clarity, a deluded stability and a fascination to be thrown off, and therefore the product of a diminution of understanding, like the delusion of an intoxication: "Dummheit ist die Schöpferin der Welt" ('Stupidity is the creator of the world').

It is, nonetheless, a natural tendency in mankind because the essential principle which negates it: "daß jeder gedachte Gedanke wahr sey" (p. 407 #1041, 'that every thought thought is true'), is constantly denied by practical experience. The necessity to raise theoretical speculation to an equal share in an undivided reality with the empirical argued for in the Jena Lectures, appears in various forms as a most fundamental message of all the writings of this period. What is urged here, in short, is that everything be assimilated to theory, and praxis as such radically demoted: "Frieden muß der Zweck jedes Krieges seyn, wie Theorie der Praxis" (p. 379 #706, 'Peace must be the purpose of every war, just as theory is of praxis'). It is in praxis that the present is inevitably separated from all other time, and the constraint of the world in which it is pursued imposes itself most forcibly as presence. This is no more than Unphilosophie, or prejudice, in Schlegel's view, but such error is recalcitrant because we will inevitably be practically active in our lives: "Daß wir Vorurtheile haben müssen, folgt schon daraus, daß wir eher handeln als denken" (p. 408 #1051, 'That we have to have prejudices follows in consequence because we will act rather than think'). The concept of world, once more, is the prior prejudice to be reckoned with: "Nicht die Dinge sind das eine ursprüngliche Vorurtheil—sondern die Welt" (p. 407 #1036, 'It is not things which are the one primary prejudice—but the world,') and its character, constituted in this way, will necessarily be material: "Der Stoff ist ein Niederschlag des Handelns" (p. 313 #1438, 'Matter is a precipitate of action').

It is important to note well, however, that this opposition between theory and praxis is not the naive distinction separating speculation from action, or thinking from doing. It is the polarity of freedom and servitude. In our uncritical usage, we usually equate the idea of an "act" with praxis pure and simple, and certainly Schlegel largely agrees with this, but only to the extent that most acts are caught up in the texture of worldly purposes and prejudices which produces servitude. The interpretations of causality, continuity, of irremediable necessity proceeding from a world that is, are chains which humanity forges for itself from the pursuit of a practical project. And while it is true that this order of certainty, predictability and exact repetition makes it possible to undertake that pursuit, to decide and act on a practical basis, that does not give it cognitive standing. We could not envisage such an undertaking, there is no doubt, without the presence of a predictable world in which a determinate end can be foreseen, chosen, and achieved, yet such a construct exists only in response to that need for action. Its philosophical foundation is no more than this motivation, and therefore no firmer than an "arbitrary positing."

This idea is not confined to Schlegel, but is widely acknowledged. For example, Heinrich Gomperz observes in his essay Limits of Cognition and Exigencies of Action:

> Pure cognition . . . is, on principle, incapable of knowing the future beforehand. But to action anticipation is essential, since to act means to realize what, as yet, is unreal. Action, then, can never be sure of its result. The man who acts must always take a risk. Action is, to some degree, always a leap in the dark, and that is why it can never have an entirely sufficient basis in cognition. In inductive reasoning, on the other hand, we, by a law of psychology, naturally expect the future to resemble the past. When, therefore, we have to act (and, as we saw, we would, in truth, act even if we did not act), what else could we do but base our action on our expectation? In other words, induction is, ultimately, not a cognitive principle at all, it is the essential principle of action. It expresses the twofold fact that anticipation is naturally conditioned by experience and that action is necessarily based on anticipation. We may say, then, that it is the exigencies of Action which, in this instance, carry us beyond the limits of Cognition.[8]

If induction is thus not a cognitive principle, it is indeed, as Schlegel argues, a diminution of cognition, and therefore opposed to the complete liberty of intellektuale Anschauung. It is both stupidity and foolishness, and so corresponds to the negative phase of intoxication: "Blödsinn (ist) ein narcotisches Uebel" (KA XVIII p. 146 #277, ('Idiocy is a narcotic ill').

The reverse of this condition of action is not passivity. Schlegel by no means takes that position, despite his notorious sympathy for Müßiggang, or idleness. It is the false praxis of a restlessly compulsive activity which must be halted by that agency, among others. As servile submission to an arbitrary and rigid construction of the world, and therefore, as it were, cognitively passive, it is more really so. (One might compare this to the views on the bourgeois work ethic voiced in Benjamin's critique of the ideology of progress, especially in the Theses on the Philosophy of History, and his characterization in the notes to that work of revolution as the "emergency brake" interrupting the advance of homogeneous bourgeois history.) Breaking out of that enclosure, by contrast, "spornet den Geist an, und treibt ihn zur Thätigkeit" (KA XII p. 95, 'spurs the spirit on and stirs it to activity'). The mode of this activity, nonetheless, is changed because the cognitive factor limiting the status of its products is undiminished in vitality. Such activity, rising above the "psychological law" invoked by Gomperz, admits no absolute basis on which to predict its ends, and therefore takes on the form of experiment: "Die wahre Magie ist ein Experimentieren mit der Fantasie auf die Gottheit" (KA XVIII p. 334 #131, 'True magic is an experimentation performed by the imagination on the Godhead').

That is, the outcome is in principle always in question, and appears only in a historical modality. The idea of a higher level of a-temporal or a-historical truths, such as the naive notion of the laws of physics, has no place here. The phenomena of physics are observations which are no less historical in this sense than any other, and thus its derived norms are not distinct from the realm of New Mythology: "Die Methode des Physikers muß historisch sein—sein letztes Ziel Mythologie" (p. 155 #378, 'The method of the physicist must be historical—his ultimate goal, mythology'). The general regularity deduced from many observations still remains provisional, and the rule joining them an analogy or allegory only. It is, consequently—and here Schlegel's position is not an idealist eccentricity, but substantially in agreement with a solid tradition in the philosophy of science[9]—an experiment itself which is constantly open to the contradiction of a new appearance in the observational state of affairs, or by another analogic construct which reorders the same condition.

But this characteristic of experimentality is not restricted to the highest and most conscious levels of methodological awareness. The leap in the dark, the "risk" which Gomperz describes, is the true disposition of all acts. If infinite variety and unpredictability are inalienable from the phenomena of nature, then the mode of experiment cannot depend solely on the deliberate epistemological standpoint of its perpetrator—this must be the original feature of any act in the natural world: "Das organische Experiment des Thiers ist das Essen, das chemische die Zeugung, das abstrakte (mechanische) ist der Sinn, die Wahrnehmung. Dieß ist das göttlichste Experiment der Animalität" (p. 146 #275, 'The organic experiment of an animal is eating, the chemical one is procreation, the abstract or mechanical one is use of the senses, perception. This is the most divine experiment of animality').

The concept of experiment preserves not only speculation and reflection as the realm of "theory," but also any human activity at all, provided it is not drawn into the false sphere of an uncritical, "unphilosophical," evaluation of its status. This, praxis, is a specifically human form of evil because only mankind is capable of erecting the idea of world which can then enslave the liberty of thought. There is, however, a mysterious equivalent to that evil in nature since Schlegel diagnoses an obscure correlative constraint existing there too: "Giebt's nicht ein immanentes böses Prinzip in der Natur, wie die Unvernunft in der Menschheit und welches kann dieß sein?" (p. 162 #466, 'Is there not an immanent evil principle in nature, like unreason in humanity, and what could this be?') This is certainly a mysterious entity, but it is the basis of Man's role in the universal scheme of things as an active agent, for it is here, in the operative capacity of "helpmeet to the gods" (see KA XII p. 42), that he sets the full liberty of the theoretical mode against such a resistance. Thus, as I will show, the "historicizing" moment of physics, or any other such study, is to go beyond even the apparent orderliness of natural phenomena, and question even those laws whose "immanent" quality seems to impress itself most imperiously on our judgement.

The Evil Principle

The "system" of Transcendentalphilosophie establishes that all phenomena are produced as self-representation of the infinite and indeterminate absolute. That is, this nothingness passes through a stage of becoming in individuation before returning to itself. This occasions what Schlegel puts forward as the philosophical question par excellence: "Warum läuft das Spiel der Natur nicht in einem Nu ab, so daß also gar nichts existiert?" (KA XII p. 39, 'Why does the play of nature not run its course in an instant, so that nothing exists?') The answer is suggested by the concept of becoming itself: "Es liegt in dem Begriff Werden die Bedingung eines Widerstandes—sonst würde die Gottheit seyn oder es würde nichts seyn" (p. 54, 'The condition of a resistance is included in the concept of becoming—otherwise there would either be the Godhead or there would be nothingness'). That is, without a factor of resistance to the fulfillment of the process, it would advance at once to that form of being which is the perfect expression of the infinite, or return at once to the origin with which that is identical.

This resistance is a sort of "first cause" of illusion: "Der Widerstand ist das böse Prinzip in der Natur" ('This resistance is the evil principle in nature'). It is, however, a peculiar and problematic entity about whose precise status not even Schlegel has a great deal to say: "Daß es da ist, weiß man; aber was es ist, weiß man nicht" ('That it exists, we know; but what it is, we do not know').

The element of the evil principle, beyond its apparently impenetrable nature, is identified more broadly as that which constitutes fixity throughout the universe, and in the allegorical cosmogony of the Transcendentalphilosophie it is also identified with weight as the most essential quality of matter, itself the most fixed form of phenomena: "Das böse Prinzip in der Natur ist die Schwere—dem Licht entgegegesetzt" (KA XVIII p. 162 #468, 'The evil principle in nature is weight—the opposite of light'). Some insight can be derived from a comparison of the metaphysics of this position and the classical Indic philosophy of the Vedanta, to which it bears certain noteworthy points of resemblance, and which Schlegel came later to study in its original sources.[10]

In the Indic form, the separation from absolute consciousness in individuation is delusion occasioned by desire, and restoration of the Real is a return to the absolute, occasioned by a form of revelation. This is a reverse factor in what would otherwise be a close parallel in the respective patterns of a phenomenal world produced by differentiation out of an original absolute and infinite unity. Revelation of original Being thus contrasts with intellektuale Anschauung because in the former situation, the production of individuation is regarded as empty and the absolute as full, whereas the latter sees the absolute as empty and individuation as full. In the Vedanta, the emptiness of existence perpetuates itself by desire, which also obscures the path back to its true origin. For Schlegel, individuation, as representation of the absolute, is not lost to the latter as such, but only by the intervention of the evil principle whose resistance prevents the representation from perfectly fulfilling itself.

The significance of the difference between Vedantism and Schlegel's view expresses itself particularly clearly in the field of ethics. His argument is not aimed at demonstrating a way to close the distance keeping man from his lost origin, but at completing the process of the universe by lifting thought, as the free and unconstrained medium of representation, to the level of perfect individuation of the infinite by becoming infinite itself—the unlimited production of infinite reality by the committed incredulity of cynicism. The concept of morality must be determined in this form also, since if it attempts to assert any particular fixed priority, it will by that token share in the evil principle as a mere prejudice. If ethics involves itself in any criterion of action, positive or negative, understood in the particular sense of responding to a fixed condition of choice or obligation, it becomes a form of praxis which Schlegel separates from his notion of morality: "Alle Moral magisch oder musikalisch (eine andere gibt's night)—was man sonst so nennt ist Politik oder Ökonomie" (KA SVIII p. 397 #921, 'All morality is magical or musical; there is no other—what one usually names by that term is politics or economics').

The idea of an ethical principle which separates the right course from the wrong, even if it avoids subjection to ordinary worldly criteria as scrupulously as does Vedantic philosophy, is still caught in the web of illusory restriction judged from the perspective of the Transcendentalphilosophie. Any consideration which is appropriate to praxis as conceived in the very broad meaning necessitated by Schlegel, must fall away. Only the principle of theory opposed to it allows the lack of distinction that must be made between uninhibited products of the imagination: "Für die Theorie ist eben alles ein heiliges Spiel, da ist das Böse nur Täuschung, nicht so für die Praxis. Und also ist das absolut Böse . . ." (p. 370 #593, 'For theory everything is just a sacred game. There evil is only illusory, but not so for praxis. Therefore that is absolute evil').

Theory and praxis are both activities in their own right, but they differ in the status they accord themselves. The evil principle is by definition a principle of finitude, fixity or being, and only an act which sets itself in alliance with that criterion may be defined as evil. In the human sphere, action undertaken in that form is the only way the principle can appear: "Nur in der Praxis liegt das Böse prinzip" (p. 371 #601, 'It is in praxis alone that the evil principle is to be found'). The morality of Schlegel's continuous revolution, then, is not anything like a conventional ethic. Its highest realization is the negation of fixed principles, the dissipation of any binding criteria whatever: "Cynismus ist moralische Genialität" (p. 100 #851, 'Cynicism is moral genius').

The status of the present is intimately bound up with the expanded role of theory, and Schlegel's special position on it shows clearly that he does not countenance a withdrawal or retreat from action, but only its cognitive revision. The complete abandonment of what is characteristic of the present, and the abandonment of those activities which ordinarily take place in it as praxis, would be "Träumerei," mere dreaming, and move closer to a naive form of romanticism, and to intoxication:

> Die Gegenwart muß anders behandelt werden als die Vergangenheit. Dieß liegt nicht in der Zeit, sondern in der Praxis. Man kann zwar auch die Gegenwart theoretisch betrachten, dann geht aber die Praxis verlohren und es entsteht Träumerei" (p. 377 #684).
>
> (The present must be treated differently from the past. This is not because of time, but because of praxis. One can also

approach the present theoretically, but then praxis is lost, and
dreaming arises in its place.')

The concept of the present may be lost, but must be reformulated so that
its particular demands and quality determined by praxis can appear within
the realms of theory: "Oder bei einem hohen Grade von Bildung kann man
neben der Praxis von ihr abstrahiren und gleich die Theorie damit
verbinden" ('Or at a high level of development, alongside praxis one can
also abstract from it and so at the same time combine theory with it'). In
this way Schlegel can argue for a completely different concept of politics,
and indeed of economics, which is based on and concordant with the
intellektuale Anschauung.

A present which is shot through with evil, but redeemed from it by
theory is therefore quite different from one which is dominated by praxis
alone. The mode of action in praxis only confirms the predominance and
constraint of the principle of fixity because praxis is enclosed in the
irremediable primacy of experience. It can only acknowledge and confront
the content of its situation, and is therefore not free, but determined by
that situation. The "action" of theory does not ignore and deny the
present, but only transmutes its modality to counteract its privilege, and
so break out of the boundary this imposes. The horizon of praxis is always
enclosed by the limits of experience.

Theory is freedom, for it is the realm where invention and
combination proceed beyond the limitation of any situation in the world or
empirical time. To submit to the far more resistant exigencies of
experience in the present is to sacrifice one's freedom; and the sense that
there are changes which demand to be made in the visible world is the
result of those prejudices endemic to praxis, or characteristic of Dummheit,
which thinks what it sees: "Dummheit ist indirekte Verrückung; Vorurtheile
sind Verrückung in Masse. Verwechslung der Theorie und Praxis ist schon
eine Art Verrückung" (p. 370 #596, 'Stupidity is an indirect derangement;
prejudices are derangement in mass. The confusion of theory and practice
is certainly a kind of derangement').

The very thought of political engagement in the way that Benjamin champions it is therefore excluded at the outset. The practical contradictions and conflicts of the world are to be dissolved immediately into the harmony of theory. That task devolves on those whose superior understanding fits them for it: philosophers, scholars and artists, but most especially the last named. Schlegel observes: "Künstler sind Menschen in höherer Potenz, nur durch sie eine Hierarchie möglich" (p. 403 #987, 'Artists are people at a higher power, only through them is a hierarchy possible'). Their activity, he believes, is the one most purged of an erroneous immanent truth, and the hierarchy set up by their influence, as the most sharply opposed to practical politics, should cause the latter simply to wither away in human society:

> Republik ist nur ein mittlerer Gährungszustand, ein Notbehelf.
> Familie und Hierarchie sind die einzigen Formen der wahren
> Gesellschaft. (Also hat Fichte Recht—die Republik solle sich
> selbst vernichten). Alle jetzige und überhaupt die modernen
> Staaten tappen um diese beiden Ideen herum (p. 397 #916).
> ('Republic is only an intermediate stage of ripening, a makeshift.
> Family and hierarchy are the only forms of true society. Thus
> Fichte is right——the republic should destroy itself. All
> contemporary states and certainly the modern ones are groping
> their way around these two ideas.')

It is particularly interesting to read this in conjunction with another note, representative of several in the same vein: "Republik der Gelehrten der protestantische Begriff; Hierarchie der Kunst der katholische" (p. 375 #666, 'A republic of scholars is the Protestant concept; the hierarchy of art is the Catholic one'). The later stage of reactionary Catholicism is therefore by no means unprefigured at this point, although this anti-political stand had still to be hardened into the subsequent overt arch-conservatism. That, however, required the separate addition of a full-blown concept of revelation and of the world as manifest image of divine will. Then, in the name of that revelation, the world as political sphere would be given over to the activity of the Romantic hierophant, who would at that stage completely displace the Romantic revolutionary.

Polemic and Politics

Schlegel's position in the Transcendentalphilosophie or in New Mythology is vulnerable to the most characteristic criticisms of historicism made by Benjamin in the Theses on the Philosophy of History. Even though his idealism is completely radical and overt, rather than put in the guise of a doctrine of social progress, it nonetheless corresponds, as a neutralization of the present, closely to the pattern Benjamin describes. The idealism of Romantic progressivity, until it begins to take on a Messianic cast through the concept of revelation, is still really very much a refined, abstract form of the political ideology of progress—but this refinement is also a critique. By eliminating the privilege of the present, of the presence of the material and political instant which imposes itself in practical life, Schlegel opens up the panorama of history in the universal equality of thoughts and forms. At the same time his uncompromising rigor denies eclecticism, that philosophierende Unphilosophie, the right to apply its compendious historical perspective as a practical or political optic.

Eclecticism, like Schlegel's Romanticism, is necessarily a methodological attitude of "indifference," ("Der Eklektizismus führt zum Indifferentism; Beispiel an Goethe" KA XVIII p. 12 #92, 'Eclecticism leads to indifferentism; Goethe is an example'), for it applies equal dignity to the full variety of phenomena, including a possible extension to past, present and future. This is also, it follows, the spirit which gives fullest recognition to continuous and sovereign history: "Der Synkretismus und Eklektizismus sind der historische Geist" (p. 100 #852, 'Syncretism and eclecticism are the historical spirit'). Indifferentism is similarly a mark of the cynic, but in freeing it from the dogmatic taint of its uncritical form in eclecticism or empiricism, he also purges it of its political or pragmatic admixture: "Der Cynismus ist Naturphilosophie und classisches, ethisches Genie, mit annihilierender Polemik gegen die Oekonomie und Politik; absoluter Indifferentismus" (p. 99 #848, 'Cynicism is the philosophy of nature and classical, ethical genius, together with annihilating polemic against economics and politics; it is absolute indifferentism'). That is, eclecticism is not counter-present <u>enough</u> in its historicism, and deludes itself with a concept of the accessible and useful—proper to the public, political domain—as a criterion of the material it accumulates: "Die Mittheilbarkeit und Anwendbarkeit ist das Kriterium des besten Eklektizismus" (p. 14 #109, 'Communicability and utility are the criteria of the best eclecticism'). These are still criteria drawn from the <u>present</u>.

The cynic's polemic is a philosophically necessary movement, defeating the evil principle which otherwise frustrates any higher purpose: "Wenn der Eklektiker <u>nach dem Absoluten strebt,</u> so endigt er mit Verzweiflung—unendlicher Leerheit, Ekel, Langweile. So die besten unter den verdorbenen Weltleuten" (p. 9 #62, 'When the eclectic strives for the absolute, he ends with despair—infinite emptiness, disgust, boredom. Therefore these are the best among the corrupted worldlings').

Schlegel's critique thus parallels Benjamin's to the degree that he also regards the equivalent politics of his own time much as Benjamin regards the politics of social democracy—as dangerous and ultimately empty forms of utopianism. His response is, of course, <u>politically</u> quite opposite, ultimately seeking resolution though idealism in a reactionary posture. And yet, philosophically, the more rigorously upheld void of a neutralized present will later lead, in the Köln lectures, to the full universal moment of an idealist revelation which replaces the worldly present with one that is a complete plenitude of time. Even though Schlegel moves in the reverse direction from the emphatic instant of the materialist dialectic, this produces a unity of opposites with the compressed present which is a model of Benjamin's Messianic time in the <u>Theses</u> (<u>Thesis</u> XVIII). It also finds a distinct echo in Benjamin's universality of redeemed history (<u>Thesis</u> III). Insofar, however, as the focus of attention here is devoted to the non-Messianic moment in each, that aspect belongs outside the equation we must now attempt to formulate and resolve.

New Mythology, generating no political differentiation, indeed no differentiation in the status of its images at all, functions, from the historical materialist point of view, only as an auto-critique of eclecticism, demonstrating the sterile abstractness of an ideology which does not allow full emergence of a direct and undimmed impact in the material dimension. It removes itself, by its own dynamic agency, out of the sphere of life because it directs all its investment to the intellektuale Anschauung of an absolute which is infinitely removed from the living world. The sphere of pressing needs which is elaborately diluted and obscured by the ideology of progress, is denied and rejected entirely here. To the extent that life itself is the locus of immediate exigencies, life itself is disparaged in the Transcendentalphilosophie, where it is established as axiomatic that "Das wahre Leben ist nur im Tode" (KA XII p. 40, 'True life is only in death').[10]

Although this might begin to sound like something of a gambler's choice in the sense used to designate Benjamin's Messianism in Chapter Two, and could indeed be read as an early suggestion of that tendency in Schlegel, we should be wary of overstepping the indicated interpretation of pure negation at this point. The true life in death here is not the invocation of an obscured true being, a higher realm for which the visible is to be exchanged in a restoration of the object of Messianic desire. This is not a question of a choice between alternatives, as in Christianity between earthly life and a higher afterlife achieved via a physical death. Nor does the "true" life introduced here correspond to the Surrealist positing of an occult or subconscious hemisphere of experience opposed to the everyday, and reached by a metaphorical death, or a flight into the complementary world of intoxication. The passage invoked here is not a singular one equivalent either to death per se, or the "romantic" sacrifice of the sober realm for the ecstasy of a dream-life. It is the idea of movement itself, without any implication of ascent to a fixed state of given privilege: "Der Tod ist die Neutralisation entgegengesetzter Lebensarten" (KA XVIII p. 182 #669, 'Death is the neutralization of opposing forms of life').

A positive (or dogmatic) alternative to life is not suggested, then, only the concept of cancellation or transition as such. Nevertheless, there is an aspect in the privileging of theory over praxis which is equivalent to arbitrary positing ("willkührliches Setzen"). Of his own procedure, Schlegel notes: "Die Aufsuchung der Elemente ist eine Destruction. Bei der historische Analyse ist das Auffindung der Dominante (des herrschenden Prinzips)" (LN 1001, 'This seeking out of the elements is a destruction. In historical analysis this is the finding of dominants, of the ruling principle'). Not only is this clearly part of the process of New Mythology, but it also stirs a striking, and surely not insignificant echo of Jacques Derrida's method of deconstruction. If we apply it to Schlegel himself in the question of his opposition theory-praxis, we discover a principle implicit there whose contradictory effect imposes a limitation on the entire body of thinking which depends on it. It follows, too, that there may well be sufficient force in this principle for an extension of its influence to include a similar limitation on the method of deconstruction.

At the point of radical distinction between theory and praxis, the progressive relativization and absorption comes to a halt. New Mythology cannot absorb its opposite and eliminate all "dogmatisms," just as "death" cannot exist without life, even in the mode of pure passage without the arrest of a privileged condition or presence. Thus, the "true life" of this pure negation is dependent on the false one of fixed states. If the work of neutralization was completed, and there were no more "forms of life" left, death (or "true life") would have nothing remaining to constitute its function. The entire system would then return to the overt phase of nothingness, or the ultimate convergence of the exoteric and esoteric. If we remember that the essence of nature conceived without its center in presence is never different from nothingness except for this paradoxical development into exoteric forms: "Das letzte Resultat der Dynamik, daß die Natur nur eine ins Unendliche unendlich verschieden potenzierte Null ist . . ." (KA XVIII p. 165 #496, 'The final result of this dynamic is that nature is only a zero infinitely potentiated in variety into the infinite . . .') then it surely follows that the disappearance of all becoming would be the immediate consequence if the resistance which holds the process back from completion were finally overcome.

Similarly, if there were no opposed counterpart to theory, it would repeat the fate of the universe---resolving itself instantly into nothingness, a passage completed. Praxis, or the evil principle, may not be excluded from the order of things, then. Both are, on the contrary, completely indispensable. The evil principle is not really evil in the absolute scheme, even though it may appear to be so to mankind: "Und also ist das absolut Böse, doch nur für uns Menschen absolut böse" (KA XVIII p. 370 #593, 'And therefore it is absolute evil, yet only absolute evil for us humans'). Without it there could be no mankind, no human activity, no history, and to wish it away is to wish nothingness. To affirm any condition or activity is to affirm the evil principle, and to affirm the possibility of theory is to affirm the necessity of praxis.

This formulation can be expressed in terms derived from the analysis of intoxication and soberness, because, just as that polarity may be shown to have no immanent power, so the contraries of theory and praxis may be revealed as determined by context and function rather than content, in a very similar perspective. By lifting this opposition out of the restricted, uncritical, commonplace application, we can remonstrate that no element, no utterance, text, act or whatever, simply belongs in one zone or the other by virtue of what it **is**, but by the character of the foundation on which its meaning is given it. This argues that the opposition still remains an obscure prejudice which perpetuates our inability to measure its significance with an unconstrained hand.

Certainly, it cannot be maintained that there exists any conscious activity free of a context of meaning and interpretations which determine its quality— voluntary human acts are inalienably references to the interpretation their instigator puts on them, their context and the intention they enclose. Therefore we can, in the spirit enunciated by Schlegel, understand that where any particular act may belong in the realm of praxis by virtue of the "prejudice" which is the nexus in which it is caught up, the same act, where the nexus is denied, may be resolved in the direction of theory. Theory asserts itself as such by recognizing and refusing the cognitive foundation of the pragmatic world as the criterion of its own significance. Conversely, the structure within which the pragmatic world (under Schlegel's distinction) reflects on itself and theory, reverses that moment by assuming an inductive certainty which, as Gomperz argued, is quite unphilosophical and unfounded.

In a general formula, it might be put as follows: experience or thought may regard its territory as integral or absolute, bounded by a necessary or natural limit permitting no passage beyond it; alternatively, that boundary may be considered only historical, drawn across the possibilities of what may be experienced or thought, and therefore liable to be revised and enclosed on both sides by a new line. To clothe this highly abstract skeleton in the flesh of a concrete case, we illustrate it with the example of Surrealism—and reveal thereby what a shifting, protean, treacherous distinction we are attempting to bring to light.

Thus, where Surrealism regards the dream-world of the subconscious as constituting a new "objective" reality, and "when it broke over its founders as an inspiring dream wave, it seemed the most integral, conclusive, absolute of movements. Everything with which it came into contact was integrated" (Reflections, p. 178), it also regards itself as praxis, with real possibilities for the transformation of life. Where Benjamin regards it as deluded in that respect, but as having introduced the "dialectic of intoxication" by which bourgeois rationalistic determination of its (false) praxis is negated, it is allowed a positive theoretical moment. The sphere of integral actuality ushered in by that dialectic is, of course, a realm of praxis, but from its viewpoint the failure of Surrealism to overcome the false division between itself and "soberness" in realization of that dialectic, is theory in a negative sense of being without substance or connection with reality.

Any sphere of praxis necessarily regards any other defining the same region as erroneous, and therefore Benjamin considers that of Surrealism to have reduced "the methodical and disciplinary preparation for revolution entirely to a praxis oscillating between fitness exercises and celebration in advance" (p. 189). The positive aspect of theory from the prospect of such a sphere is its capacity to enlarge that realm of praxis by coalescing with it. The Surrealist project to "win the energies of intoxication for the revolution" (p. 189) will only be a real gain if the territory it encloses by the "theoretical" act of transgressing the boundary of meaning established by bourgeois rationalism is then annexed by the larger realm of materialist praxis, so that Benjamin asks whether they are "successful in welding this experience of freedom to the other revolutionary experience we have to acknowledge because it has been ours, the constructive, the dictatorial side of revolution?"

Any theory, by contrast, reduces all spheres of praxis whose territory it crosses to theory also. So long as it resists the gravitational tendency to change its character, it remains a medium of compatibility in the area it negates as praxis. Praxis is identifiable with "myth" in the old sense of self-enclosed system, and it might appear that this not only precedes New Mythology historically, but that it is also prior to any form of theory methodologically. The fact that Schlegel draws his New Mythology from myths constructed in the old spirit, transforming them in the way described for Spinoza (who was to "put off the warlike accoutrements of the system") suggests not only that he is dependent on what is already to hand, but that it could not have come into being except in that form. Observation of any of these elements themselves indicates strongly that the focus and concentration of constructive effort in the evolution of an area of meaning, draw their energy from a conviction that human force belongs here rather than elsewhere.

The creative concentration of such powers is a function of privilege in its chosen sphere over others, so that the full establishment of a "myth" can only advance positively if it is grasped in that privileged guise. Productive energy is generated by conviction that what is produced has a unique validity, and is therefore in some way indispensable in its own terms. All the bodies of meaning which Schlegel incorporates in the theoretical constellation of New Mythology were established that way originally, and this includes fictions also. The authority and dignity which sustain the fictional texts of Homer or Dante or Shakespeare can be brought into this descriptive pattern no less than the metaphysics of Spinoza, because they are founded in a context of social and ethical meanings which are a thoroughgoing praxis in the sense indicated.

At the same time, this methodological order is not without parity. The definition of praxis as mythic enclosure means that it is equally necessarily preceded by theory. No text is born ex nihilo, full blown and complete, since all its constituents must be arrived at historically: "Alles Neue ist nur Combinazion und Resultat des Alten" (LN 678, 'Everything new is only a combination and result of the old'). The moment of production or combination is possible only as theory, and if it is to continue to grow and evolve, to remain responsive and adaptive, it must maintain the contact with theory. Otherwise it is simply a husk, corresponding to Novalis' description of Nature: " . . . nichts als lauter Vergangenheit—ehemalige Freiheit . . ." (KS III p. 580 #197, 'nothing but pure past—former freedom . . '). A real systematic priority between theory and praxis is therefore an impossibility. The two co-exist in history as a sort of diastole and systole of human vitality. Each contributes to the force which maintains the movement of the whole—the capacity of mankind to meet the constantly changing demands of life.

This relationship also reveals the fundamentally political nature of interpretation of the experienced world, for the "systolic" phase of praxis, focusing reality in one sphere, must impose itself by persuasion in the political or institutional modality of ideology. The "diastolic" phase of theory must counter that established position by means which are similarly political. And yet, as with the relativity discovered in the question of intoxication, the perspective governs where such terms as "political" may be applied. Theory, as exemplified in Schlegel's case, regards itself not as mere persuasion on one side of a mutually indispensable progress, but as "philosophy," as the necessity of liberated thought and uncontradictory vision. Praxis, on the other hand, does not consider itself a dogmatic imposition confining thought, but as the necessity of nature, of what is.

It is thus characteristic to find each side "depoliticizing" itself, claiming the natural authority of the necessary order of things, in order to errode the position of the other.

An instance which comes to mind at once is Schlegel's polemic against "politics" in the name of cynicism. When his theoretical phase reveals itself as originating a right-wing posture as praxis in its later form, the political quality of that counter-politics is revealed too. An equivalent from the other side can be seen in the bourgeois response to Benjamin's "politicization" of literature. The objection arises because the texts concerned reflect an order which is interpreted as natural, or apolitical, within the integral perspective of bourgeois ideology—but by that token eminently political from without.

A depoliticized moment also appears in Benjamin's "world of universal and integral actuality," to the extent that this is projected as an essential presence. The kind of language he uses to denote "the methodical and disciplinary" aspect, or "constructive, dictatorial side of revolution," exposes the inner gravitation of praxis to mythify and enclose itself, to raise itself above the necessity of critique. Even as he radically politicizes the issues vis à vis the status quo, he stabilizes or depoliticizes the character of the revolution. Nevertheless, it is striking, indeed quite remarkable, that this process is not taken all that far. The contradiction between political materialism and physical nature, between metaphysical and anthropological materialism, maintains a political dynamism or continued element of theory to interact as a permanent fecundating factor in the manifestation of this sphere of images.

That rare and very impressive fusion of the two factors is the situation most favorable to effective generation of meaning whose vital agility may constantly re-create their contact with the demands of lived human life---and it is that consideration which everywhere motivates us to take the cognitive risks of motion in theory, or of arrest in praxis.

NOTES

[1] From the "Lehrbrief" in Book 7. J. W. Goethe, <u>Gedenkausgabe der Werken, Briefe und Gedanken,</u> Hrsg. Ernst Beutler (Zürich: Artemis Verlag, 1949), Bd. VII, p. 533. 'Only a portion of art can ever be taught, and the artist needs all of it. Any who only half-knows it, is always wrong and talks a great deal . . .'

[2] This occurs in a letter to Friedrich Schlegel sent by Novalis on December 26, 1797, (<u>Preitz</u>, p. 108), in which he describes an afternoon of lively discussion about Friedrich with his brother, August Wilhelm and the latter's wife, Caroline.

[3] Walter Benjamin, "Surrealism—The last snapshot of the European intelligentsia" in <u>Reflections,</u> p. 189.

[4] André Breton, <u>Manifestoes of Surrealism</u>, trans. Richard Seaver and Helen R. Lane (Ann Arbor: University of Michigan Press, 1972), p. 10. This source henceforth indicated as <u>Manifestoes.</u>

[5] The term <u>Welt</u> is explicitly distinguished from <u>Natur,</u> to specify that the latter is the philosophically correct concept of the phenomenal sphere. In the Jena Lectures, he observes: "Wir unterscheiden <u>Welt</u> und <u>Natur.</u> Die Welt ist das Ganze als System des Mechanismus gedacht. Die <u>Natur</u> ist das Bild der werdenden Gottheit" (KA XII p. 54, 'We distinguish between <u>world</u> and <u>nature.</u> The world is the whole, thought of as the system of its mechanism. <u>Nature</u> is the image of the Godhead in its becoming'). See also the philosophical notebooks, where he writes, for example: "Von der Natur wissen wenige, sie meinen die Welt wenn sie von der Natur reden" (KA XVIII p. 192 #784, 'Few know anything of nature, they mean the world when they speak of nature').

[6] The nostalgic dream of a redeemed language, restoration of the pre-lapsarian Edenic state, is a tendency arising quite naturally in relation to what we earlier noted as the "protest against terminology" (see KA XVIII p. 5 #15) Schlegel observes in dogmatism. A sense of the imperfection of language with respect to presence produces a conception of, and longing for, its redemption. Friedrich Schlegel himself will later respond to that dogmatic "protestantism" in a different way, and one curiously interconnected with his Catholic conversion. As the intellektuale Anschauung, which he quite early called "gleich das KATHOLISCHE Phänomen" (KA XVIII p. 406 #1025), changed from a neutralizing intuition of absence to a consciousness of revelation, it became the foundation for a concept of perfectibility, and thus the basis of a Messianic restoration within which the undivided, absolute order of the Church is prepared for.

[7] Benjamin himself was actively involved in research into the effects of hashish and mescalin over a considerable period. Documentation of many experiments undertaken with Drs. Ernst Joel and Fritz Fränkel is available with other materials in Walter Benjamin über Haschisch, Hrsg. Tillman Rexroth (Frankfurt/M: Suhrkamp, 1972).

[8] In: University of California Publications in Philosophy, XIV (1939), p. 68-69.

[9] The past of this idea reaches, say, from Heraclitus to Ernst Mach. The contemporary situation offers us a range of authoritative views such as that represented in the collection Criticism and the Growth of Knowledge, ed. Imre Lakatos and Alan Musgrave (London: University of Cambridge Press, 1970), where the possibility of elucidating permanent or absolute truth is not defended in any of the competing arguments, the issue of controversy being only the conditions most likely to produce "successful" experimentation and the generation of a "workable" theory. Few are quite as eager to carry the element of proliferation and instability to the forefront so forcefully as Schlegel, but those who would like to see the risk factor taken out of knowledge will not be reassured by the discussion there.

[10] This relationship between oriental metaphysics and German idealism is a much-discussed topic, of course, not only with regard to Schlegel and his

contemporaries, but the later generation, notably Schopenhauer, also. The element of will or desire as constituting individuation is also well-represented in Spinoza, who, with Fichte, is one of the two major antecedents Schlegel acknowledges and brings together in the Transcendentalphilosophie. (See Spinoza's Ethics, for example, in Book III, Proposition 6). In a letter from Paris dated September 15th 1803, after he had begun to study Sanskrit with an Englishman named Alexander Hamilton, Schlegel wrote to Tieck that this was "die Quelle aller Sprachen, aller Gedanken und Gedichte des menschlichen Geistes; alles, alles, stammt aus Indien ohne Ausnahme" ('the source of all languages, all thoughts and poems of the human spirit; everything, everything originates in India without exception'). The Köln Lectures reflect this growing interest, as do entries in his notebooks, e.g. KA XIX p. 42 # 18, p. 44 #35, p. 45 #36.

[11] In this connection one can draw attention, once more, to the quotation in which Schlegel rejects the "romantische Vergötterung des Lebens"—the romantic deification of life.

CHAPTER IV

THE HISTORY AND PROPHECY OF PHYSICS

Cette manière de sentir est choquante, peut-être. Elle fait de la "création" un moyen. Elle conduit à des excès. Davantage,— elle tend à corrompre le plaisir ingénu de croire, qui engendre le plaisir ingénu de produire, et qui supporte toute lecture.

Si l'auteur se connait un peu trop, si le lecteur se fait actif, que devient le plaisir, que devient la Littérature?

Paul Valéry, Au Sujet du 'Cimetière marin'[1]

The Unifying Medium of History

It is by no means immediately apparent how one should set about evaluating the status of Schlegel's New Mythology, for it seems to lay claim to no authoritative foundation at all. From the perspective of those traditional warring factions among which we are used to taking sides, an approach which can so easily accommodate the (negated) forms of any of them must strike us as weak, flabby and pointless, if not downright outrageous. From Schlegel's point of view, however, if the Blödsinn of prejudices derived from the world is really a narcotic evil, the opium of philosophizing non-philosophers, as it were, then the question becomes an issue of how he would persuade the individual ensnared and misled in this direction to lay down his pipe.

We may take it that this is implied by the concept of the hierarchy of artists or the notion of absolute ethics, as the direction of progression and the aim of revolution. There is quite clearly a nexus of persuasion here, a dialectic of enlightenment, a **task**. Nevertheless, the logical character of this persuasive project is quite different from that which holds between traditional contraries. The central criterion here is not a moment of exclusion, as in the conventional modality of persuasion which is directed against falsehood by a corrective contact with an authoritative truth, but, as has been illustrated by many references now, the annihiliation of such authority altogether by the mutual cancellation of opposed claims to that mode of truth.

The polemical nature of such an enterprise is, of course, quite fundamental and explicit: "Jeder wackre Mensch, jeder ächte Cyniker fängt einmal an mit absoluter Polemik. So fing ich entschieden an, gegen meine Lage und gegen die ganze Modernität" (KA XVIII p. 80 #613, 'Every gallant person, every genuine cynic starts off with an absolute polemic. That is decidedly how I set out, against my own situation and against all of modernity'). Yet it is also different from all positions which are less than absolute in this regard, because he is engaged in far more (or less) than proposing one construction and opposing another. It is not a complementary process of doing and undoing, but of undoing as such. "Ich philosophiere ruckweise" (p. 56 #371, 'I philosophize in jolts and starts'), he observes. That is, his thought moves forward as a sequence of disruptive shocks, breaking out of the web of what has already been settled. The text of New Mythology is thus not so much woven as, to refer back to the image applied by Benjamin to the "Penelope labors" of Proust, unraveled. The new process of mythologization is one of upending, reversal, to turn back the way language is knit up into the authoritative illusion of world. The unraveling will also, however, bring **back** what has previously condemned itself through the delusion of authority to the darkness of past prejudices: "Kommen die alten Philosophen in der modernen Poesie etwa rückwärts wieder? (LN 1106, 'Do the ancient philosophers not perhaps come back reversed in modern poetry?') The historical aspect of this mythologizing activity is therefore pre-eminent.

Schlegel early establishes that "Historie=Realphilosophie" (KA XVIII p. 97, #818, 'History is philosophy of the real'), indicating that this is the appropriate and necessary focus of cynicism's polemic. The reading of the past here is its rewriting in the new modality of mythology, which means its presentation as divination or analogy. The historian's task is properly a creative one, like the divinations of prophecy, for he generates a significant construction out of the elements of the past which is more than simply an inductive interpretation. At the same time, his version is destructive, for it must contradict the coherent, homogeneous reading of the past, just as the prophet disrupts the homogeneous projection of the future: "Der Prophet und der Historiker sind beide beides, zugleich Philosoph und zugleich Poet" (p. 85 #666, 'The prophet and the historian are each both together, philosopher and poet at one and the same time'). Both are "authors" in the sense Schlegel applies to the active cynic, and both counter the illusory continuity of a coherent world process (consistent with Being), and induction as a cognitive principle.

The famous and enigmatic fragment "Der Historiker ist ein rückwärts gekehrter Prophet" (KA XVIII p.85 #667, also AF 80, 'The historian is a prophet facing backwards'), is clearly comprehensible in these terms, and also fully harmonious with its appearance in Benjamin's notes to the Theses on the Philosophy of History. The historian not only faces back towards the past while he constructs his divination of the text of events, but for Benjamin he is also a "counterprophet" in the sense that he introduces a revolutionary contradition to the bourgeois "prophet" of progress and utopianism, who asserts a form of history which is subject to causality, induction, and a concept of homogeneous time. Here the Benjaminian historical materialist saves the present from extinction within the current of progress by exercising the counterinductive moment of heterogeneity. The present which Schlegel annihilates in his polemic as a cynic against "his own situation and all of modernity" is, however, similarly that of homogeneous or inductive time from which the past and future may be projected as determinate. When he writes "es ist sehr irreligiös und sehr unhistorisch in der Historie erklären zu wollen" (p. 240 #563, 'it is very irreligious and very unhistorical to want to explain things in history'), this argues that the events which figure in the past as he reads it, are lifted out of a determined causal chain, just as they are for Benjamin.

If history is not causal and continuous, its precise nature in Schlegel's work is still obscure, as well as extraordinarily significant. Its overwhelming importance is suggested, for example, when he observes: "Die sieben freien Künste beziehen sich wohl auf die Planeten. Eine große Entdeckung wäre es die Erdkunst zu finden;

. . . Es ist offenbar die Historie" (p. 172 #568, 'The seven liberal arts can certainly be related to the planets. It would be a great discovery to find the art corresponding to the Earth; . . . Clearly it is history'). Nonetheless, a precise explanation of what he really understands by the term cannot be given so long as he is committed to his "counter-metaphysical" position of producing a philosophy without Being. It is, certainly, an example of that mystical terminology which contains a split within it, an inherent contradition. He notes: "Zweck der Historie ists, Facta zu apotheosiren. Das erzeugt den komischen Gang" (p. 230 #430, 'The purpose of history is the apotheosis of facts. That causes its odd gait'). The concept of fact, of course, is never regarded as fixed or given: "Jedes Factum ist zugleich Mysterium und Experiment. Jedes Factum ist Hypothese, das versteht sich" (p. 131 #107, 'Every fact is simultaneously mystery and experiment. Every fact is, of course, a hypothesis'). The procedure of characterization which is then predominant in discontinuous history is not a purely cognitive one, but both critical and creative: "Eine Charakteristik ist ein kritisches Experiment" (p. 141 #1220, 'A characterization is a critical experiment').

The uniqueness of facts manifested in a historical modality, and their intertwinement with the act of their characterization or presentation to the subject is representative for Schlegel of all human knowledge. Indeed, he carries that to the extreme position of dissolving any exterior "objective" constraint, as we have seen in the disturbing expansiveness of New Mythology. This produces both similarities and contrasts with Benjamin through which the presence of an objective dimension in the latter's image of truth may now be brought into a further series of critical distinctions.

The knowledge of the past is subject to an additional limitation which goes beyond even that of phenomena in a condition of becoming, so that Schlegel finds it necessary to mark a restriction on the mystery of Charakterisieren itself: "Nur das Vergangene ist Stoff der Historie, daher erhält man statt der gesuchten Charakteristik des Zeitalters stets nur eine große Symphilosophie mit dem Zeitalter" (p. 141 #222, 'Only what is past makes up the stuff of history, and because of that instead of the desired characterization of the age all one gets is a great symphilosophizing with the age'). This structure is repeated by the historical materialist when he "grasps the constellation which his own era has formed with a definite earlier one" (Thesis XVIII A). The temporal dimension in which this occurs is termed _Jetztzeit_ or the "time of the now"—a dramatically foreshortened order of time through which a moment is not chronologically but historically bound up with the present. Thus, for example, "to Robespierre ancient Rome was a past charged with the time of the now. . . . The French Revolution viewed itself as Rome incarnate. It evoked ancient Rome the way fashion evokes costumes of the past" (_Thesis_ XIV).

This sense of repetition, of the present calling up a connected image out of the past, is expressed by Schlegel too: "_Echo_ ist ein Hauptbegriff der höhern Historie" (p. 307 #1362, 'The _echo_ is a primary concept of higher history'). Both, therefore, agree in separating themselves off from the cognitive delusion that history is simply "there" to be recovered, the fixed entity of "wie es eigentlich gewesen," in the phrase Benjamin quotes from von Ranke. Therefore Benjamin distinguishes the two tendencies from his own materialist standpoint where he writes that "Historicism gives the 'eternal' image of the past, historical materialism supplies a unique experience with the past" (_Thesis_ XVI). Schlegel's _Symphilosophie_ with a previous age is, of course, unique also, but nonetheless quite different in quality because of the nature of the present involved. As Benjamin writes: "A historical materialist cannot do without the notion of a present which is not in transition, but in which time stands still and has come to a stop" (_Thesis_ XVI). This restores all cognitive authority to the presence of his own time, which asserts itself as material constraint in the immediate demand of praxis. Such authority exerts itself on the past with which it stands in constellation in equal measure also, for it "gives that configuration a shock, by which it crystallizes into a monad" (_Thesis_ XVII).

The crystalline fixity of that historical perception is as distant as dogmatic historicism from the supple and poetic relationsip of Schlegel's "provisional" and "interimistic" readings of history. In place of the uncompromising "monad," there is a more fluid astrology at work in his constellations: ". . . statt einer Charakteristik, ein sich verständlich machen, Orientieren" (p. 141 #222, 'instead of a characterization, a connection of intelligibility, an orientation'). Schlegel, like the historical materialist, is motivated by his own time in recuperating history, but it is a poetic motivation, not the kind of cognitive basis which Benjamin finds in his material situation. Yet, in agreement with Benjamin, he does not interpret it like the historicist whose scrutiny approaches a past that is completely separate, unconcerned with his particular present: "In der Poesie wird die ganze Vergangenheit als Gegenwart gesetzt. Historie als bloßes Studium zu betrachten, ist unheilig und albern, ja höchst langweilig. Alle Historie wird Rhetorik" (p. 293 #1178, 'In poetry the entire past is posited as the present. To regard history simply as a mere topic for study is sacriligious and silly, indeed most boring. All history becomes rhetoric').

The status of each of these three constructions of history rests on a different basis of persuasiveness. In historical materialism it is the illuminating urgency of an imperiled concrete present; in historicism it is the idea of an autonomous and universally valid reality accessible as permanent truth through the means of consistent and causal evidence. Surprisingly perhaps, what these two have in common from the Schlegelian point of view, lies in their political character. Although they are opposed programmatically in this regard—one is aimed at change, the other at continuity—they each exert their political leverage from a fulcrum which is held to be independent of the persuasive process; which is to say, from the methodological perspective, depoliticized. The material present and the eternal past are in essence both posited as simply there.

This distinction between the methodological basis and the programmatic aspect reveals a great deal about New Mythology as it contrasts with the other two tendencies described. In New Mythology they are, for any significant purpose, already separated, whereas in the other two they are intimately bound up together. Putting them apart is extremely damaging in both cases. That is, questioning the validity of either basis, whether it be the causal, continuous necessity of things as they are, or the demand for a particular form of change in things as they are, is immediately apparent as a challenge to the program. Schlegel's reversed philosophizing sets this structure upside down. The persuasive factor does not derive its force from a metaphysical position, prior and depoliticized. Any such foundation as this resides entirely in what corresponds to the "program" itself, which sustains itself by the élan of its own forward movement in invading and incorporating everything which is established as natural or necessary authority elsewhere. This is read, from the standpoint of our ordinary expectations, as a lack of authoritative force altogether, but that is an uninformed response, lodged in inapplicable and uncritical categories.

That which would conventionally stand as the foundation or <u>origin</u> of the body of meaning which justifies the program is the <u>goal</u> for Schlegel, and is, furthermore, a goal which can never be fully attained: ". . . er ist unendlich wahr, aber die Unendlichkeit dieser Wahrheit wird nie vollendet" (p. 406 #1028, 'it is infinitely true, but the infinitude of this truth is never to be completed'). When he uses the term <u>Gott</u> in a context implying such centrality as the prior origin of all things, it is most definitely <u>not</u> to be understood other than in that sense of an ongoing project, rather than as the traditional onto-theological anterior entity: "Gott kann nur geschaffen werden. Sie sollen nicht von Gott eingegeben sein, sondern im Gegentheil ihn eingeben" (p. 330 #74, 'God can only be created. They should not be inspired by God, but on the contrary they should infuse him'). The concept of divine Being possessed of priority or orginarity as a basis of knowledge is quite explicitly denied in forthright terms:

> Endliche Geister ohne einen unendlichen nichts—aber der unendliche ist durchaus nicht gegeben, so wenig wie eine Offenbarung. Gott ist eine Aufgabe der Geister, so sollen ihn machen. Er ist nicht in, aber er wird in der Welt—aber er ist außer der Welt freylich nur auf eine apokalyptische nicht scientifische Weise (p. 301 #1277).[2]
>
> ('Finite spirits are nothing without an infinite one—but the infinite spirit is in no sense given, any more than a revelation. God is a task for spirits, who are to make him. He is not in, but his process of becoming is in the world—though he is also outside the world in a purely apocalyptic sense, and not in any way of knowledge.')

The finality and authority of the "scientifische Weise," a way of knowledge, is replaced by something whose "truth" must always remain postponed and unrealized—represented only allegorically or analogically: "Es muß für den Idealismus unendlich viele Analogieen geben, darum kann man von seiner Wahrheit fast nicht ohne Ironie reden" (p. 406 #1028, 'There must be infinitely many analogies possible in Idealism, and therefore it is almost impossible to speak of its truth without irony'). This situation makes "Gott ein Werk der Willkühr" (p. 330 #71, 'God a work of arbitrariness or caprice'), and allows for no limit on constructed meanings, in consequence of which it does not fulfill the same function as the methodological or epistemological keystone of the other two doctrines of history. Nor is that restricted to questions of history per se, but to all kinds of knowledge whatsoever, so that even the natural sciences have no "eternal" basis in immutable aspects of presence. Physics itself, as noted earlier, is "historical" and "mythological." That is, it has no point of leverage from which to impose itself as constraining choice. Not one element of physics is permanent or necessary, and therefore beyond the absolute admissability of endless variety.

It is thus also political inasmuch as it must depend entirely on persuasion, and for Schlegel science is never depoliticized in the sense that any factor belonging to it could be held by systematic necessity outside the legitimate field of plural constructions. The ground of choice or acceptance in this uncurtailed multiplicity cannot be one of recourse to a fixed component exterior to the forum in which the different possibilities present themselves and compete. Whatever theory we choose or continue to uphold, it must be for the immanent quality of the construction itself and the circumstances in which it appears. Persuasive force is then a question of attractiveness, not necessity, and so the scientist stands on the same ground as the artist: "Die Physik ist eine Kunst—Witz und Glauben gleich sehr darin herrschend. Nichts ist erbärmlicher als ein Physiker ohne Witz" (p. 154 #378, 'Physics is an art—wit and faith both rule equally there. Nothing is so miserable as a physicist without wit').

The attractiveness of a scientific interpretation has its source in the same fittingness as any other analogy; it is an inventive, witty combination like astrology ("Alle Physik ist Lumperei die nicht auf Astrologie ausgeht"—'All physics is just trumpery if it does not strive to become astrology') and a divination of precisely the same character, the finding of forms which belong together on the basis of their evocative capacity in the enrichment and _Bildung_ of humanity. It is the expansion of the harmonious sphere of human consciousness which is constantly free to invent itself and re-invent itself without oppressive constraint. What enters and contributes to this is absorbed, by that token, into New Mythology. And this "fittingness," which is the criterion of the paradigmatic figures of astrology (Schlegel writes: "Die Astrologie ist die Kunst des Schicklichen" p. 253 #721,—

'Astrology is the art of the appropriate'), is also the theme of its political aspect: "Die Politik ist die eigentliche Kunst der Weisheit––die Wissenschaft des Schicklichen" (p. 307 #1363, 'Politics is the real art of wisdom––the science of the appropriate').

This, of course, is not the politics of Gemeinheit, by which the world of closed prejudices is organized and administered, and against which the cynic mounts his critical polemic, but the absolute aspect of politics described when Schlegel notes: "Alle Politik ist astrologisch und divinatorisch" (p. 358 #455, 'All politics is astrological and divinatory'). It is therefore the opposite of the false concerns of Ökonomie, or the incorrect evaluation of the empirical realm as presence, which stand in the way of the full development of humanity: "Constitution der Menschheit als Gegengewicht gegen Empirie und Ökonomie, weil durch diese eben die Menschheit immer zerstückt wird" (p. 301 #1276, 'The constitution of humanity as counterweight to empiricism and economics, because it is through these that humanity is constantly broken apart'). This is the religious moment of politics: "Religion ist das was alle Antinomie der Bildung auflößt und zu Einheit bringt" (p. 301 #1288, 'Religion is that which dissolves all antinomes of development and brings about their unity'). The concept of God which belongs to this form of religion is precisely the opposite, also, of that which appears among mankind as the Messiah. It is the progressively created unity of mankind itself: "In der großen Person der Menschheit ist Gott Mensch geworden" (p. 320 #1534, 'In the grand person of mankind, God becomes man').

This is the real foundation of the programmatic universality of New Mythology as set out in the Gespräch über die Poesie. The divinely human unity and community of mankind are all that New Mythology expresses, and it is manifest where all the prejudices which obscure it are dissolved. When they are negated by "religion," the integrity of consciousness itself, as both the nature and collectivity of humanity, remains. This is the sphere in which the productivity by which man creates himself can proceed:

> Eine Geschichte des Bewußtseyns ist zwar nothwendig, aber sie
> ist noch nicht die Kenntniß des Menschen, weil die einzige höhere
> Kraft zersplittert wird. Wer den Menschen ganz kennen lernen
> will, der muß ihn betrachten in Gesellschaft, da er hier mit seiner
> ganzen Kraft handelt (KA XII p. 46).

('A history of consciousness is certainly a necessity, but it falls
short of being the full knowledge of Man because the single higher
power is fragmented there. Who would know Man in his entirety
must consider him in society, since it is here that he acts with
his power entire').

This is indeed what man i̲s̲: "Der Mensch soll betrachtet werden als
menschliche Gesellschaft; oder das Verhältniß des Menschen zum Menschen"
(p. 44, 'Man should be regarded as human society, or the relation of person
to person'). And it is from this principle that the form of unity identified
above as God can appear within the mode of historical reality: "Die
historische Harmonie des Instinkts beweißt, daß die Menschheit wirklich
schon Eine Person ist" (KA XVIII p. 123, 'The historical harmony of instinct
proves that humanity is really already one person').

Religious/political effectiveness now operates in place of the
exclusive moment of truth in finding the signifying measure of invented
meanings, so that New Mythology is kept from expanding into an
overburdened, chaotic mass: "Was hemmt die Explosion der Produktivität?—
Daß die Natur Gott ausdrücken soll" (p. 155 #385, 'What controls the explosion of
productivity?---That nature is to express God'). What at first sight seemed a
disabling permissivity, may now be seen to preserve itself both from arbitrary
exterior justification, and from irrelevance to the human condition, since Schegel
has indicated that "God" here is the collective life of free human society.

The assertive spirit with which Schlegel breaks down the perimeter of
conventional truth is thus not carte blanche for any nonsense, no matter how
outrageous and eccentric. The poetic/political/religious criterion which takes its
place is not passive before worthless claims, but critical and active. And it
discriminates at each point from within the material itself, from the locus of its
contact with the dimension of historical community. Thought becomes active and
creative by contradicting interpretations of images of the universe in which it
experiences itself, not by ignorance of them. This would be equivalent, Schlegel
argues, to a purely private arithmetic which is quite void and pointless so long as
it is sequestered in that insular condition. It cannot be thought fully until it
achieves the power to enter the "political" sphere and form a persuasive

combination with the universe that is the medium of connection between person and person.

Schlegel observes in the Jena Lectures: "Nach unserem System ist Wahrheit das Reelle, in so fern es mit Bewußtseyn und Kraft gedacht wird" (KA XII p. 95, 'According to our system, truth is the real, so far as it is thought with consciousness and vigor'). Clearly, not everything <u>can</u> be thought with consciousness and vigor. What is simply denied by induction, however, or the demand for consistency with established forms, is not necessarily weakened as thought on this principle. Those restraining criteria would transfer the commanding factor to the prior Being of the universe, whose fixity may be discovered in "laws" of nature. This would no longer be historical, but transcendent and eternal, before which man's position must ultimately be one of passivity or servitude. The contrasting capacity proper to thought is the unlimited ability to generate immanent phenomenal connections, parallels, equivalences and correspondences which are vested in consciousness as allegory, symbol and wit.

While this is akin to the aestheticization of the universe, it is essential to remember that it is focused in a political or communal subjectivity, not a private one. Schlegel does indeed go on to make the point that the conventional differentiation no longer stands between "beauty" and truth, for he writes: "Die gewöhnliche Erklärung (der Wahrheit) ist: Übereinstimmung des Subjektiven und Objektiven. —Gut: aber auch Form und Materie stimmen mit einander überein, und dies heißt Schönheit. Es ist der präzise Ausdruck dafür" (p. 95, 'The usual explanation of truth is: agreement of the subjective and objective. —Fine: but form and material also agree with one another, and this is called beauty. That is the precise term for it'). Yet this clearly holds to the same implication of a necessary vigorous potential as thought to enter and move the historical or political totality: "Schönheit mit Bewußtseyn und Realität ist Wahrheit" ('Beauty with consciousness and reality is truth').

Form here refers to the structure of analogy or the moment of combination; material is experience and awareness of the phenomenal universe or historical text from which the elements to be placed in constellation are drawn. The Übereinstimmen is not the logical agreement of fixed definitions, the homogeneous extension of what has already been established, but the unpredictable flash of a new aspect, a new quality, revealed to the artist's vision like an astonishing metaphor in poetry, a new system of proportion in painting, or of tonality in music. It is "illogical" according to what has gone before, like the distortions of perspective, or playing one melody on top of another in polyphonous music, or the principle of inertia in physics and the heliocentric cosmology. On the other hand, an interpretation which does have the requisite magical or divinatory power, regardless of what it does or does not contradict, if it may be read within the community of history, belongs in New Mythology.

The problem resolves itself into one of "legibility," which is an expression of the political dimension. New combinations are not all so instantly recognizable as some witty metaphors, and much of what is now public wisdom was once as impenetrable as "private arithmetic"—it may have been as appalling as Galileo's heresy, as ugly as the Demoiselles d'Avignon, as outmoded as Democritus' atomic theory, or as inept as Lucinde.[3] Until it may be thought "with consciousness and vigor," it remains an ungerminated seed whose potential for life is uncertain—and the life of an idea is its capacity to conflict with others, to emerge from a private existence into historical activity as a public and political force.

This is the nature of our present concern with Schlegel's notebooks, emerging into critical vitality after having so long remained in oblivion, dormant.

Physics and the Text of Nature

This epistemology disbars the dangerous idea of a "scientific truth" about political life which may be imposed on others because its objectivity is a higher criterion than agreement. For the form of politics Schlegel envisages, the opening out of a universal sphere of production, this would represent a block or resistance. It would be the evil principle. In general, one can say that the idea of objective knowledge as conventionally understood always stands contrary to the political mode of agreement. If it is posited as systematically _prior_ to agreement, prior to the active historical consciousness or relations betwen man and man, and therefore prior to politics, it overrides and cancels all of these things. It then belongs side by side with Messianism and revelation as the source of violent oppression, for if its reality is not constituted by the inclusiveness of its power to unite thought in structures of concordance, then it justifies the power to assert its dominion by those who hold it as their partial and exclusive possession, on any who do not. This will be the implacable justification of one side which has defined itself as right in opposition to wrong, where the urgency of conquest is always implicit.

There are two contrary conceptions of universality offered here. One is progressive, that of humanity in a condition of _becoming_, an organic nexus characterized only by paradox, experiment and infinite variety of contact. The other is determinate as Being, and so may allow its true nature to be brought to an ultimate, conclusive realization. This may appear in many guises, and be expressed in varying degrees of overtness or concealment, but even where they are not explicitly Messianic in form, these are derived from or associated with an effectively Messianic image of redemption. From the opposed point of view, nonetheless, so long as one refuses to accept that any fixed, quintessential face may ever be stamped on a universal man, the Messiah himself must have a double face as relative as the concepts of soberness and intoxication. What appears as the blessing of salvation in one sphere, will be the fury of the Antichrist in that complementary to it.

Therefore, when we earlier noted that an idea of justice in the exoteric and explicit sense of a fixed criterion could not appear in New Mythology, we may now argue that this is a strength rather than a weakness. As a "depoliticization," such a fixed and absolute notion becomes oppressive, or unjust, if it is raised above the intuitions of the community required to submit to it. Whether it is theologically or scientifically based, the depoliticization of justice leads to its imposition in what may be described as Messianic violence in order to achieve conformity. The rationalization of oppressive violence is necessarily a principle of unsurpassable "objectivity" in this form, and it will be found disguised as a factor in the relations between person and person, yet alien to precisely those conditions in which its authority occurs. The class oppression of capitalism and the abuses and humiliations visited on the Soviet proletariat are in this respect ideologically identical, and differ only tactically in the details of the myth by which each system protects itself and keeps its victims from the full status of political subject.

The stories which are told to this end are, most typically, scientific rather than directly theological, and it is consequently a pressing issue that the success of science as a branch of knowledge not be permitted to translate itself into a Messianic counterknowledge or counterpolitics. It is the particular character of what is drawn on in the construction of scientific ideas, the empirical realm, that it is liable to create the impression of absolute determination. In consequence it is characteristic of the scientific mode of representation, far more than those of literature or even narrative history, to acquire the aura of transcendent certainty and authority. Even though scientific modalities are often very successful in predicting patterns in phenomena with an impressive degree of quantitative accuracy, this does not alter the fact that the interpretations of why these phenomena occur, and explanations of what they really consist of in themselves, are no less bound within metaphor and analogy than any other genre of representation. Schlegel's resistance to this tendency, and the vigor with which he upholds the theoretical or experimental quality of all scientific conclusions, is of great moment in this dangerous situation. Through him, we may be able to restore scientific principles to their true methodological standing, which is, in a very real sense, that of "stories."

Schlegel does indeed state that "Die höchste Darstellung der Physik wird nothwendig ein Roman" (KA XVIII p. 155 #379, 'The highest representation in physics will necessarily be a novel'), which to our conventional sensibility sounds like wilful absurdity, and a threat to what all will agree are genuinely impressive achievements. Benjamin, too, from his materialist standpoint, associates himself with that conventional prejudice in his essay on Surrealism, when he takes issue with the Surrealists' "romantic" protestations on this question:

> If, however, Apollinaire and Breton . . . complete the linkage of Surrealism to the outside world with the declaration, "The conquests of science rest far more on a surrealistic than a logical thinking"—if, in other words, they make mystification . . . the culmination of which Breton sees in poetry (which is defensible), the foundation of scientific and technical development . . . then such integration is too impetuous (Reflections, p. 184-85).

The idea of physics as a novel in Schlegel must be judged very carefully, however. It reflects on the theory of the Romantic novel as well as on physics. In the section of the Gespräch über die Poesie entitled Brief über den Roman ('A Letter on the Novel'), he is at pains to stress that the element of imagination in a romantic book (his definition of the novel) is not the creation of fictive characters and circumstances, but a concern to represent "das Höhere, Unendliche, Hieroglyphe der . . . heiligen Lebensfülle der bildenden Natur" (KA II p. 334, 'the higher, the eternal, hieroglyphs of . . . the sacred plenitude of life in formative nature'). It follows, therefore, that it deals with historical reality, unlike the writings of Antiquity, which are constrained within the singularity (or false objectivity) of old myth:

> Die alte Tragödie sogar ist ein Spiel, und der Dichter, der eine
> wahre Begebenheit, die das ganze Volk ernstlich anging,
> darstellte, ward bestraft. Die romantische hingegen ruht ganz auf
> historischem Grunde, weit mehr als man es weiß und glaubt.
> ('Even ancient tragedy is a game, and the poet who presented a
> true topic of serious concern to the whole nation, was punished.
> The Romantic, on the other hand stands entirely on a historical
> basis, far more so than one knows or believes.')

This reflects the character of modern poetry described in LN 991 which
appears subjective, but is objective in the sense that it corresponds with a
natural or historical reality that is infinite. The productive imagination
can represent the universe precisely because it is able to respond to it
freely, and make it apparent as an entity of infinite variety. The finite
reality of old myth, which seeks to set out a world which is integral and
uncontradictory, must avoid and protect itself from real history, or from
the concrete phenomena of life themselves: "Phänomen ist was abweicht von
einer Hypothese" (KA XVIII p. 306 #1345, 'A phenomenon is what deviates
from an hypothesis'). Old myth is thus prevented from saving the
phenomena since it is committed to concealing itself as hypothesis, which
is equivalent to what I earlier termed depoliticization. The imagination,
on the other hand, is able to reveal the paradoxical as such, and is
harmonious with the multifarious phenomena of nature or history in that
respect: "Nur die Fantasie kann das Rätsel . . . als Rätsel darstellen; und
dieses Rätselhafte ist die Quelle von dem Fantastischen in der Form aller
poetischen Darstellung" (KA II p. 95, 'Only the imagination can represent
the enigma . . . as an enigma; and this enigmatic quality is the source of
the fantastic in the form of all poetic representation').

The "active cynic" is, then, indeed like the poetic author who offers
a construction or interpretation of the world in order to show its
mysterious, contradictory quality and inherent variety. Poetry and
criticism (that is, productive criticism in the manner of Schlegel's Über
Goethes Meister) are thus not essentially different in their function.
Whether the text is history, or poetry, the task is production of another

text which constructs an order of relationships between the parts of what is surveyed. This is done with perfect justice to what is visible—where the word justice is understood as belonging to that mystical terminology whose meaning is made good in the sphere constituted between man and man. The poet/critic expands the realm of heterogeneous possibilities in his subject matter through his characterization, but does not impose this as final (transcendent) knowledge of it. The physicist operates the same way in the empirical sphere. He respects its phenomena: "Consequenz ist die Tugend der Empirie" (KA XVIII p. 306 #1351, 'Consistency is the virtue of the empirical domain'), because without this virtue his theory would have no persuasive force or relevance. Yet theory is not constrained by a transcendent reality revealed in the phenomena, to be elucidated as present in and "behind" them. As with a literary text, there is no singular meaning by virtue of whose presence all theories should be consistent with one another. Therefore the physicist approaches nature in the imaginative spirit of the critic: "Der Physiker, der Skepsis und Empirie in sich vereinigt, wird dadurch schon zum Kritiker, die Natur wird ihm Text, er interpretirt die Natur mit dem Sinne als der große Kritiker den Autor" (p. 165 #498, 'The physicist who combines scepticism and empiricism in himself becomes thereby a critic. Nature becomes a text to him, he interprets nature with his intellect the way a great critic does an author').

Benjamin's blunt, not to say undialectical, dismissal in the Surrealism essay of any alternative to the now conventional view of a rationalistic scientific reality is all the more odd in the light of our certain knowledge that he was aware of, and apparently impressed by, the two major representatives of Romantic science, F. X. von Baader and J. W. Ritter. It is true, of course, that his comments are directed at Surrealism, which was in no way as philosophically grounded as early German Romanticism. Nonetheless, since the scientific orthodoxy with which Benjamin aligns himself is incontestably a product of bourgeois history in the age of industrial technology, it is very striking that the Marxist view should approach its ostensible opposite so closely on this issue, that any other tendency should be allowed no validity whatever.

It is a matter of historical fact that the Romanticism of the Jena Circle was intimately involved with natural science at its highest level of contemporary achievement—probably more so than any literary or philosophical movement for centuries. The approach it represented did not, admittedly, survive with much vigor beyond the first years of the nineteenth century, and it may in retrospect be considered the late efflorescence of an outlook already long threatened by the opposed tide,[4] but to judge its serious standing by that criterion would itself be "impetuous." Benjamin himself begins to mention F. X. von Baader, the first of the two great names cited in this connection, when writing to Gerhard Scholem in April 1917 (Briefe I, p. 134, 135) and the following month (p. 137, 139). He became familiar with Ritter's work in 1924, while working on Der Ursprung des deutschen Trauerspiels ('The Origin of German Tragic Drama'), mentioning the Fragmente aus dem Nachlasse eines jungen Physikers ('Fragments from the Papers of a Young Physicist') in a letter to Scholem where he notes that his own method is that of the Romantic concept of philology. Among other enthusiastic comments, he oberves: "Das Buch von Ritter ist ferner unvergleichlich durch seine Vorrede, die mir ein Licht aufgesteckt hat, was eigentlich romantische Esoterik wirklich ist. Dagegen ist Novalis ein Volksredner" (p. 143, 'The book by Ritter is moreover incomparable for its preface, which made me realize exactly what Romantic esotericism really is. By comparison Novalis is just a popularizer').

This letter, dated May 10th 1924, was written immediately before his momentous meeting with Asja Lacis, first referred to in that dated June 13th, through whom he was introduced to the radical Marxist concerns he presents in the essay on Surrealism, and which he was to develop for the rest of his life. We can conclude, therefore, that Benjamin's position on the Surrealists in this context is most unlikely to be merely the reflection of a general prejudice regarding science, or an unthinking response in which a complex reality is simply passed by. It must indicate a definite change from a quite adequately informed vantage point.

Counterinduction

Baader and Ritter were both introduced into Schlegel's circle by Novalis. The correspondence indicates Schlegel was first made aware of the former by reading references in Novalis' notebooks (see letter of 8th July 1798 in Preitz, p. 119, and previous footnote). Subsequently, Novalis wrote to him:

> Einen wünscht ich noch in unsre Gemeinschaft—Einen, den ich Dir allein vergleiche—-Baadern.
>> Seine Zauber binden wieder
>> Was des Blödsinns Schwert geteilt.
> Ich habe jetzt seine ältere Abhandlung vom Wärmestoff gelesen—Av. 8f. welcher Geist! Ich denke an ihn zu schreiben. —Könnte er nicht zum "Athenäum" eingeladen werden? Vereinige Dich mit Baadern, Freund—Ihr könnt ungeheure Dinge leisten (Preitz, p. 133).
> ('There is one man I would like to see in our community—one whom I can compare only to you—Baader.
>> His magic spells bind once again
>> What idiocy's sword divided.
> I have just read his early discussion of caloric—what a mind! I think I will write to him. —Couldn't he be invited to join the Athenäum? Get together with Baader, friend—you two could achieve wonders.')

The letter to Schlegel which accompanied that to Caroline in which the idea of "das Nüchterne" is discussed, also refers to Baader's Über das

pythagoreische Quadrat in der Natur ('On the Pythagorean Square in
Nature'), calling it "nichts wie derbe, gediegene Poesie" (Preitz, p. 151,
'nothing but utter, thoroughgoing poetry'). The passage in Caroline's
letter containing the thoughts on soberness is immediately followed by a
reference to Ritter, in which he remarks: "Schreiben Sie mir bald von
Ritter und Schelling. Ritter ist Ritter, und wir sind nur Knappen. Selbst
Baader ist nur sein Dichter" (p. 219 'Write to me soon about Ritter and
Schelling. Ritter is Ritter, and we are just shield-bearers. Even Baader is
only his poet').[5]

Ritter is particularly interesting in this connection because his work
continues to stand as a major contribution to the development of his
discipline, even in the context of today.[6] He is credited with being a
founding father of electro-chemistry, having achieved significant
preparatory work in the discovery of the Mendeleev periodic table of
elements, and—appropriately for a scientist whose interests did not halt at the
boundary of the occult—is regarded as the discoverer of ultraviolet rays. Although
we cannot look more closely at the details of this impressive record here, it is
certainly sufficient to lend a stamp of legitimacy to the approach he represented,
and the principles underlying those studies.

Many of the remarks on method in the book of Ritter's referred to by
Benjamin in his letter to Scholem, Fragmente aus dem Nachlasse eines jungen
Physikers, show a strong and clear relationship with Schlegel's philosophy. This
therefore gives most emphatic support to the view I have argued, that the open and
uninhibited character of New Mythology is not an impediment to its power as a true
or significant understanding of our universe. In the introductory section of the
book, Ritter observes:

> Mit dem wirklich wahren (Einfall) gehe es nahe wie mit dem
> Traum; man wisse allemal erst um ihn, indem er sich bestätige—
> wie dort, nachdem er (der Traum) einem im Wachen wieder
> einfalle—wobei man aber, im einen, wie im andern Falle, ganz
> bestimmt wisse, daß er jetzt zum zweyten Male, also ein erstes
> Mal früher, da gewesen sey, und auch zu der und der Zeit.[7]

('Things stand with a genuinely correct idea much as they do
with a dream; one really only knows about it for the first time
when it is confirmed—just as, in the case of the dream, it only
comes back to one in waking—so that in one case as in the
other, one knows for sure that it is now there for a second time,
and was thus there once before, and indeed at such and such a
time.')

The confirmation of an idea, that is to say, takes place in the public
sphere, the realm of waking in which the intersubjective or political
criterion must be satisfied. Yet, at the same time, it originates, as a
divination, in the mysteries of the night. Productive thinking in physics
does not, therefore, proceed inductively, or by conformity with the
established evidence of the daytime world, but by the inventive appearance
of heterogeneous ideas whose source is in the imagination.

It is especially interesting that the idea of the unconscious at work
here is further expanded in agreement both with Schlegel's notion of
philosophical method ("An genialischem Unbewußtsein übertreffen die
Philosophen die Poeten doch sehr weit" KA XVIII p. 94 #785, 'In their
genial unconscious philosophers outdo poets by far,') and with Surrealism.
The image that follows the cited section confirms the Surrealist claims
regarding science in that it presents a picture strongly suggestive of their
technique of automatic writing:

Ueberlasse man sich seinem Gedankengange mit der Feder in der
Hand, und wo man nun eben wahrhaftig nicht sonderlich über das
reflektire, was man schreibe, weil man ganz nur den Ergüssen
seines Herzens und Gemüths, und mit möglichstem Wunsche nach
Vollerhaltung derselben, folge, . . . wo also nicht die Feder,
sondern der Gedanke selbst, schreibe, und gleichsam erst
geschrieben gedacht seyn wolle, weil diesmal überhaupt nicht
anders gedacht werden könne (<u>Ritter</u>, LXIII).

('Just give yourself over to the current of your thoughts with a pen in hand, and do not reflect particularly on what you are writing because you are simply to follow the flow of your heart and feelings with the strongest possible desire to capture these in full . . . so that thus it not the pen, but the thought itself which writes and as it were is only thought as it is written, for what comes about in this manner could not be thought any other way').

Scientific knowledge for Ritter is largely the product of a dialectical interpenetration of what are sometimes called "natural interpretations," (ideas so imbedded in the foundations of traditional inheritance in knowledge that they are not ordinarily touched by critical light), through which they interrupt and contradict one another. This means a principle or pattern derived from one situation or moment as a commonplace observation, becomes an active tool for understanding when taken "out of context," and applied where, by the rules established through the ingrained habit of ordinary usage and the accepted norms of scientific definition, it does not belong. This is the method of analogy. It is not a logical process, but one of inspired inventiveness.

A typical example may be given from the Fragmente, where he writes:

Läßt sich wohl ein Electrometer empfindlicher (für Electricität durch Vertheilung) machen, wenn man über der Spitze desselben eine Loupe von Metall anbringt, deren electrischer Focus dann die Spitze trift. Dies würde besser, wie alle Condensatoren, seyn. Auf gleiche Art müßten sich auch (mit Linsen von Eisen oder Stahl) Magnetoscope construiren lassen (Ritter, p. 163 #253).

('An electrometer may be made more sensitive—for electicity by distribution—if one sets a loop of metal over its point, whose focus coincides with the point. This is better than any condenser. In the same way, it must be possible to construct magnetoscopes with lenses of iron or steel.')

The principle of refracting lenses in optical microscopy is logically the domain of light and transparent media. It is illogical, and for many years after that was written would have seemed senseless, to make the leap from there to electricity and magnetism. Nevertheless, this is the basis of the electron microscope, one of the major inventions of the 20th century. The freedom to present such an idea cannot be necessarily subject to its Popperian falsifiability, nor must it even be born out by any empirical evidence. It is purely a question of opening out the possibilities of thought.

The effectiveness of the ideas in Ritter's fragments in this regard is clearly not determined by a singular objective truth to which we have any access. They depend on their historical context. Some were much more potent in their time, some much less. Some seem absurd to the commonsense of the present, others brilliantly prophetic. It is impossible to predict which might emerge in the future. Some of them are still in the stage he referred to as that of the dream, not yet confirmed by the acquisition of persuasive force; others have returned to that condition after their day has advanced once more into night. And it is the task of the physicist to awaken what has been brought into our first, or dreamlike awareness, by history, into its second life with the power to rise and fill out the sphere of light constituted by responsive and vigorous consciousness.

As a scientific procedure, it rests on the assumption that there is more to nature than meets the eye because all that can be visible in that way is inevitably determined by the form in which the world is built up in "natural interpretations," or the basic prejudices about what is real. These tell one where to look, and what to expect, and in consequence tend to perpetuate the system of things which follow consistently from them. Thus, the scientific world investigated by methodological orthodoxy is also a dream or an "intoxication," in the sense of old myth. It does not stand by its attractive quality of persuasion in relation to a free or enlightened consciousness, but rather through conformism and the authority of inertia in Schlegel's "evil principle." Therefore it is also a condition of darkness.

Nor is this judgement merely to be found in the history of Jena Romanticism. Respected and influential thought in our own time may be found which is equally supportive of this conviction. Philosophers of science with impeccable credentials argue very plausibly against the ideology of rational scientific method, and in favor of the view that in fact all scientific innovation has in reality depended on heterogeneous thought in the manner Romantics have described. For example, Professor Paul Feyerabend writes in his book Against Method, that "prejudices are found by contrast, not by analysis."[8] The question science must confront is then how to produce that contrast in order to expose the unreflective, unexamined system of patterns and presumptions in orthodox reasoning:

> The answer is clear: we cannot discover it from the inside. We need an external standard of criticism, we need a set of alternative assumptions or, as these assumptions will be quite general, constituting, as it were, an entire alternative world, we need a dream-world in order to discover the features of the real world we think we inhabit (and which may actually be just another dream-world) (Feyerabend p. 32).

Such alternative assumptions are an integral part of the disintegrated New Mythology, in which truth arises out of the mutal negation of complementary errors. That is, once the principle of unlimited progression in the possible configurations of the world is admitted into the system, all facts in the natural realm appear as interpretive figures rather than observed truth, and as such their meaning is "hieroglyphic" or "symbolic," and may be applied wherever the inventive mind can find a new constellation for them. The facts of optics are therefore brought by Ritter to bear on magnetism or on sound (Ritter p. 153 #253, p. 162 #251 respectively), the relationship of vegetable and animal life is compared to that between speech and hearing (p. 41 #430), and the activity of "galvanism" determining movement in animals is related to the way electricity produces growth in dendritic precipitates (p. 32 #412), and so on.

This potentiality of endless combinations and interpretations creates a progression of harmonies which is discontinuous, but where the parts which form an exoteric paradox are by that token set in an esoteric harmony overall. This does not, of course, in any way resemble that of the conventional image of discovery, in which a universal system of nature whose proportions are <u>there</u> to be made visible precedes and dictates the line of advance. The universality of an "esoteric" mode of science is "elastic." Its ultimate harmony which permits all others is that of the <u>intellektuale Anschauung</u>, which Schlegel calls "nichts als das Bewußtseyn einer prästabilierten Harmonie, eines nothwendigen, ewigen Dualismus" (KA XVIII p. 280 #1026, 'nothing but the consciousness of a prestabilized harmony, a necessary, eternal dualism,')---that is, the infinite separation between consciousness and the Absolute. It admits all other harmonies into knowledge because of its own perpetual and irreducible distance. If it could itself be drawn into the realm of knowledge, and that necessary dualism infringed by presence as exemplified in the conventional structure of science, the process would be cut short and lose its exhilarating freedom: "Ein großes Unglück wäre es, wenn <u>Gott</u> sich wissen ließe, dann ginge die reine Wissenschaftliebe verlohren" (#1025, 'It would be a great misfortune if God were to let himself be known, for then the pure love of knowledge would be lost'). Ritter, too, expresses the necessity for an esoteric principle of harmony which must subsist <u>outside</u> the world of things, so that its effect may be sustained <u>inside</u> the process of their representation:

> . . . zeitliche, beschränkte Rücksichten blos machen Etwas zu diesem oder jenem; von einem höheren Standpunkt aus löse Alles sich wieder in Friede und Eintracht und gleich nothwendige Mitgehörigkeit zum Allgemeinen Einen Organismus der Belebung unseres, und des Daseyns überhaupt, auf (<u>Ritter</u> VIII).
>
> (. . . only temporal, limited considerations make something into this or that; from a higher standpoint everything is dissolved again into peace and unity and a necessary participation in the one universal organism which vivifies our existence, and existence in general.')

Feyerabend argues, with considerable historical evidence, that real scientific advance, the enrichment of understanding through change and innovation, depends on two "counterrules" which support his version of that endlessly admissive elasticity of thought when he contends "that there is only one principle that can be defended under all circumstances and in all stages of human development. It is the principle: anything goes" (Feyerabend p. 28). The first of these counterrules encourages the introduction of hypotheses which contradict well-established theories, and by now this will give us no new difficulties; the second "favours hypotheses inconsistent with observations, facts and experimental results" (p. 30-31). The latter may appear at first sight to go beyond what I earlier suggested should be admissible, but once again the paradigm of reading will make it clear what is really at stake here.

The persuasive power of a scientific theory requires that its relationship with the phenomena to which it brings meaning should be perceived in a certain way, to which we can apply the word "consistency" or agreement. This is, as Schlegel observes, the "virtue" by which empirically based claims justify themselves ("Consequenz ist die Tugend der Empirie"). But there is a certain emptiness in the term consistency itself, for the presence of any virtue depends on how it is judged. It is, for example, consistent with observations that the sun moves overhead and the earth remains solid and steady underfoot, but what one calls consistency here is (that is: was) only a particular "natural interpretation." The experience of ground under our feet and a disc of light in the sky are potentially consistent with an enormous variety of statements about them, each with its own implications for cosmology. The disc of light, after all, need not even be a luminous body, but might be a window through which a central fire is visible, or a reflection, or a series of discs which appear and disappear.

Armed with a suspicious mind, or prompted by new information, one can construct tests which modify the status of any such claim, but whatever conclusion one arrives at: "there is not a single interesting theory that agrees with all the known facts in its domain" (Feyerabend, p. 31). The result is not "truth" or "proof." No collection of facts can ever be consistent with only one theory, though it is possible the others might be less succinct and economical. The state of information accumulated on a particular question will in practice produce a choice which is not only slanted by the more or less conscious desire to support rather than deny the consoling integrity of one's world, but that choice in turn slants the accumulation of data. More insidiously (since the process will normally be unconscious) the language in which the evidence is brought together is necessarily predetermined by what is already "known." Feyerabend points out that "observational reports, experimental results, 'factual' statements, either <u>contain</u> theoretical assumptions or <u>assert</u> them by the manner in which they are used" (p. 31). The basis on which something will be judged "in agreement" with evidence is already implicit in the phenomena as they are constituted: "Experience arises together with theoretical assumptions, and not before them" (p. 168).

Therefore we can agree with Schlegel that the definition of truth, "Übereinstimmung der Vorstellung mit dem Gegenstand" (KA XII p. 4, 'agreement of the idea with the object'), does not give an automatic and absolute meaning to phenomena which follows by a transcendental or universal principle of consistency: "Dies sagt nicht mehr und soll auch nicht mehr sagen, als was ein Zeichen sagt von der Sache, die bezeichnet werden soll" ('This says no more, and should say no more, than what a sign says about the thing which it is to designate'). The meaning of a sign depends on the rule applied to its signification. Counterinductive theories do not contradict evidence in the sense that they depend on <u>fictive</u> phenomena, but in that the significance of any phenomenon as <u>evidence</u> is not absolute. It may indeed be contradicted if one introduces a new rule of correspondence through the new theory. It emerges, therefore, that the pattern of relativity discovered for other central terms applies here too, for what is rationally consistent according to the sphere of principles established by one theory, is inadequate or contradictory in another complementary to it. The "counterinductive theory" must attempt to re-order the basis of the old theory, even though it need not transform itself in turn into myth in the process. As long as it does not succeed in setting up its own persuasive basis, however, it remains in the condition of Ritter's dream-ideas. It is only _potential_ as an active, political agent, whose realization will remain an uncertain prophecy until historical circumstances change and favor its achievement.

The world of critically (counterinductively) approached phenomena is thus the equivalent to a written text in its status as a given concatenation of written signs—printed words on paper. It does not correspond to the world portrayed in the book. That would be the result of a singular and contingent reading, a particular series of historical choices in their interpretation. At the same time, the bare text is never approached as such, in a state, as it were, of primal innocence. Reader and text are both always imbedded in a cultural matrix of readings and interpretive strategies without which neither could have reached the point of confrontation or critical conflux in question. As Schlegel says: "Das künstliche Lesen besteht darin, daß man mit andern ließt, nämlich auch das Lesen andrer zu lesen sucht" (LN 2016, 'Artistic reading consists in reading with others, that is, in attempting to read the reading of other people'). No reading is thus an originary or pristine act, but it asserts its independence where it resists or becomes a critique of the situation it finds. Precisely the same holds for the phenomena as they appear in a particular, historical, scientific sphere. Principles of interpretation have been applied, the "facts" have been given quite specific meanings. A world has been built up consistent with the theories prevailing in that context. And here, too, that consistency is not the virtue of innocence, but of obedience.

In the ideology of conventional science, consistency is equated with reason as the inalienable precondition for all truth. In application it is always "political," however—that is, contingent, motivated and particular. In its propagandistic self-representation as indefeasible, it becomes myth. The perception of consistency is an acceptance of a particular line, and the rational scientist is brought into the servile position, by conventional mythology, from which he is unable to criticize the view which holds sway over him, precisely because the depoliticization intrinsic in the principle of rational consistency makes him "quite unable to discover that the appeal to reason to which he succumbs so easily is nothing but a _political manoeuvre_" (Feyerabend p. 25). The counterinductive principle which Feyerabend urges is nothing more, if one might express it this way, than a counter-depoliticization.

Accordingly, he redefines the role which science plays in society or the culture as a whole:

> The task of the scientist . . . is no longer "to search for the truth," or "to praise god," or "to systematize observations," or "to improve predictions." These are but side effects of an activity to which his attention is now mainly directed and which is "to make the weaker case the stronger" as the sophists said, and thereby to sustain the motion of the whole (p. 30).

The Path Which Prevails

Feyerabend goes to some lengths, and produces a plausible though scarcely conclusive body of evidence, to support this contention, mainly through the example of Galileo, whose tactical skill is summed up when he writes:

> Galileo prevails because of his style and his clever techniques of persuasion, because he writes in Italian rather than Latin, and because he appeals to people who are temperamentally opposed to the old ideas and the standards of learning connected with them (p. 141).

A natural concern arising from the legitimization of this "sophistry" is that it might move "the whole" in the wrong direction—one would not be so enthusiastic about this form of activity if it stood in the service of genocide, imperialism or social oppression. The short response to this, of course, is that motion in such a direction is far more likely as a correlative of myth than of any hypothesis, theory or sophistry which presents itself in the modest and humane spirit of "anything goes." The monstrosities which cause one to shudder when surveying the passionate convictions of the past did not arise out of the sophistry with which we now judge their case to have been argued, but the fact that they succeeded then in protecting themselves from appearing that way.

Since the Fall, none of our knowledge escapes the epistemological limitations entailed by that sad event. We can neither aspire to divine insight into the nature of things, nor to divine perception of justice and righteousness, so the argument by which we support our judgements can never be advanced from a position of certainty, but must share the same basis as the exposed sophistries of previous convictions. The only error, and the only danger we can be sure of avoiding, then, comes from a misplaced arrest of movement, the imposition of a conformity on those who would not accept it without constraint.

Nevertheless, the lesson we learn from Galileo seems to suggest a further complication to this situation, since Feyerabend has a tendency to confuse two different kinds of movement, or two different kinds of revolution. For reasons which can be discerned in Schlegel's comment that one can no more have a private politics, than a private arithmetic, we must distinguish here between a logical and a historical power of significance. There can be no serious objection raised against what Feyerabend calls his "anarchist epistemology" on logical grounds. In the private sphere of invention, the idea that "anything goes" meets no opposition. In the public, historical or political sphere, there is a new factor indicated by the need to "prevail." As Feyerabend notes, Galileo had to appeal to a "temperament" turned against the old teachings—that is, attract the support of a prejudice. This necessarily constrained his choice.

That public tenor may not be equated with the private inventiveness of the creative individual. The interest of the group or class from which Galileo could draw support was "diastolic" only incidentally, because possession of the field was not in its hands, and the dominant cosmological myth part of a totality opposing it. The aim of that section of the population to which he appeals is not the permanent dismantling of the epistemological bulwarks of order, but reinstatement of a more congenial structure in place of the old. What appears to be a step away from myth is only a step away from a particular myth, prior to establishing another which fits changing needs and the redistribution of power and influence. Without wishing to pretend to a more exact knowledge of this change than is implied here, one may describe it as part of the class-struggle between bourgeois and feudal elements. The appeal to a new spirit which enabled Galileo to prevail was not that of continuous revolution as in New Mythology or anarchist epistemology, but of continuous progress of the kind which Benjamin criticizes as "historicism." The pragmatic experiment, observation and scientific progress here will produce a mythic order in its own right.

The advance from a feudal and theological science to a bourgeois and rational one is not the passage from confusion to clarity, intoxication to soberness or dream to waking, but from one enchanting myth to another. Feyerabend is quite correct to point out the naivety of believing the old familiar tale about Galileo as the ancestor of our present majority doctrine, its hero and justification. The precise process of his discoveries was certainly at variance with that simple picture. The degree to which he is identified with the rationalistic experimental spirit is, however, neither spurious nor fortuitous. Both the theory Galileo championed, and the method he adoped to justify it, were dictated by historical conditions in a complex symbiotic relationship.

To a certain extent, the innovative potential of a discipline like physics will be made use of by the growing power of a new order to challenge the old, and to an extent make use of that in turn. The former case resembles the way revolutions have traditionally taken advantage of the alienated masses. They are mobilized to take to the barricades by the intoxicating call of liberty, and then left as excluded from the new regime as they were from the old, once the "anarchist" power of mass uprising has performed its task of moving the whole. Similarly, the intellectual sphere has its "anarchist" component which may be used to jar the foundations of the established condition. As Schlegel writes: "Es giebt so eine Art von Gedanken wobei alle übrigen in einen Zustand des Schwankens gerathen" (KA XVIII p. 226 #387, 'There is a kind of thoughts whereby all others are brought into a precarious state'). Such ideas, like the turbulent proletariat, are as potentially dangerous to the victor in the struggle as they are to the vanquished. Consequently, if a new thought is to be accepted into the rising order, it must be harmonious with the wider realm of the latter's influence. Epistemological anarchism would have been as difficult to incorporate into an intellectual regime in Galileo's time as the masses into an administrative structure. Only certain ideas, which might indeed have been born and devised within the implicit logic of "anything goes," but which have acquired a different and more reassuring, "useful" or stabilizing face, could count on finding that kind of favor, however.

Nevertheless, epistemological anarchism is not an impossible approach at all today. It does not imply the corruption of knowledge and the deluge of barbarism. It may suprise some, and irritate many, but, like Galileo's heliocentric theory, it is more remarkable for the ease with which it promises to work and the contradictions it promises to resolve, than for the old values it takes away. But that is the situation today, and Feyerabend is on shaky ground when he claims that there was a missed opportunity in Galileo's success. This criticism centers on the idea that the "propaganda" and "psychological tricks" employed "obscure the fact that the experience on which Galileo wants to base the Copernican view is nothing but the result of his own fertile imagination, that it has been <u>invented</u>" (<u>Feyerabend</u>, p. 81), but not because this means it was untrue. It should, on the contrary, have provided an exemplary case to reveal the untruth of all such evidence, so Feyerabend argues.

If the fictive character of science had been thematized <u>then</u>, Feyerabend states, instead of being camouflaged as consistent with what is "known and conceded by all . . . the most obvious expression of truth" (ibid.), a far more radical upheaval would have been brought about in the approach to knowledge. The claim here reminds one of a similar idea postulated in Bertold Brecht's play about Galileo to the effect that a more resolute stand against the Inquisition would have unleashed a social revolution. Feyerabend writes: "These tricks are very successful: they lead him to victory. But they obscure the new attitude towards the experience that is in the making, and postpone for centuries the possibility of a reasonable philosophy."

The issue here is the change of discourse, the transformation of the common coin of history, and Feyerabend's position suggests that Galileo was able to make two perceptions: 1) that the state of astronomical knowledge had reached a point where an alternative to the Ptolemaic model could be made plausible, and 2) that the arguments for that, the alternative he could propose, and any other, were all equally based on imaginative leaps to which no methodological limit could be set once they were in motion. The problem is that these two propositions operate by quite different historical dynamics. The first involves replacing an observation language appropriate to the authority of canonical texts, to one based on instrumental measurement and comparison of heavenly and earthly data. The second concerns the comparison of many observational languages.

As Feyerabend himself argues:

> . . . we must emphasize that a comparative judgement of observation languages, e.q. materialistic observation languages, phenomenalistic observation languages, objective-idealistic observation languages, theological observation languages, etc., can start only <u>when all of them are spoken equally fluently</u> (p. 80).

Galileo's situation was that the world of science knew only one such language, and he had discovered that a certain body of texts could be made comprehensible in another, and proceeded to apply and teach it. Since the language was new and in the process of dissemination, there would not have been any context available in which it could be perceived with assurance as "tricks and propaganda." Those terms, as applied by Feyerabend, are drawn from a comparative perspective impossible to Galileo. As established early in Against Method, "prejudices are found by contrast, not by analysis," and a polarity of two views is not sufficient contrast to reveal that the new position itself is a prejudice within a larger context of possibilities. Feyerabend's viewpoint is based precisely on the historical accumulation of many more developments whose record now exposes what was invisible to Galileo except, perhaps, as an intuition impossible to communicate in any available historical terms.

The political, that is, persuasive, nature of Feyerabend's "reasonable philosophy" finds a congenial medium in the current condition of contemporary pluralism. The contradictions of the many approaches and theories operate like the assembly of many images and systems in New Mythology. They demand and favor a viewpoint which moves easily across their boundaries and speaks all the different observational languages with equal comfort. The production of a coherent sense out of this requires an added factor, however, just as New Mythology requires the Transcendental-philosophie. Feyerabend expresses this in terms of an opposition between a vision of humane attitudes in which the imagination is set free, and the "abstract monsters" which are "used to intimidate man and restrict his free and happy development" (p. 180). This is a mystical idea as it stands. It is a conviction that stands outside and at the head of the arguments against method, just as the conviction that the workings of the scientist's imagination would coincide with and uncover the workings of the universe stands at the head of Galileo's justification of his findings.

Perhaps one day the polarity of counterinductive science and observational languages of rational truth will appear in a historical situation where Feyerabend might be chided by some future writer for having missed an opportunity to begin a revolutionary development in scientific mysticism. Yet that would be wrong. The potentiality of such an idea is obscured by its historical impossibility, and it remains extraneous to the counterinductive revolution proposed. The issue at hand is a "reasonable philosophy." No politician will ever point out objections to his arguments which lie outside the field of view of those he is working to persuade. Those are best left unspoken and unthought, just as the "reasonable philosophy" of "anything goes" was unspoken, and probably unthought, by Galileo. Thus, Feyerabend today concentrates his polemic on the issue at hand, not one which has yet to announce itself and reveal its outlines.

The questions concerning such an issue must wait until the means are present by which a purely intellectual or imaginative possibility can build itself into a historical one. It must find the data, the fragments it can knit up into language which can sustain its claim on the attention of significant aspects of the culture at large.

Then, like the heliocentric theory, or Ritter's once absurd speculations about universal electromagnetism, their time will have come, and they will be received into the public sphere. In choosing which idea is most likely to be adopted and sustained, one must take a gamble. Those whom history judges to have been the great innovators are not those who have entertained the most impressive number of new thoughts, but those who have been most successful in placing their bets.

The political arena is the battleground in which an idea will live or die. The power to survive and prevail there distinguishes what may later become a monument of sound judgement from what may with luck be remembered as a noteworthy oddity, or more likely sink into oblivion. The gamble which Galileo took was not simply counterinductive in the one-sided sense that it went against the established current. It also contained the historical perception that it could be made to stand and endure. That implies a reading of the ongoing text of history in which a counter-current could be discerned whose influence would take his idea out of the sphere of private eccentricity and into the daylight of decisive and persuasive action. To have an effect, the position one opts to champion must be one which has the strongest chance. Galileo prevailed because he was a skilful prophet who could divine the way the historical wind was blowing, and let it roll the dice his way.

NOTES

[1] Variété III (Paris: Gallimard, 1936), p. 60.

[2] Novalis expresses a similar thought in Das allgemeine Brouillon, when he notes: "Gott hat gar nichts mit der Natur zu schaffen. Er ist das Ziel der Natur . . ." (KS p. 250 #60), but the radical reconstruction of the concept of God as generated by nature is not pursued here. It remains a separate being with which contact is created by inner harmony: ". . . dasjenige, mit dem sie einst harmonieren soll."

[3] Schlegel has his narrator, Julius, refer to himself as an "Ungeschickten," a clumsy or inept person, at the opening of Lucinde.

[4] The history of that change is, naturally, a profoundly complex pattern of events, but insofar as it affected the points of relationship between science and literature, both Ritter in Germany and Humphry Davy in England illustrate this change in climate during the first decade of the new century. These years established the restrained, patient studies of empiricism in a firm ascendency, for its solid, utilizable gains were most fitted to attract support in a milieu where tangible benefits of innovation had become as impressive, and much more in evidence, than any other kind of wonder. Ritter's career suffered a dismal eclipse when he failed to respond to the reaction against speculative science, but Davy embodies the change in his own person. Coleridge, who had worked closely with Davy in the Bristol years, and admired his imaginative insights, was thoroughly appalled when he accepted a knighthood and began to profess the Daltonian atomic theory—regarded by Coleridge as intimately connected renegade gestures.

There is an informative account of this relationship in: Richard Haven, Patterns of Consciousness (Amherst: University of Massachusetts Press, 1969).

[5] Preitz adds an interesting footnote here, indicating that Ritter's influence even among literary figures was not restricted to the Jena Circle, or even to Romanticism: "vgl. Clemens Brentanos "Frühlingskrranz," Bd. 1, S. 70 (Leipzig, Insel-Verlag, 1909): ". . . dem großen Physiker Ritter, von dem Goethe sagt: Wir alle sind nur Knappen gegen ihn" (p. 219).

[6] Many works have been devoted to this remarkable figure, a recent example of which, Arnim Hermann, Hrsg., Die Begründung der Elektrochemie und Entdeckung der ultravioletten Strahlen (Frankfurt am Main: Akademische Verlagsgesellschaft, 1968), also contains a lengthy bibliography of other studies.

[7] Johann Wilhelm Ritter, Fragmente aus dem Nachlasse eines jungen Physikers, Hrsg. Arthur Henkel (Heidelberg: Verlag Lambert Schneider, 1969), p. LXII. The quotations from this source henceforth indicated Ritter.

[8] Paul Feyerabend, Against Method---Outline of an Anarchistic Theory of Knowledge (London: New Left Books, 1975), p. 31. This source henceforth cited as: Feyerabend.

CHAPTER V

FROM WRITING, NEW MYTHOLOGY AND THE NOVEL, TO NEW HISTORY

> One statement at any rate I can make in regard to all who have
> written or who may write with a claim to knowledge of the
> subjects to which I devote myself,—no matter how they pretend to
> have acquired it, whether from my instruction or from others or by
> their own discovery. Such writers can in my opinion have no real
> acquaintance with the subject. I certainly have composed no work in
> regard to it, nor shall I ever do so in the future; for there is no way of
> putting it in words like other studies.
>
> Plato, <u>Epistle VII</u>[1]

Misuse of Language

What is the function of a work like <u>Against Method</u>? What is the effect of
Schlegel's proposals for the New Mythology? Does the polemic in either affect the
practice of science or literature, or is it restricted only to arguments in a quite
separate sphere, the commentary of spectators removed from the game? While it is
true that Feyerabend is able to offer an effective critique of the rationalistic
picture of science, it is equally true that, by his own arguments, the advance of
science as a corpus of ideas has proceeded regardless of ideologies of order where
they have held sway over our intellectual life. To put the question another way,

would the uncontested rule of rationalism as the only explanation of science, have the capacity to prevent the unpredictable and heterogeneous jumps or changes in direction which keep knowledge alive? And if not, where does the power which brushes it aside come from?

The counsels of critical epistemology which we find in Schlegel and Feyerabend, and which crop up regularly in a variety of forms throughout the ages wherever there is speculation, are a part of history like the counsels of any virtue. And like any virtue, theirs has to compete with other virtues, or vices, for the support of the culture at large. It is not the novelty of the ideas as such which makes any of these more effective, but more likely the renewed guise in which they are propagated. After all, since Jesus of Nazareth, who has anything new to say about charity? Yet, in changing times, the same principle is advanced with renewed images in a renewed context, to meet the expectations of a transformed situation. Just as Galileo's cosmology or Dalton's atomic theory were old ideas brought back in a new form better adapted to the temper of their times, so the critical essence of Schlegel or Feyerabend is not a new revelation, but the heart of the most ancient of revolutions. And just as Galileo took care to represent his shattering "new" proposals in a form most apt to attract support, so the primary aspect of this or any revolution is its appeal to the circumstances presented by history.

To prevail, to be heard and accepted, an article of counsel must find a form in which it may appear as the strongest and most likely road to take. The criteria are not absolute. They depend on what the audience is willing to credit as valid, and the audience is constituted in that function by the totality of its historical experience. The history of the moment is the medium of representation which the bringer of counsel has to fashion according to his intention. And while "anything goes" as a private instant of speculation, no such instant is of historical moment until it is represented and transmitted in the quite distinct modality of collective understanding. No matter how inspired or far-reaching or unprecedented an intention the individual may have, it is conditioned by the considerations of representation, of "translating" a vision into a collective image which will have significance for the historical rather than private subject.

What holds for specific ideas within the body of knowledge, holds also for the overall principles of method and epistemology. Those works which proclaim that the world is not knowable as integral finality, base their arguments on demonstrations of the potentialities for change which have already been realized. Announcing the logical principle on its own, or to declare that alterations will come though they have not yet, has no great power. But change will lead to more change, just as stability will lead to more stability. The significance of those who propagate theories of change is limited, because no matter how forceful the prophet's voice, it will not be heard by a tradition in the sleep of continuity. More importantly, the writer is a reader of his own age, and if he does not read the possibility of change in it, he cannot write of it either.

This last interdependence of reader and writer also allows us to determine the systematic limits of innovation even where it is favored and in motion. Both the writer and the reader which implies also the innovator and his public, function from and within the same collective medium of representation; as Schlegel says "Lesen und Schreiben nur dem Grade nach verschieden" (KA XVIII p. 133 #130, 'Reading and writing are different only in degree'). Consequently, if there is inadequate stability to sustain reading, writing suffers in proportion. While it is true that a completely static tradition cannot avoid impoverishment and decay as it loses the element of response in favor of repetition, it is also true that if the central body of repetitions is reduced below a certain point, the peripheral or frontier areas of responsive innovation have no basis against which to render themselves legible. That is to say, if the area of stable knowledge or conventional meanings is so eroded by overwhelming changes that the map loses its frame of orientation, no new paths can be plotted. No translations from the impressions of the inventive personal subject to the medium of history can be made, and the tradition dissolves.

The possibilities for revolution are rather limited in the picture I have described. The "movement of the whole" does not really happen, in fact. It is somewhat like the way the great belts of vegetation shift as the climate changes. A forest might move as the ice-sheet advances in the North, and the cyclone tracks swing to the South, but the trees do not change their ways and walk. Seeds are able to germinate in places where they once dried up, others wither in the cold where formerly they might have flourished. This is the stability we observe in our great systems of signification. A revolution adds an area here, and extinguishes another there, but the body as whole stands more or less still. In language, we can change some words, forget others, add new possibilities, but without the continuity of the vast majority, the system would disappear and there would be nothing.

Feyerabend notes the changes at this level which Galileo effected, and writes that in general, "existing forms of speech . . . must be distorted, misused, beaten into new patterns in order to fit unforeseen situations (without a constant misuse of language there can not be any discovery)" (Feyerabend, p. 27). Yet, of course, most misuses of language do not produce anything new, any more than most instances of eccentric behavior or irrational viewpoints. It is certainly true that one cannot predict with certainty which will genereate movement, or when, but that does not mean that there is no difference a priori between misuse and heterogeneous innovation. The skill in divination is a special feature of the contact between the intuitive and historical subject, or individual and collective modes of experience. If one prefers to put it in such terms, I am arguing here for a criterion to distinguish between the erratic incompetent and the radical, innovative genius.

Ordinary language is a system which constructs the possibility of repetitions. A symbolic representation generated by a word is the production of an equivalency between impressions or constellations of impressions. Without the word or some other symbolic mark, the aspect joining two separate phenomena does not appear, and that meaning does not exist. Although metaphoric meaning does introduce a change of focus and emphasis in the way the world operates, it remains within this described formation. The metaphor adds a new possibility to the words it connects because it draws them out of the continuum of their established grammar, but this pattern can only occur because of a factor whose operation permitted the appearance of the grammar in the first place. This is the "translation"—which, like the word metaphor, means 'carrying over' in its etymology—from the hidden zone outside language, outside the realm of "to be."

The signifying token is able to produce something as phenomenon in the sphere of Being, out of a complementary or prior sphere which Schlegel will characterize both as Becoming and Nothingness, according to the aspect involved. This difference of spheres is the agency whereby the "original" is given a form which is repeatable and therefore accessible. On the other hand, the "original" is properly a nothingness. But "nothing" must be understood here as quite distinct from the naive conception which arises as a result of the way the word for nothing functions in language. There it signifies that which contains no being, and from which no being can come. "Nothing" within the system of language is simply a halted signification, a blank. The idea is built only on a bare principle of negation. To say X is not, generates an emptiness defined and enclosed within language. Nothingness as the sphere outside language, or outside any system of coherence and regularity, must be grasped quite differently because it exists in relation to that system, and indeed is prior to it. Schlegel notes: "Nichts ist absolut transcendent; alles hat seine Sphäre. Was absolut transcendent wäre kann nicht existieren" (KA XVIII p. 82 #634, 'Nothing is absolutely transcendent; everything has its own sphere. Anything that would be absolutely transcendent cannot exist'). Nothingness, in the sense of das Nichts, must not be confused with the linguistic blank, but thought of as it is given through the distinction between Being and Becoming.

The factor which divides the latter from Being is that its sphere is characterized by a disparate (and fragmented or chaotic) temporality. The "original" which finds its representation in Being as phenomenon, is lost in its absolute uniqueness or absolute incommensurability. It disappears endlessly because there is no basis in it for repetition. The grammar of languages establishes itself by registering a similarity in its own sphere. This is what Schlegel means by creation out of nothing, and the phenomenal universe which we call world is thus the representation or signification of nothingness. But this is no longer the sterile blank from which nothing can come. It is, on the contrary, the field of all possibilities, from which everything has come and will continue to come. And in the term field, we recall the relationship alluded to, in the introduction, of mathematical interchangeability between field and particle in microphysics. The field only appears by its expression in the nature of the particle's behavior, while the particle is only comprehensible within the field. They are antithetical, and yet each is inconceivable without the other. It is on this basis that Schlegel rejects Being as a metaphysical concept independent of nothingness. As an appearance, it can only be a representation, and cannot be regarded as final and in itself, except in that unphilosophical thought where the nature of signification is ignored.

The culture, as a nexus of systems of signification, each of which is involved in its relationship with the others, is the closed historical image of what was constituted by preceding acts of translation both from the sphere of nothingness, and from one to the other. The systems include, in addition to language as such, social organization, knowledge of the natural world, traditions of values, metaphysics and so on. One can deduce that even though one strand might lead the others, the hierarchy among them is not a permanent absolute, but a function of power which is historically determined. That system will be dominant in a given area, where it has been rejuvenated by the appearance within it of something new. Schlegel writes: "Jede Uebersetzung muß eine Verjüngung sein" (KA XVIII p. 204 #87, 'Every translation must be a rejuvenation'), but, to draw on an image from the model of living entities, the point at which the culture "feeds," or appropriates material and energy as opposed to transferring them within itself, is the point of contact with its "outside." Where something is registered in the organization from what is not already part of the historical totality, its annexation from the non-historical exterior of nothingness is a (real or qualitative) historical change.

An obvious and easily decipherable point of such innovation is in economic practice, and in its technology. It is not necessary, however, that it be restricted to that zone. Whatever is liable to an equivalent disturbance or disruption in the process of human life, is capable of this renewal and therefore this autonomy. The vitality of historical change is dependent only on the capacity to suffer irruption from the alternate sphere, the capacity to function as a recipient medium of translation. Since all forms of cultural systems must be mediated through individual consciousness, and all are liable to the contact with private subjectivity there, the historical system is implicitly always open to tensions from that source, or to "mutations," in the terminology of life-forms. This is the guarantee of continued life for all historical signification: "Nur durch eine fortdauernde immer wiederholte Störung ist Leben möglich" (p. 419 #1181, 'Only by continued, always repeated disturbance is life possible').

It should be stressed once again that the changes can only be manifest in the historical medium, and never appear in a prior form. The field of possibilities can have no visibility as itself ever. Only the reality of historical change enables us to speak of it, and yet nothing may be said of it. Furthermore, the "hierarchy" of innovation is substantially indeterminable for the same reason. Once a change is established in one system of the culture, the uneven development will precipitate commensurate changes throughout the nexus. For example, a technical invention may necessitate a long sequence of corresponding modifications in economic activity, class structure, in language and science. But it is impossible to say that the invention was not preceded by some other change which altered perception and facilitated it. All systems must be assumed to act on one another constantly in ways which are sometimes more and sometimes less radical, sometimes more and sometimes much less discernible, and to do so in ways which are not causal, that is determinate, but historical, which means imaginative, inventive, hetereogeneous and unpredictable.

The question of the source of change within the overall nexus, therefore, neither determines the precise form of the response, nor does it permit that one might predetermine the correlative responses subsequent to it. That is to say, one cannot predict the viability of an innovation. The idea of viability here is defined very simply as the possibility that something may be added as a new factor to the body of what is already familiar. This will depend on the condition of all the other signifying systems complementary to that in which the change occurs, because the single system in a culture cannot long sustain a "private" meaning contradictory to the others, any more than an individual can maintain a private use of language. It must either be consistent with the totality, or capable of entering and modifying the complementary systems. By this proposition, one can regard Galileo either as introducing a cosmology which worked because it was capable of re-organizing other areas of the culture, or as being the enactor of an impulse to produce commensurate change in natural science in a historical process which began with social and economic forces. Not only is it quite unnecessary to decide between the two, it is also impossible to limit the complex to these, or any closed range of factors.

All such changes, whether in science, language or whatever, are enlivened by promptings from elsewhere in the culture, proceed by creative interpretation in their own area, and survive by sucessful modification of the whole. This motion is potentially continuous and unlimited because neither language nor any mode of signification rests upon the final foundation of what "is," where that implies Being outside them. The meanings contained within the historical totality, by which predication is possible, require stability to function, and as passive inhabitants of those systems, we depend on and believe in their solidity. But to rejuvenate them, we must see them quite differently. In the act of imaginative invention, we have to deal with systems of meaning as provisional, not as the determinate reflections of the world we repeat in "ordinary usage."

Mystical Grammar

There is a quite easily perceptible difference between the terminology in Ritter's and Schlegel's speculative fragments, and that in the language at large. The whole concept of the items they discuss operates in a way whose fluidity alters the usage of the verb "to be" itself. In ordinary speech, this mediates the connection between a word and all that a grammatical definition sets out as its agreed upon territory. Their approach, on the other hand, is enlivened by the recollection that a constellation of phenomena suggests itself by repetition of experience, and it is only this constellation which is marked by the token of a word and conceived as a "thing." Thus the observed properties of the materials called metals suggest that they exist as a group, and the group has members which are distinct among themselves, but Schlegel insists that such associations should be appraised astrologically. The appropriateness of other combinations is always to be sought.

The boundaries of those phenomenal series are ordinarily determined by grammar, and are therefore not "real," but only one of an indefinite number of possible determinations. Mystical terminology or grammar ("Die Magie ist mystiche Grammatik" KA XVIII p. 253 #719, 'Magic is mystical grammar') opens a new realm beyond ordinary grammar, where the verb to be is a magical fomula conjuring up altogether new correspondences. This means the negation of the present in the sense of a disruption of the synchronic grammatical order by introducing a fluidity among terms, although, equally, the structure itself is indispensable for that procedure: "Ohne Buchstabe kein Geist; der Buchstabe nur dadurch zu überwinden, daß er fließend gemacht wird" (p.344 #274, 'Without the letter there is no spirit; the letter can only be overcome by making it fluid').

Ritter was, for example, able to project the concept of iron into a significance greatly exceeding that simply of one metal or chemical element among others. Its magnetic quality, and the magnetism of the earth, suggested a far more central role. Accordingly, he applied a series of "magical" additions to its meaning, to claim, among other things:

> Alle Stoffe auf Erden scheinen zerlegtes Eisen zu seyn. Eisen ist der Kern der Erde, "der sichtbare Quellgeist der Erde" (Jac. Boehme) . . . Es ist der dynamische Aequator der Erde, unter ihm steht die Sonne des Magnetismus senkrecht. —Alle Stoffe auf Erden zusammen genommen müßten zum Produkt Eisen geben müssen. Dieses ideale Eisen herzustellen ist die Tendenz aller chemischen Action. Denn das dynamische Mittel der Erde muß sich immer wieder neu herstellen, der Repräsentant desselben aber ist das Eisen (<u>Ritter</u> p. 34-35 #51).
>
> ('All substances on earth appear to be decomposed iron. Iron is the core of the earth, "the visible source-mind of the earth" in Jacob Boehme's phrase . . . It is the dynamic equator of the earth, and beneath it the sun of magnetism stands vertically. — All substances on earth put together would have to come out as iron. The tendency of all chemical action is to produce this ideal iron. For the dynamic center of the earth must always generate itself anew, but its representative is iron.')

The identities and equivalences invoked here are "nonsense" by the standards of ordinary expression, and even by the language of rational science. Yet these ideas did not come to be written down because Ritter was a fool, or a liar, nor were they even picked out at random. They were the intuitive synthesis from long experience with the chemistry, physics and biology of electricity, magnetism and galvanism. In modern times, the magnetism of iron is regarded as the result of the orderly arrangement of its atoms, which permits the electromagnetism characteristic of all atoms in all elements to be united as a single force apparent at that large scale.

Since this universal quality is represented for common observation only in such an instance, its central status is not so nonsensical after all. It may as easily be regarded as an early, but significant, step towards a theory whose authority is now paramount.

The intuitive synthesis here is directly parallel with that which enabled him to say that iron bending electromagnetic lines of force "is" a lens, to create a new concept for the term microscope, and a similar leap produced the first thought of what is now realized as the radio-telescope: "Sollte es magnetische, electrische, Telescope geben können? —Spiegel für Magnetismus, Elektricität? —Linsen, Telescope und Spiegel für alle Kräfte?" (Ritter p.161 #249, 'Should it not be possible to have magnetic or electrical telescopes? — Mirrors for magnetism and electricity? —Lenses, telescopes and mirrors for all forces?')

These ideas, as Feyerabend argues for all scientific discovery, are not "rational." They are, nonetheless produced by something containing more coherence than the mere rejection of an established norm. They are readings of the text of phenomena, a text which is made up of all the previous readings and rereadings gathered in the historical inheritance. As was stressed earlier, the conception of a pure phenomenon is ideal only, with no real existence, but the "astrological" or "divinatory" critic's reading can use the body of order established before him, through which all phenomena appear, as the starting point from which his innovation can begin, and on to which it will be grafted. It is that alone which makes the universe legible, instead of an overwhelming, inchoate chimera beyond all recognition.

If his new construction is powerful enough in its own form, it may enter the inheritance of science itself. That difference between a powerful critical reading and a random rejection, therefore, is in essence the same as the distinction between an inept misuse of language which loses meaning, and a poetic transformation which overcomes or exceeds grammar to generate a new meaning and a new limb for grammatical language itself. Anything may be the source of a scientific idea, just as any slip of the tongue or random juxtaposition may produce a fine metaphor, or a found object may be exhibited as a sculpture—but the realization depends on the finder, who is the reader of its text. Without the reader, the meaning has not yet been written.

The delay in the change from impenetrable "nonsense" to intriguing prescience may be an enormous interval of time, as it was with some of these ideas of Ritter's, demonstrating that there are two distinct kinds of reading possible. While the collective or "rational" modality of meaning in the culture at large requires a lengthy procedure of assimilation, there is an "irrational" foreshortening in the time-scale of the innovative and rejuvenating spirit Schlegel calls "wit," which forestalls that labor: "Witz ist abbreviirte Weisheit" (KA XVIII p. 89 #711, 'Wit is abbreviated wisdom'). The transformation of witty meanings into rational consistency is not automatically guaranteed by its reference to the prior order, even though in deviating from it, the new formulation must have begun from there. The modality of wit is sui generis, neither rational nor random. It is a flair, an autonomous sense which finds its object without any visible track to lead it there: "Die Römer wußten, daß der Witz ein prophetisches Vermögen ist; sie nannten ihn Nase" (LF 126, 'The Romans knew that wit is a prophetic ability; they called it nose.') And this same sense, this "flair" (Witterung in the German), is what for Walter Benjamin characterizes that perception of history which breaks out of causality and universal continuity:

> Fashion has a flair for the topical, no matter where it stirs in the thickets of long ago; it is a tiger's leap into the past. This jump, however, takes place in an arena where the ruling class gives the commands. The same leap in the open air of history is the dialectical one, which is how Marx understood the revolution (Thesis XIV).

The condition which permits the operation of wit is that of an imperfect signifying system. The quality of a redeemed language, or of the prelapsarian Adamic language, where words belong in an indissoluble and perfect union with their objects, permits no tampering or astrological reconstruction. Thus, Ritter could not have extended and contradicted the meaning of a lens to cover a magnet if he had been working in the Garden of Eden (nor would he have wanted to). The divine order names all that a lens is, all that a magnet is, in the bestowal of the term. No change is possible in that perfection. Wit is poised between illusion and chaos, dependent on the order it finds, yet able to act only because that order is illusory where it appears to be final. Wit is an impulse which awakens consciousness to the reality of its situation.

Yet, as Schlegel, Benjamin and Feyerabend all argue, there is a tendency always for sleep to supervene, an "evil principle" of conformist inertia, which not only keeps mankind from realizing its best potential, but may preserve the dream until it has become a horrific nightmare. The hypnotic power of illusion even expresses itself through the longing for a dream from which no rude awakening can shock us, in the image of redemption of which Benjamin refuses to despair. For him, that longing is the force which should pull history out of its illusions, but surely it is the most dangerous of means to such an end. Nevertheless, the question of how Schlegel's and Feyerabend's proclamation of the never ending revolution should affect the "narcotic evil" which afflicts history, still remains unclear.

If it is true that all innovation is destined eventually to enter the synchronic system of collective culture and disappear into the dream-world of general agreement, do their writings offer any resistance? That is to say, hope of a change from the sequences of the past? Their analysis suggests with great persuasiveness that the sleep can never be total, that it is always more or less fitful, and always liable to be interrupted so that a new dream may begin. But that says nothing of their capacity to change or add to this pattern. Is it possible for their arguments, or polemics like theirs, to disseminate an art of awakening? Can they influence and potentiate the powers of invention, or diminish the thralldom of illusion?

Archaeology

Schlegel asks: "Wer hat denn das Erfinden erfunden?" (KA XVIII p. 126 #40, 'Who was it that invented invention?'), and clearly there is no answer—it is quite as old as time. It has always been there, and similarly it cannot be re-invented, or isolated and augmented:

> Eine Erfindungskunst ist wohl eine Chimäre; nicht weil alle Erfindung, wie der Pöbel wähnt, Zufall wäre. Es gibt ein Erfinden welches historisch nothwendig und transcendental betrachtet frei ist. Dieß ist das eigentlich ächtes Erfinden; alles andre ist nur ein Finden und Entdecken. Es ist freilich über alle Kunst hinaus; es zeigt sich da von selbst, wo einer den Geist einer ganzen Wissenschaft oder gar mehrer hat (p. 88 #706).
> ('An art of invention is certainly a chimera; not because all invention, as the vulgar crowd imagines, is accident. There is invention which is historically necessary and considered transcendentally is free. This is actually genuine invention; everything else is only finding and discovery. Certainly it goes beyond all art; it appears by itself, where a person possesses the spirit of an entire science, or perhaps of several.')

It is, therefore, immanent, part of the weave of history, the spontaneous accompaniment of the human enterprise of knowledge. And yet he concludes: "Die Kunst sich und andre zu solcher Erfindung zu bilden ist die Philosophie" ('The art of educating oneself and others to such invention is philosophy'). The question, then, since he has repeated several times the principle that "es soll keine Philosophie geben als Historie" (p.226 #385,

'There may be no philosophy other than history'), is how history can be used to augment what is an intrinsic quality of itself. That is, since imaginative invention is already the heterogeneous element dialectically interwoven with the historical process, how does one potentiate history so that the spontaneous factor within it is potentiated?

The standpoint of the historian is in history to the extent that what he reads and writes is "historisch nothwendig" ('historically necessary') and thus Schlegel refuses the position that there is a universal optic available to him: "Gewöhnlich unrichtiger Gedanke, daß die Historiker die Begebenheiten aus einer gewissen Entfernung ansehen, und daß diese Entfernung das Wesen des historischen Gesichtpunktes sei" (p.24 #67, 'Commonly false thought: that historians consider matters from a certain distance, and that this distance is the essence of the historical point of view').

On the other hand, to be "transcendentally free," and not caught within a determinate and predictable necessity, he has to be able to bring an interpretive moment to bear on his situation, and so he concludes for the historical standpoint: "Es ist Abstraktion, aber nicht diese übersichtige Allgemeinheit und Flachheit" ('It is abstraction, but not this overviewing generality and dullness'). That abstraction and its role can be clearly identified in a variety of facets in many notes, but the idea of how it can be favored, and the Bildung of mankind advance, seems to remain trapped in circularity so long as the emphasis is with human velleities. Erfindung, Poesie, Kunst, Religion, Fantasie, are all countermoments poised against that fixed synchronic system whose transmission is only half the historical dialectic. History itself must already include them, for it cannot be considered separate from change: "Die Historie nur da möglich wo etwas geschieht" (p. 260 #802, 'History is only possible where something happens').

The term used to distinguish the fixed image from the heterogeneous principle together with which it represents the changing process of history, is culture: "Der Gegensatz der Religion ist Cultur" (p. 334 #130, 'The opposite of religion is culture'). Invention cannot be lost to the dialectic, except where culture breaks away into the doomed sterility of an a-historical condition. At the same time it cannot be raised to clear hierarchical supremacy by its own volition or conscious project. It is confined within the dialectic of its history, or to the optic of its perspective. "In der Historie ist die Erkenntnis wieder so wie die Anschauung—auch in der Historie sehen wir nur das Nahe und das Nächste" (p. 372 #625, 'In history perception is just like intuition—even in history we see only close by and nearest to us'), Schlegel concedes, and yet, of course, this is in no way a historical determinism, but only the recognition of how creative possibilities are situated: "Wie viel Gesetzmäßiges in der Geschichte ist, so ist doch auch sehr viel freyes darin, die Fantasie hat Spielraum genug" (p. 350 #360, 'However much regularity there is in history, there is still a great deal in it that is free. The imagination has enough room for its free play').

The historian does have this free play, yet only as an immanent factor in a situation he does not have unrestrained command over, and to which he is born: "Um die Geschichte von etwas zu schreiben, muß man noch in derselben Sphäre leben" (p. 385 #770, 'In order to write the history of something, one has to live in the same sphere'). As discussed already, imaginative free-play is the task of the artist, or artistic spirit, whose activity is like a lever against the determinate aspect, working from the "hierarchy" of its special function in mankind. Nonetheless, it remains within that given sphere. Philosophy, about which Schlegel wrote: "Philosophieren heißt die Hierarchie beweisen" (p. 420 #1198, 'To philosophize is to confirm the hierarchy'), is no less confined. There is, however, a break in the circle: "Historie ist durch die Immanenz verschieden von Archäologie" (p. 385 #770, 'History is distinguished from archaeology by immanence').

By this argument, the revolutionary perception whereby republican France saw itself reflected in republican Rome, which Benjamin introduces in Thesis XVI, was not conditioned only by an immanent change in the sphere of the present. It was not solely an act of imagination which seized on the image of Rome that had been latent in the culture long before the revolution. It was, equally, the "archaeological" penetration of the antique past into the present which brought about the sudden change in historical understanding. The form in which this could have taken place is not to be conceived only as archaeology in the plain sense of excavations, but also as the spread of a particular knowledge into areas where it had hitherto been vague or inaccessible. Primarily, this indicates the effect of popularizers of knowledge and their use of the printing press. The appearance of books, such as the encyclopaedia, in which a great rush of alternate constructions of social life is thrust into the culture, is a precise expression of the extended sense implied by Schlegel's distinction between archaeology and history.

Therefore, despite the "indifferentism" of encyclopaedic or eclectic knowledge, it may still transform the actual immanent dialectic of historical happening through its capacity for interference—it enters and complicates the historical dialectic on the "cultural" side. The stable picture of truth which these complications jeopardize, depends on the enclosure which is characteristic of conformist historiography. Its images are universalized and projected back on the past because it has systematized criteria which account for all that the historical subject surveys from the vantage point provided by a culture. The autonomy of the data is repressed to produce a conformity in their interpretation with the demands of the integral present. The system is capable of this because of the frailty of the record, and the briefness of memory. This limits and simplifies the situation of the data with which the interpretive dynamic must contend, so that the system is able to maintain its harmony with them. Its projection will thus be reflected back by the conformation of the past to sustain the present.

The nature of the present is bound to be a direct expression of the demands made on it by the record of the past. To justify its form of order, it must be adapted to provide an adequate response to what is known about the past, so that it can propagate itself into the future, and not dissolve. The demands of history manifest themselves partly through the actual character of events, of course, but inasmuch as the sphere of prior states will ultimately always extend into realms which contradict the situation of the present, the crucial factor to consider is the force with which it penetrates the curtain of time. The vulnerability to repression of the past will establish the degree to which the present must produce structures of assimilation, and temper the singularity or rigidity with which it represents what has gone before. And the frailty of the record, or alternatively the concrete evidence which survives and achieves visibility, therefore becomes paramount in the formation of a particular mode of history in a particular present.

The ideology of progress, for example, differs from the theocratic system which preceded it precisely in that it was produced by the shock of a measure of "archaeological" intrusion into the latter. It was, in part, the new awareness of the pagan inheritance in Renaissance Europe which helped to tear it free from that myth of a plenitude of truth which had fed the theocratic Messianism of the medieval age, and thus set the modern period in motion on its characteristic course. The dissemination of elements which resisted the dominant authoritative images had, to take an important juncture in the history of the notion of progress, become a flood in the years when Galileo first became active, and that breached the channels by which the system had for centuries contained the flow of ideas. The restrictive order failed, and gave rise in its place to a system of criteria which does not determine the content of knowledge directly, but rather its methodological basis only.

The criterion of rationality which appears here does indeed lay claim to the "form" of knowledge, which is to say it claims to provide and describe the legitimizing mode of access by which it is acquired. It does not, however, attempt an absolute or pre-emptive determination of those contents in the inheritance which may be possessed now, or added to in the future. This introduces a criterion of potential knowledge whose actualization is then a universally ordered process, as opposed to the Messianic universalization of an integral actuality.

Since few cultures are ever completely free of intrusions, the nature of the change between modes of history, such as that characterized by the advent of "progress," or the further stage represented by Romantic Progressivität, is initially one of quantity. The accumulation which Benjamin regards as a never-ending, empty process in bourgeois historiography, may threaten itself with disruption at a certain point, according to this argument. While his analysis is certainly accurate where it diagnoses an enormous digestive capacity on the part of historicism—which remains serene, lucid and coherent after engulfing astonishing volumes of the knowledge that flows from its multitude of sources—yet in order to account for Benjamin himself as a historical phenomenon, or for Marxist history more generally, there is a strong case to be made for this same flood as the stimulus.

One would agree that there are certain biographical, or immanent, features of his situation which make him less tolerant of the amount and kind of knowledge to which he was exposed. Nonetheless, hypertrophy of the historical record until it reaches a quite unassimilable quantity must be taken seriously as the condition of that knowledge, and as a decisive factor in causing the collapse of the bourgeois interpretive system in his thinking. As a scion of the prosperous middle class, he was not prompted to reject historicism by any directly experienced economic interest. The revolutionary intellectual of bourgeois origins and traditional education will quite typically accept privation, and renounce rewards and comforts otherwise within easy reach, even as he commits himself to a struggle for the material benefit of interests other than his own.

Since his personal motivation cannot then spring solely from the exigencies of his material, or even political, predicament (although the latter is not discounted as a factor), it is not clear why the distant images of revolution should exert such a profound fascination on him. I suggest it may be traced to the sheer pressure of accumulated "archaeological" evidence, the weight of a record too concrete and jagged in the detail of its own outline, too extensive in its minute documentation and authentication, for the vessel of historicism to resist while it sets about the all-too-slow process of rationalization and orderly assimilation into the sphere of homogeneous knowledge. Thus, it collapses, and quantity gives rise to a qualitative change. Accumulation at a certain point has exceeded the old mode of absorption, and this must ultimately destroy it.

This seems to have been the situation within which Schlegel experienced history also, for he observed that the explaining activity of history, its transformation into the mythic order of the present, had ceased to function: "Was wir jetzt Historie nennen, ist eben nur Compilation, eine Art und Theil von Philologie" (KA XVIII p. 376 #671, 'What we now call history, is actually only compilation, a kind and branch of philology'). Because of this essentially unassimilated form, it has greater potential in the sphere of "transcendent freedom"—it produces the contradictory accumulation of myths which he turns into his New Mythology. Eclectic truth brought to this point cancels itself to yield a source for poetry: "Die compilatorische Historie ist Nahrung der Poesie und Philosophie" (p. 377 #681, 'The compiling history is nourishment for poetry and philosophy'). It has this effect because the distance between the archaeological presence and the integral cultural sphere will itself generate a form of critical leverage, or abstraction: "Archäologie ist nur eine Art Historie wie Kritik eine Art Kunst" (p. 384 #767, 'Archaeology is simply a kind of history the way criticism is a kind of art'). Quite obviously, this does not only refer to evidence drawn from outside our time, but also our cultural geography. The effect of contacts with other traditions on the Western imagination in Schlegel's day, and throughout the modern period, has functioned in precisely this "archaeological" role. This may be presumed to be what Schlegel means when he writes: "Romantisch ist die Oberfläche der Erde" (LN 1262, 'The surface of the earth is Romantic').

There is also a counterpart to this archaeology in relations with the future. Where the image of future time is more than a continuation perpetuating, necessitating and justifying the present in an inductive forward projection, it too exercises a disruptive effect on the way the present is read. As Schlegel noted in Athenäum Fragment 218 (see Chapter Three, p. 146-7) the obscurity of the future and the precariousness of prophetic divinations about what will be, also affects what **is**, because our understanding of what a thing is cannot be detached from what it contains as potential for its own alteration or development. In the theories of natural science, Feyerabend's positions reflect the perception acquired through the study of history that nothing can be depended on because of what has previously been determined to be—that which is sustained by evidence can give way, that which is discarded can return. The confident assurance about the way evidence and the explanations one might hold to in the present will look to a perspective in the future, disappears. Similarly, the assured dismissal of what one decides to reject or abandon has no basis of strength as it looks to the future. Thus the phenomena of the present have changed the nature of their presence among us. We know they owe us no loyalty when they pass on into another time.

They have thus acquired an aspect of foreignness through this tie to the future which is equivalent to the potentially alien character of an object belonging to the past. There is, of course, nothing corresponding to the intrusion of an actual artefact which can come from the future. No concrete erratic presence like an object or written witness from the past can penetrate **backwards** in time from a future which has no concrete existence. The indeterminate future does, on the other hand, change the nature of objects in the present by this transformation of the cognition through which they appear as what they "are."

Present objects are ancestors to the unpredictable progeny of the way they and their circumstances may develop in the future. There are qualities in them which will prove to be the dreams that are recalled in the future as the discoveries of a waking knowledge still to come, in Ritter's formulation of the "Einfall." Describing the unfamiliar atmosphere with which the intuition of this possibility can charge an object, an utterance, or a situation, Benjamin compares it to the sense of déjà vu, but here it is not a feeling that one has returned to something known before, but that something will be returned to and only then really known.

Through this changed cognition, there may be something already perceptible in the present that it will return in the future as a déjà vu, something which Benjamin describes as apparent in the incompleteness of the present, a discernible gap which awaits fulfillment in the future recollection. That is also part of the necessarily self-concealing and contradictory divisions in the ideological world of class-society, which has to deny itself to itself. The resources of the present, so he argues in the notes to the Theses, are sometimes only adequate to register the reigning situation like a photograph which will not be developed until a later opportunity. Even the nineteenth century French historian Jules Michelet suggests something of this process with the formula "chacque âge rêve la suivante" ('each age dreams the next').

There are explorations of such experiences in Benjamin's collection of autobiographical reminiscences Berliner Kindheit um 1900 ('A Berlin childhood around 1900'). Certain things are, he writes in the section entitled "Eine Todesnachricht" ('Announcement of a death'), like the muff left behind in a room which reminds one of the woman who forgot it. Except that in the special cases he describes, it is not an absent visitor now drawn away into the past whose atmosphere is carried in a particular scene, a certain situation, certain words spoken, but a future moment in which the recollection will return and be understood for the first time in an illumination of déjà vu: "Wie uns dieser auf eine Fremde schließen läßt, die da war, so gibt es Worte oder Pausen, die uns auf jene unsichtbare Fremde schließen lassen: die Zukunft, welche sie bei uns vergaß"[2] ('Just as such an object lets us know there was some unknown woman there, so there are words or pauses, which make us aware of that other invisible stranger, the future, who left them with us').

The death in the passage he relates was that of a cousin he scarcely knew. Benjamin was about five years old at the time, and his father came to tell him specially when he was already in bed. He is told in every detail about what a heart attack is, but pays little attention. The information is a matter of indifference to him. Instead, something else impresses itself on his awareness: "Wohl aber habe ich an diesem Abend mein Zimmer und mein Bett mir eingeprägt, wie man sich einen Ort genauer merkt, von dem man ahnt, man werde eines Tages etwas Vergessenes von dort holen müssen" (ibid., p.47, 'But I committed my room and my bed very carefully to memory like a place to which one pays especially careful attention because one has a feeling one will one day have to return there to retrieve something one forgot'). This is like the special form of consciousness he later describes in The Work of Art in the Age of Mechanical Reproduction as characteristic of the public formed among the masses by the medium of film. It is distracted, and yet it examines and tests the world with renewed critical perception by identification with the probing, exploring agency of the camera's lens.

In "Eine Todesnachricht" distraction from the elaborate story and explanation he is told parallels and prefigures the scepticism on the larger social and historical scale which will loosen the hold of bourgeois ideology on the critical and revolutionary masses. It is accompanied by the sense that something else, another world of more solid truth is beginning to manifest itself through the widening cracks and unsteadiness of a bourgeois edifice growing ever more precarious as an account and picture of the world. In fragmentary interruptions of the continuity and apparent naturalness of that ideological tale, a hidden and dangerous domain of reality threatens to undermine its rule. But only the future reveals to the little boy what the vague trembling he detects in that seismic intuition will later prove to have signified: "In diesem Zimmer hatte mir mein Vater ein Stück der Neuigkeit verschwiegen. Nämlich der Vetter war an Syphilis gestorben" ('In this room my father had hushed up a part of the news. For this cousin had died of syphilis').

The personal reminiscence takes on a broader significance, and becomes part of Benjamin's larger critical project in uncovering the processes of history and historical cognition which lead to revolutionary critique. It reflects a world in which the singular ideological view of his class is cracking before the pressure of those very contradictions and social forces it exists to smother and hide from view. That contradictory experience interrupts the bogus inductive continuum of a future constructed to guide a singular dimension for action, providing epistemological rails for the train-journey of history in which, as he comments in the notes to the Theses, revolution is the emergency brake. The failure of that continuity admits many other possibilities for action which lack the apparent guarantee of outcome, but which open up new chances and new hopes for desires which had previously been excluded as irreal and absurd. These are hopes which are heterogeneous with the present. They open the door of history on new directions which follow the reawakened forces of human life and human desire.

These are not arbitrary plans, but potentials brought into existence when the restriction of a partial view and the arbitrary plan to impose it universally, founders. The change in consciousness which Schlegel, Benjamin and Feyerabend each manifest in a different form, is the product of a change in the reach or recollection of the historical culture in which they find themselves. This was not created by the imagination which it sets free, but by the technology of communication, the means of representation and of dissemination, which constitute the memory and range of history at the most undifferentiated level.

Phaedrus

One can go back as far as Plato to find an explicit statement on the disturbance of the harmony of the present by this extension of historical memory. In the Phaedrus, for example, Socrates warns of the dangers of a written text which "drifts all over the place, getting into the hands not only of those who understand it, but equally of those who have no business with it; it doesn't know how to address the right people, and not address the wrong."[3] The written text maintains one dimension of inviolable integrity, for it never compromises or adapts itself to circumstances. That is not to say that it always means the same thing, for its significance is inevitably subject to the manner and motives of its interpretation. Nonetheless, as an archaeological object, it cuts across the divisions of time in a way that the spoken word, or the memory of the spoken word, cannot.

Written words have a sort of fanatical quality, persisting in their testimony regardless of all appropriateness to the moment or the situation. Though their readings may explain or justify them, they themselves have no talent for tact. Even where they contain an apology, it will quickly become the wrong apology, and then requires that an apologetic reading be found for that: "They seem to talk to you as though they were intelligent, but if you ask them anything, . . . they go on telling you just the same thing forever" (Phaedrus p. 158). The spoken word, on the other hand, is that which always belongs. Plato calls it the legitimate brother of writing because, unlike its inept and ill-bred sibling, its sense of appropriateness can be depended on. It goes together with knowledge of its milieu, and "knows to whom it should speak, and to whom it should say nothing" (p. 159).

Socrates says that one "must be exceedingly simple-minded . . . if he imagines that written words can do anything more than remind one who knows that which the writing is concerned with" (p. 158). That is, to refer back to Schlegel, one can only read the history of the sphere in which one lives. But if one comes across a text which does not belong in that sphere, which speaks illegitimately, one cannot use it as a mere reminder. Instead, one constructs a meaning from its statements which is not legitimate in one's own sphere either. And one may either regard this as bastardizing the purety of one's inheritance, or as introducing invigorating, fecundating fresh stock. Plato of course takes the former view.

The myth of Theuth and King Thamus which Socrates relates to Phaedrus contrasts real memory to the record of writing, for when Theuth reveals his new invention the king protests:

> If men learn this, it will implant forgetfulness in their souls: they
> will cease to exercise memory because they rely on that which is
> written, calling things to remembrance no longer from within
> themselves, but by means of external marks; what you have
> discovered is a recipe not for memory, but for reminder. And it
> is no true wisdom that you offer your disciples, but only its
> semblance; for by telling them of many things without teaching
> them you will make them seem to know much, while for the most
> part they know nothing; and as men filled not with wisdom, but
> with the conceit of wisdom, they will be a burden to their fellows
> (p. 157).

As a reminder, writing can only _point_ to the substance of thought, whose proper medium and locus is the mind. Since it is dissimilar from mind, the relationship can be no closer than that.

Thamus' objection covers two complementary points, one distinguishing telling from real teaching, which involves the shared moment of instruction, the contact of direct presence; the other opposes two ways of maintaining possession of wisdom once it has been imparted. If men use writing as the receptacle of what they know, rather than memory which is "within themselves," they will lose it, because in translating knowledge into writing, which is heterogeneous with thought and experience, its real quality is lost. What makes teaching so much more felicitous than telling in the haphazard transmission of writing, is the homogeneity of media. The thoughts which flourish in the bearer of wisdom may be transplanted into the mind of his student because the two resemble one another. The recipient medium of the pupil's understanding is apt because it conforms with that of the master, and thus offers a congenial home to which his knowledge may easily and safely pass:

> The dialectician selects a soul of the right type, and in it he
> plants and sows his words founded on knowledge, words which can
> defend both themselves and him who planted them, words which
> instead of remaining barren contain a seed whence new words
> grow up in new characters; whereby the seed is vouchsafed
> immortality (p. 160).

The coherence of individual existence is likewise a guarantor that the moments of recollection will be similar to the original moment of experience since both are produced in the singular sphere of one person's consciousness. When knowledge reappears as its image in memory, it does so in an instant of consciousness which will be compatible, though temporally distinct, with that in which it was acquired. The separate but related instants of consciousness sustain the truth of memory like the separate but compatible figures in the "dialectic"—the souls "of the right type." The truth of memory resembles that of the image of received teaching because it is supposedly still in contact with the trace left by the original impression. The continuity of consciousness closes the gap of time, the contact of instruction closes the gap of separate existences. Thus memory enjoys a kind of supporting connection which would be lost if it were translated into writing. The function of this connection is like that of the supporting parent whose presence always benefits speech, unlike writing which "when it is ill-treated and unfairly abused . . . always needs its parent to come to its help, being unable to defend or help itself" (p. 158).

Thus writing is said to threaten continuity, despite the apparent dependability of an objective, unvarying text which Theuth thought such a boon. Translation of memory into writing cancels the contact through consciousness with the experience, and transposition into writing of the spoken word cancels the protective contact of master and student. Since Plato does not elsewhere show signs of ignorance or stupidity, however, one may assume he is not unaware of the distinction between consciousness in the moment of an experience, and the necessarily quite separate moment of its recollection in memory, and therefore the distinction between the recalled image and that which it represents. Equally he is not unaware that even the wise instructor's words heard by the pupil are only indications of his thoughts, not the experience of those thoughts themselves. These forms of discontinuity are always in effect. Nevertheless, there would be an inescapable foolishness in entirely rejecting the idea that such forms of communion do constitute unitary spheres despite their contradictions.

There _is_ such a thing as consciousness, there _is_ such a thing as teaching, and there are even traditions of wisdom. But since these are enclosures which include and sublate contradictions, it follows that writing itself may also constitute its own enclosures, with its own characteristic sublation of those contradictions to which Plato quite correctly refers.

It is in the nature of oral tradition that integrity of the inheritance is in the most direct competition with variability, because the medium of transmission is so intimately involved with the medium of invention. That is, memory and invention are both functions of intention. To preserve a memory intact requires a care of it which writing may dispense with. Precisely because it has that rude and rugged persistence, the written record can endure centuries of orphanage without harm. Its ill-bred tactlessness is also the startling insensitivity which it displays to being "ill-treated and unfairly abused." It may be misread, given meanings and influence quite opposite to the intention of its author, and yet live on unchanged as an object. On the other hand, each generation must become parent in turn to the oral teachings. If the custodian of spoken teachings becomes sceptical or indifferent to one part of what he has received through following his own thoughts, that part is most likely to die out, for it will not be passed on in its full vigor, if at all, to the next generation. No-one knows what ideas of Socrates have disappeared forever because Plato considered them unimportant and they never found any response in his dialogues.

The orally preserved tradition is ordinarily fearful of variations; it gravitates to formulae which are resistant to confusion in being mutually confirming, and it is economic in its architecture. Like the synchronic system of grammar in spoken language usage, it preserves very little that is marginal, very little which does not justify its survival by contributing to the seamless texture of the whole. As antagonistic variations occur, one formula will assert itself and the displaced version vanish into oblivion. There is no access to the past which was, only the derived form which remains. The synchronic system offers the condition of the present as the unity which contains all that has gone before. Bounded in this way, it becomes what Schlegel terms an "individual." All the possibilities enclosed within it are united by that singular form. The written text, however, may also define an individual, but one with an added dimension.

It unifies all the possible readings made of it throughout the extent of its existence, just as oral wisdom unites all the personal experiences which share in its formulations, but because the response to writing in turn may be written, those readings can form a family which cuts across the synchronicity of a historical present. All the writings on the Phaedrus through the generations, for example, and of course the writings on them as well, form a community, no matter how abused and ill-treated by misconstruction they may be in the absence of their parental authors. Wherever they survive physically, readings which once were eccentric persist independently of memory and interest, one day to emerge again, perhaps, when re-read in yet another way. The book, as a genre of historical awareness, develops gradually as these communities grow through more and more heterogeneous changes. As various readings of the Book of Life—the mythic interpretations of the human condition—are brought into written form, they begin to grow in the historical dimension, whereas before they were restricted to their own present.

They collect about them a literature of criticism and comparison. As writing, they can be carried between cultures and times, and so produce structures of connection and fusion. The origins of any writing, since they lie in personal experience and personal memory, are of course lost. The text may represent, it

246

does not contain them. But this is only a further stage of the loss of experience which is only _represented_ in memory, and the loss of personal memory, which is only _represented_ and not contained in the transmission of oral teachings. A form of contact which parallels those which Plato admires in memory and teaching, _is_ preserved in writing—preserved by the presence of the object of the text itself.

Each and every reading is a unique experience with the writings that are gathered up by history and brought to each concrete present, but each is part of a community founded by the text and marked by the relationship with it. Each reading can be put into writing, which then establishes that community as a historical entity whose links penetrate in visible form beyond the boundaries of personal presence. The ties with books spun by books weave history into a texture which is no longer restricted by the limitations of the fabric of memory. The horizon or reach of the present is thus extended both forward and backwards. In reading it communicates with the past, in writing with the future. The saturation point of each capacity is potentiated far beyond what was possible before. What can be remembered is dwarfed in range and quantity by what can be read in a lifetime, what can be written dwarfs what can be taught in a lifetime as the text is disseminated to a spatially and temporally unlimited readership.

If we look again at Schlegel's use of the terms _Roman_ and _Prosa_, which exceed and comprise all genres, it is clear that they represent the new character of history in the "Zeitalter der Bücher" (KA II p. 332, 'age of books'). The "novel" for Schlegel is not only a translation from the writer's own incommensurable experience, which is then lost, into a point of origin for subsequent readings, but is itself a reading. Since the experience of the writer's present is filled with the presence of texts, is a composite of what he has read, the novel is the continuation of the life of those other writings, and they are all partial origins of its own life. The medium of Romantic prose is the dynamic agent by which the mythic forms of the past have become historical in the form of the novel. This is, for Schlegel, how those forms may penetrate into the continued weave of historical time from the point of their existence _outside_ it, where they were previously restricted and protected by the special sphere of privilege they enjoyed within their own particular tradition:

Die Vermischung und Verflechtung sehr heterogener Bestandtheile und selbst Mythologien ist eine nothwendige Aufgabe des Romans. Eine antiquirte Mythologie kann nur im Roman behandelt werden. Auch die Verbindung mehrerer Mythologien ist nur im Roman möglich (LN 1565).

('The mixing and weaving of very heterogeneous components and even mythologies is a necessary task for the novel. An antiquated mythology can only be treated in a novel. Even the combination of several mythologies is only possible in the novel.')

It is prose which gathers together the strands of history. Its combining or associating power is political in the sense that it is through the mediation of such writing that disparate elements may be brought to bear on one another: "Die Grundlage der Prosa ist dialektisch d.h. logisch politisch" (LN 584, 'The basis of prose is dialectical, that is logical and political'). This political role is inner-textual, and is the essential constitutive moment of the novel: "Der Roman muß politische oder satirische Totalität haben. Jede andre wäre Fehlerhaft" (LN 9, 'The novel must have political or satirical totality. Every other would be erroneous'). This is a position he establishes early in his notebooks, and sustains throughout. Even the elaborate analyses of different tendencies and directions are all subtended by this original perception of the novel's essence. That political character takes precedence over the possible kinds of Romantic novel because those are the result of a preponderance of one element, which militates against the combining moment of such a work:

Alle diese Extreme sind Fehlerhaft weil dadurch das Wesen des Romans selbst nämlich die Mischung zerstört wird eben darum schon. Es ist also gar kein Roman. Dieß Uebergewicht ist gegen die politische Totalität (LN 20).

('All these extremes are wrong because it is precisely through them that the essence of the novel, namely the mixing, is destroyed. Therefore it is not a novel at all. That preponderance is contrary to the political totality.')

The task of redeeming the past in Proust's novel-writing, which Benjamin compared to a Penelope-labor of forgetting, can quite easily be brought into this perspective. Writing, in Proust's enterprise, is indeed, much as King Thamus protested to Theuth, the unraveling of the ordinary memory recalling the past to the present. The act of remembering merely brings back the image of the past, which we can recognize only because it reminds us of the absence of that which it represents; the act is wholly weighed down with the motive of the present, which is consciousness of that absence. Though there is nothing which can return the experience of the past as such to Proust, this is not the center of his quest. The longing is for happiness, or redemption of the present's chilling emptiness. And this is the promesse de bonheur of writing. The involuntary memory which wells up spontaneously at the taste of a madeleine, or the catch of uneven flagstones, is like reading because the meaning of those objective presences is taken from them afresh, renewed as it is each time a text is read. The astonishing pleasure he experiences is not the re-appearance of the original present, but the unity of experiences within the history of readings of those profoundly potent objects. They carry the past inscribed on them like the written record.

The flavor of the madeleine dipped in tea can be repeated, found again, though a particular moment when it was first tasted in the past may not—just as the written text survives, even though the originating desire of the author associated with its first appearance is lost. At a certain moment in the present, Proust reads that renewed sensation, and through it discovers a mode of contact richer than that which voluntary memory can bring. The same contact is brought about by his writing. By transmuting feeling into the images of a novel, the works then gather up all the never-ending series of moments which they have the power to produce as readings. The readings all look to the text as a parental sun which returns to the noon-sky each time the book is opened. The event which takes place in time, on the other hand, is doomed to fall with its moment into the past, and even though it may be mirrored in some form by the activity of the new presents which follow and replace it, the new light excludes the old. Therefore, the communion of readings marked by a single text has for Proust a more secure integrity than the sphere of the individual personality whose continuity encloses and links memories and their origin. As he turns all his memories into prose, they become accessible in the promise of the text that it will remain.

For Feyerabend's anarchistic epistemology, too, this kind of historical recollection situates what has grown possible for him, and yet never was for Galileo. The body of scientific knowledge has become knit up, through the compilation of long and detailed records, into a vastly articulated organism. One can see the justice of Schlegel's claim that "Die höchste Darstellung der Physik wird nothwendig ein Roman" (KA XVIII p. 155 #379, 'The highest account of physics necessarily becomes a novel'), for scientific work can no longer perceive itself as an authoritative reading of the Book of Life, but as a political engagement with theories from the past through the criticism of new speculation and experiment. The historical dimension is uppermost in Feyerabend's new consciousness of natural science:

> Plutarch, or Diogenes Laertius, and not Dirac or von Neumann are the models for presenting a knowledge of this kind in which the history of a science becomes an inseparable part of the science itself—it is essential for its further development as well as for giving content to the theories it contains at any particular moment (Feyerabend p. 30).

Like New Mythology, the inheritance of a historically conscious science whose records are read, rather than consumed by the image of the present, is "an ever increasing ocean of mutually incompatible (and perhaps even incommensurable) alternatives" (ibid). It abandons the economy and synchronicity taken as the ideal by a rationalist view of knowledge which regards itself as moving ever closer to the truth, and as carrying the distillate of all discovery within its system. Such science considers that it has culled all that is valid from past labors, and exhausted its history in the process. The system of the present is the universal image which may project itself back with unchallenged authority over the past. For Feyerabend, however, the past is never exhausted. It continues to exert itself, and compete with all alternatives in perpetuity: "Nothing is ever settled, no view can be omitted from a comprehensive account" (ibid). The texts of previous theories and previous research live on to give birth to an endless series of new readings.

Therefore the significance of <u>Against Method</u> is not as exhortation, nor as one more description of method, or one more epistemological theory. It is the recognition of a changing historical situation which was not brought about as his, nor anybody's deliberate project, but by the political transformation of history itself through its own growth.

New History

In Lyceum Fragment 119, Schlegel writes about the mythic quality which veils the distinction between the personal intimacy of experience and the exterior aspect which is expressed in lyric poetry, exemplified for him above all by Sappho. The possibility of truly lyric poetry depends on a sense in both writer and audience for the reality and the dignity of what is expressed. This, in his view, no longer exists:

> Sapphische Gedichte . . . lassen sich weder machen, noch ohne Entweihung öffentlich mitteilen. Wer es tut, dem fehlt es zugleich an Stolz und an Bescheidenheit. An Stolz: indem er sein Innerstes herausreißt, aus der heiligen Stille des Herzens, und es hinwirft unter die Menge, daß sie's angaffen, roh oder fremd (LF 119).

> ('Sapphic poems . . . can neither be composed, nor publicly disseminated without desecration. A person who does so is lacking in both pride and modesty. In pride: because he tears out his innermost self from the sacred silence of his heart, and tosses it out to the crowd so that they may gape at it, rough or estranged.')

Only a mythic view of _truth_ about human nature, a garment of universal validity to hang about the intimate sphere, permits the personal realm to be made public in the guise of collective significance. Without this basis for sincere conviction, there is nothing to redeem what is then a presumptious and immodest kind of writing: "Unbescheiden aber bleibt's immer, sein Selbst auf die Ausstellung zu schicken, wie ein Urbild" (ibid.,

'Immodest it will always be, to send oneself off to the exhibition like an ideal image'). That has become unacceptable now that such nakedness is not protected, as it might once have been, by the aura of special privilege conceivable within the certainties of a mythical antiquity:

> Gäbe es aber auch noch eine Natur so konsequent, schön und klassisch, daß sie sich nackt zeigen dürfte, wie Phryne vor allen Griechen, so gibt's doch kein olympisches publikum mehr für ein solches Schauspiel.
> ('Even if there were still a nature so resolved in its principles, so beautiful and so classical that could show itself naked, as Phryne did before all the Greeks, there is no longer any Olympic public for such a spectacle.')

The change this has produced in poetry written under conditions closer to those which now obtain, no longer permits that approach, nor that designation:

> Und sind lyrische Gedichte nicht ganz eigentümlich, frei und wahr: so taugen sie nichts, als solche. Petrarcha gehört nicht hierher; der kühle Liebhaber sagt ja nichts, als zierliche Allgemeinheiten; auch ist er romantisch, nicht lyrisch.
> ('And if lyrical poems are not entirely unto themselves, free and true: then they are worth nothing as such. Petrarch does not belong here; this cool lover says nothing but dainty commonplaces; he is Romantic, not lyrical.')

The hardihood of the cynic is altogether different from the ideal innocence of Phryne. He can expose himself with serene assurance because he knows that what is put on view is nothing of himself. His interior being is absolutely separate from its public expression. Only the mythic modality of forms asserts the coincidence of the inner reality with its representation as an outer appearance. Freed of this illusion, there is no longer any sense for the cynic that the private sphere is in need of protection. The division between inner existence and appearance leaves it sequestered in absolute security and isolation. That leaves no basis on which representations of the most intimate experience should be felt to lie any closer to the reality of his private realm, and thus in need of protection from the vulgar, uncomprehending public. Protected by this division between the personal and the explicit, he can expose any part of his life with impunity: "Nur Zyniker lieben auf dem Markt" ('Only cynics make love in the market-place').

Even though the two tendencies might cover the same subject-matter, the distinction between them is complete: "Sapphisch ist nie zynisch" ('Sapphic never means cynical'). It is, however, not to be construed as the difference between literary and non-literary expression. Cynicism changes, but does not exclude, the possibilities of poetry: "Man kann ein Zyniker sein und ein großer Dichter: der Hund und der Lorbeer haben ein gleiches Recht, Horazens Denkmal zu zieren. Aber Horazisch ist noch bei weitem nicht Sapphisch" ('One can be a cynic and a great poet: the dog and the laurel have an equal right to ornament Horace's grave. But Horatian is far from the same as Sapphic').

Even though Schlegel's novel Lucinde shocked and appalled his contemporaries by its transparent exhibition of his private life with Dorothea Veit, he personally remained quite undismayed by the vituperation directed at him. "Gefahr übermütig zu werden, weil das Gesindel mich so sehr verabscheut" (LN 1941, 'A danger of developing an overweening pride because the rabble loathes me so much'), he noted. This certainly indicates that he had the courage of his cynical convictions—"Mythologie durch die That zu constituiren" (KA XVIII p. 376 #679, 'Mythology is to be constituted by the deed')—in carrying out the full implications of his enterprise in New Mythology. The playful revelations of Lucinde are not to be read as demonstrating the thing-in-itself. They are not the outward form in which an inner reality is present and manifest, but are abstractions from the personal sphere, a translation into a wholly separate medium, and therefore a wholly distinct image. It is, in short, ironic, a parabasis.

Novalis was quite incapable of grasping this, and saw only the difficulties the book would bring on itself. In his letter to Caroline from February 27th, 1799, he is particularly anxious about the response the subtitle, <u>Cynische Fantasien oder Sataniken</u> ('Cynical Fantasies or Satanisms') would evoke: "Viele werden sagen—Schlegel treibts arg . . . dies ist ein falscher Messias des Witzes—kreuziget ihn! (KS IV p. 280, 'Many will say—Schlegel is up to no good . . . this is a false Messiah of wit—crucify him!'). Like so many other readers, though with infinitely less justification, he shows no comprehension of the new territory into which the novel has cut a path: "Nun ist das Postulate—Sey cynisch—noch nicht gang und gäbe—und selbst sehr innige Frauen dürften die schöne Athenienserin tadeln, daß sie den Marckt zur Brautkammer nähme" ('The postulate—be cynical—is not yet common and current.—and even women with very passionate hearts might reprove the beautiful Athenian that she chose the market-place to be her bridal chamber'). The significance of <u>Lucinde</u> in exploring the possibility that the novel might pass beyond fictions eluded Novalis.

Schlegel clearly considered that it was unnecessary, indeed self-defeating, to construct a novel out of fictitious subject matter because the portrayal was already "fictive" in being <u>categorically</u> separate from any indicated "truth." The idea of the "real truth" of his experience, or Dorothea's, was necessarily infinitely exterior to any representation. It could exist only in its own sphere, an absolute wholly indeterminable from within the novel. As an origin whose modality situated it outside the novel, it could not figure as the goal to be realized within it. Schlegel writes: "Der Roman strebt nicht nach dem Unendlichen, sondern aus dem Unendlichen heraus" (LN 1378, 'The novel does not strive to reach the infinite, but rather to draw itself out of the infinite'). The finite text of the novel is produced by negation of the infinite reality which it excludes as a nothingness relative to the historical sphere.

This reverses the more commonplace direction, which adopts a fictive image as a negation of the lived historical realm, and constructs its narrative world in place of that as a noumenal literary truth. This purports to penetrate to a deeper level, or at least to present an essential meaning in a more general and extensive order. The idea of literary fiction which is based on the attempt to penetrate to the "real" in that way, will naturally also deny the significance of full attention and seriousness in the way we think of the concrete aspects, the surface of real things, in shared <u>historical</u> existence. It deprives the concrete phenomenon of meaning and impoverishes it as a presence in the political weave of human life. Novalis, however, did not recognize either the limitation or the function of representation as it was demonstrated by Schlegel's novel. This is most amply illustrated in his own, <u>Heinrich von Ofterdingen</u>.

There, he still leans toward myth as a reflection of universal truths. <u>Heinrich von Ofterdingen</u> is filled with the conviction typical of the later and more commonplace notion of Romanticism, that the truths which lie behind the visible may be brought into view by the revelations of poetry—that the veil of Isis may be swept aside by the privileged command of the hieratic initiate, and its treasures of wisdom carried back into the presence of the visible sphere. Novalis' novel sets itself free of the images of concrete life and experience in order to lay claim to the wisdom beyond them. As fictions, its strands weave themselves beyond the everyday frame to make contact with the transcendent truths of the Book of Life. Schlegel builds the visible sphere by translations from its opposite, which nonetheless remains beyond visible reach. That which transcends the historical medium remains a nothingness. His concern is to form real events into history by the creation of a text out of them. His work will not use fictive images to present the privileged, a-historical wisdom which transcends the concrete presence of the text. Similarly, he cannot expect to achieve the sublime harmonies of form which become possible where a text preserves itself from an unmanageable entanglement in a contradictory burden of reference to the impenetrable incalcitrance of any concrete image or event.

Schlegel follows that interest in the truth of the day, the writing that takes up the concerns of the moment and situation in which it is composed, which he describes as characteristic of Romantic literature in his <u>Brief über den Roman</u>. The poetic image that is created in this way need not conform to some prior reality outside its own sphere. It constitutes itself quite separately from that vision of truth. Its presence as a text is what defines its truth, for that is the power by which it generates history, not as the channel by which something other than itself is summoned up. It is true the way its own situation is true—purely as appearance in its own sphere, on which nothing that is absent may press a claim of presence. Hence he writes: "Alle Bilder der Dichter sind buchstäblich wahr" (KA XVIII p. 146, 'All images of the poets are literally true'), and in the same spirit: "Behauptung daß alle Religionen wahr sind" (p. 328 #44, 'Insistence that all religions are true'). The potential field of literary significance is therefore expanded far beyond the boundaries of traditional privilege.

The political contact established by the text is appropriate to the public face of a real situation because it furthers the historical project of _Bildung_ in which all of mankind becomes one person. The medium of literature unites all readers within the sphere it creates, and if that sphere is the real, historical one, then the continuity of history becomes identical with the formation of humanity into one infinitely varied individual.

The illusion that reading is like a window into the writer's interiority, rather than a mirror of the reader's present, collapses with the myth that would present the transcendent origin of the act of writing as manifest within its representation. Schlegel's separation of those spheres changes the criterion of literary dignity. Since the work of art, in his account, blocks out the light of the origin which stamps its form, the task to which it must be equal is the enhancement of the variety and intensity of the readership's own illumination of itself. The capacity to be read which distinguishes the textual object is its closeness to the present, not its rootedness in a distant sphere. The text understood in this way eclipses the light of myth, and fills the solar position in the sky of its readership only as an optic which gathers up and organizes the fire that is brought to it, and without which it would remain dark. Its "archaeological" significance depends on its power to generate a response in the present which transforms or extends the spectrum of that time. It does not carry the distant past into the present as a freight brought in from afar; it is a vessel which arrives empty, but gives new shape to what fills it.

The concept of Romantic prose which Schlegel opposes to the poetic forms of the mythic condition, and the opposition of cynical to Sapphic poetry, show a revealing parallel to the changes registered in Benjamin's theory of the loss of "aura" which affects art in the modern world. The genre of narrative Benjamin described in _The Storyteller_, for example, which is represented as giving way to the quite different form of the novel, has an essentially oral wisdom at its core. The storyteller, Benjamin writes, "has counsel," he is the custodian of a kind of timeless truth extending its weave through a common bond of life which is now on the point of extinction:

> But if today "having counsel" is beginning to have an old
> fashioned ring, this is because the communicability of experience
> is decreasing. In consequence we have no counsel either for
> ourselves or for others. After all, counsel is less an answer to a
> question than a proposal concerning the continuation of a story
> which is just unfolding (Illuminations, p. 86).

The communicability of experience depends on the mythic order which is revealed in it, common to all who share in its world, but this is exposed as illusion where the complexity of life increases, as its rhythms become ever more fragmented and contradictory. The story of life grows too confused to represent in the story-teller's counsel—the continuation of that story is impenetrable.

Aura is defined in The Work of Art in the Age of Mechanical Reproduction as "the unique phenomenon of a distance, no matter how close it may be" (Illuminations, p. 222). It denotes the sense that a work of art is suffused with a sacred quality which shines out to the beholder from within it. This transforms the object from that which is simply close at hand to an image of the distant sphere of divine luminescence by an optical sensation akin to the way one's gaze appears to pass through the surface of a mirror into the space behind it. Benjamin argues that the reproducibility of privileged objects strips away their aura because it reasserts their absorption in this world. It affirms that they are truly objects, their surfaces real and substantial. The unique hand-crafted object, or the tale told of a unique experience are thus make to speak and speak and speak again, until it is clear they do not "have counsel." A limitation is brought into focus like that of written words as Plato criticizes them in the Phaedrus: "They seem to talk to you as though they were intelligent, but if you ask them anything about what they say, from a desire to be instructed, they go on telling you just the same thing forever."

In extinguishing the light of aura, Benjamin aims at the denial of what he calls "cult value," but this is in no sense a diminution of the significance of such works. It only asserts that their value is not eternal, but always to be realized, always to be made anew. Without this distance, the work of art holds nothing back. It has nothing to lose, no special status in relation to another sphere to protect. Therefore its effect on the living present is maximal. In this spirit Benjamin praises André Breton for having made Nadja "a book with a banging door" (Illuminations, p. 180). Its forthrightness is like that of Lucinde, for Breton also sees the fatuity of marking off literature as a sacred preserve which is uniquely fitted to the privileged role of signifying the ineffable. Even though Surrealism regards signification in its works as actually rendering visible the ultimate workings of the subconscious, it shares with Schlegel the more important concept that the charge of this significance is potentially manifested in all aspects and moments of lived life—a lesson it learned from Freud's Psychopathology of Everyday Life.

The purpose of counsel is to protect the image of life from the threat of chaos. It takes the form of "a proposal concerning the continuation of a story" because a story has a coherence in its sequence. Life just has to be transformed to make it appear that way, and that transformation is its projection into the eyes of wisdom. This is the function of auratic art—to create the image of life as it appears in the perspective of a timeless transcendent truth. Only from a point of view outside time is it possible to check the overwhelming flow of events, to overcome the unpredictability of that real world which offers no security at all. The exclusion of forbidden intimacies, and the retreat from the historical situation are both reflections of the incompatibility between "the epic side of truth, wisdom" (Illuminations, p.87), and concrete reality. The idea that the poet of antiquity was punished if he confronted a real topic of his day, to which Schlegel refers in Brief über den Roman, expresses this necessity.

Where history has no power to impose order on the domain of happenings, art finds a realm of harmonies beyond their reach. Fiction, wisdom or myth all represent a point of security on which to step outside the vortex of time. Schiller's line "Ernst ist das Leben, heiter ist die Kunst," sets those two realms of life and art apart in just that sense, and yet, at the sme time, there is a sense of the price to be paid—the melancholy collusiveness of gaiety which is always threatened by its emptiness compared to the implacable reality which will not go away. Schlegel's negation of such illusion is expressive of a quite different gaiety, one which knows and looks squarely at the world itself: "Logik das correlat des Romans. Logik ist Kunst der Philosophie. Roman ist gaya sciencia, Wissenschaft der Poesie" (KA XVIII p. 293 #1175, 'Logic is the correlative of the novel. Logic is the art of philosophy. The novel is the gay science, the science of poetry').

The essence of this gay science is clearly that it does not fear the turmoil of events. Consequently, one would conclude that Schlegel is able to dispense with a mythic wisdom either because the character of events has changed, and is no longer fraught with disorder, or the capacity of a historical mode of apprehension to deliver orderliness and harmony within events has created a new standpoint within history itself. The latter is, of course, more plausible. The power of Romantic prose, or the Romantic novel, to breast the turbulent flow of time is a transformation of history as a mode of representation. The functions of art and history are no longer split apart.

The decay of communicable experience which Benjamin diagnoses, the disappearance of that wisdom which is "counsel woven into the fabric of real life" (Illuminations, p. 86-87), may therefore be read in a way rather different from the interpretation he gives. Perhaps life no longer needs that alien support. Perhaps history has grown strong enough to represent all of life without the need to have recourse to myth. Benjamin argues, both in The Storyteller and in Erfahrung und Armut ('Experience and Poverty'), that it is the increasingly disastrous chaos of history which defeats wisdom in our century:

> For never has experience been contradicted more thoroughly than
> strategic experience by tactical warfare, economic experience by
> inflation, bodily experience by mechanical warfare, moral
> experience by those in power (Illuminations, p. 84).

Yet it is by no means certain that this is so. The machine-gun of the Great War was surely less incomprehensible, less indiscriminate, and ultimately less destructive than, say, the Black Death.

Benjamin voices here what is, in fact, an almost universal conviction that the loss of coherent values and beliefs in contemporary culture, for good or ill, is the result of objective misery, disorder and chaos in the modern world. The historical records, however, suggest that misery and disorder are, as far as one can tell, the rule throughout history, interspersed by occasional interludes of supineness or exhaustion. Myth, in fact, seems never to have been so secure and seamless as in the ages when whole nations could vanish as a result of invasions or famines. Now nothing and no-one disappears without trace. The historical records draw on technological means of representation and documentation so that every existence goes into the indelible images in which our new history consists.

It may be true, as Benjamin writes in The Storyteller, that the technologically organized conflict of the Great War was indeed one in which "men returned from the battlefield grown silent—not richer, but poorer in communicable experience," but this was surely not just because the events witnessed were too monstrous to relate, but rather too empty of meaning. The mythic experience of war had been supplanted by a different source of imagery. The drama of warfare itself had changed so that the individual actor is no longer required to function as the medium of the script, and the stage is filled far beyond his horizon.

The technological means of organization, telephone, air travel, the global articulation of production and supply, by-pass the mass of participants in a way that a purely verbal chain of command would not. An army without technical channels of communication uses its manpower as the means of disseminating its intention as well as fulfilling it. A front eight hundred miles long is not possible without electricity, but the messages which travel along its wires are unknown to the soldiery. Consequently, the combatants have nothing to report when they go home. The home front has access to films, newspapers, photographs. What can a civilian in the capital learn from a man who has only seen a square mile of mud for three months? What he does have to tell cannot be told; the inner sensations of fear and privation are not easily given a public form. His experience is no longer the means by which the war is communicated to the culture at large. Both the necessity and the capacity for oral representation are swept away by the newly-extended powers. The participant learns about the war in the same manner as the distant spectator. The new media of history transform it into meaningful imagery for all.

The relatively small compass of personal observation is only able to stake its claim to representation of the much vaster and more complex world in which it takes place, by the aura which suggests that it is drawn from a deeper level of meaning, an aspect of the world which is more harmonious, ordered—a wisdom beyond the storm of events. It is the emphasis on this claim which divides art from the separate practice of history insofar as the latter rests its case on facts or statistics rather than narrative or interpretation. In founding itself on "wisdom" or "myth," or "the epic side of truth," art is protected from contradiction by the concrete realm of appearances. In the modern world, however, representation has undergone a change in power from being the most laborious and specialized area of production, to the most explosively accelerated one of all.

The limitations of personal observation, and individual communication, are now left behind with memory and forgetfulness. No image has to stand alone as the epic emblem of a reality which exceeds it beyond measure. A vast multiplicity of images can rival the most polyform aspect of the world they document. There is thus an enormous reduction in the need for the special privilege of recourse to a hidden order of auratic truth. The concreteness of representing objects is restored to the way they are read, because the sense of concreteness in what they signify is no longer destructive to their function. Their quantitative power makes them adequate to a universe which we are now able to confront, far more than ever before, in its vast plurality.

It is in this way that the entire history of our times redeems itself from the need for a distant origin of meaning, because everything that is captured in a fixed image undergoes an inversion of its powers. When confronting its autonomous existence as part of our surroundings, part of the flow of time over which we have no command, any object will involve us in an insecurity which invites us to seek protection in a structure of illusion. Its appearance is always heavy with the foreboding of its share in an irresistible, incomprehensible and unpredictable rush of events. Thus, it demands to be neutralized by an atemporal dimension of reality. The face of the world is never wholly knowable, however familiar, for the moment in which we see it is perched on the edge of a future beyond the reach of temporal knowledge.

On the other hand, the power to absorb everything into reproduced appearance, out of the storm of time, will repeal that alien quality. The world captured in reproductions can no longer refuse our capacity to judge it. The enormously potentiated image-making technology of modern times establishes a powerful order into which our reality can be drawn and put at our disposal, thus setting it free from both the chaotic context of time, and the illusory context of the eternal in myth. This is a liberation whose significance may have been exceeded only by the invention of language itself for the way historical meaning is created in the course of human existence. Therefore, in his essay The Work of Art in the Age of Mechanical Reproduction, Benjamin writes:

> Our taverns and our metropolitan streets, our offices and furnished rooms, our railroad stations and our factories appeared to have us locked up hopelessly. Then came the film and burst the prison-world asunder by the dynamite of the tenth of a second, so that now, in the midst of its far-flung ruins and debris, we calmly and adventurously go traveling (Illuminations, p. 236).

The world subject to film, photography, and to the entire arsenal of electronic weaponry with which its movements, from the microscopically small to the cosmically immense, may be produced in a hundred million images, slowed down, stopped, speeded up, reversed, stored, recalled, all with equal contemptuous ease, is no longer a world through which we humbly read the signs of a divine plan. History has changed, and will continue to change, under this pressure. It demonstrates to a growing extent that same power which swept all trepidation from Schlegel's heart in writing Lucinde. The renewed awareness that arises when things are pulled out of the matrix in which they could once dominate the beholder by appearing to embody the mythic manifestation of what is and must be, becomes more and more pronouced in ever more varied ways.

Things grow old very quickly now, because all that remains of mythic aura for large classes of the objects we own and use is that of fashion, chic or novelty itself. This is the substitution we have made for the cult-value of timelessness. Objects in a mass-produced world have only the novelty of a newly-devised and emerging style to separate them from the ranks of all those others which are already exposed as nothing but part of an endless process, without any special privileges or hidden claims. This is the only escape from that raw nakedness of new history where they are all gathered up within the limitless record. For Benjamin, the tearing of this final veil of illusion heralds the emergence of clear perception of things as they are, and his discussion of Surrealism, he praises Breton for his revolutionary insight and work of exposure in this area:

> He can boast an extraordinary discovery. He was the first to perceive the revolutionary energies that appear in the "outmoded," in the first iron constructions, the first factory buildings, the earliest photos, the objects that have begun to be extinct, grand pianos, the dresses of five years ago, fashionable restaurants when the vogue has begun to ebb from them. The relation of these things to revolution—no one can have a more exact concept of it than these authors. No one before these visionaries and augurs perceived how destitution—not only social but architectonic, the poverty of interiors, enslaved and enslaving objects—can be suddenly transformed into revolutionary nihilism (Reflections, p. 181-182).

Where the contemporariness of that whose only validity was in its being contemporary fails, it indicates the feebleness of its previous self-assertion. It becomes evidence of the disappearance of an enduring wisdom, and of the abysmal emptiness which an entirely new mode of history must fill. The cult-value of novelty is the paper-thin panel on which a form reminiscent of the old illusion still stands, and on to which a succession of reconstructions is flashed in order give the barrier its only substance. Benjamin asks: "What form do you suppose a life would take that was determined at a decisive moment precisely by the street song last on everybody's lips?" (ibid., p.182), for such a situation could obviously find nothing in the song itself, but only in the gap opened up in the sequence of novelties. The result, he believes, would be a revolutionary freedom of action.

The disappearance of all cult-value is only made possible, however, by its displacement. It does not collapse from internal weakness or critical attack, but by the appearance on the horizon of a new form of order which has a more powerful capacity to generate meaning. What

Benjamin perceives as a revolutionary nihilism is expressed with that vagueness which manifests itself in the appeal to a Messianism because it is understood in a backward-looking perspective. The vanishing auratic world is Benjamin's signal that a new world is opening up, but he is unable to identify a positive outline for it. In attempting to set a describable entity in the space Benjamin fills with a Messianic image which essentially marks the limit of thought, I adopt the term New History as a reflection and extension of Schlegel's New Mythology. New History is neither a restoration of something lost, nor a transcendent dispensation, but neither is it a credo to be adopted as a matter of voluntaristic decision. It is the growth of history to a kind of universality which is based neither on a theological conception of what is real, nor on a dogmatic one.

Like New Mythology, it is primarily the result of rescuing all that could possibly be brought within its demesne from any criterion of exclusion. The means of this rescue, provided by the new technology of representation, fulfill a role directly paralleled by Schlegel's concept of the novel, and of prose. One can therefore attempt to extrapolate something of how the functioning of New History is to be envisaged from what can be ascertained about the Romantic novel as Schlegel conceives it.

The basis of New Mythology in the novel removes the fundamental criterion of a recoverable truth as a privileging element. That is to say, since all possible constructions of the world are given an equality of status as truth, the particular view or views which are written into the text are a matter of indifference from that standpoint. The book is representative of its own particular origin as the creation of its author and his circumstances, and it is solely the relationship between the two which makes it legible. The value of the book is in that legibility, which is its own truth, and is capable of infinite interpretation since origin and text are at an infinite remove from one another. It is therefore inexhaustible as a moment of true interest: "Wenig Menschen haben Sinn für allen repräsentativen Werth den es giebt. Es gibt in dieser Hinsicht kein langweiliges Buch und jedermann ist interessant" (KA XVIII p. 89 #718, 'Few people have a feeling for all the representative value there is. In this regard there is no book that is boring and everyone is interesting').

The privileged "communicable experience" of storytelling, by contrast, only occurs against the background of empty experience which is lost to history altogether. The epic side of truth is a restrictive category which is able to take in only part of the world it divides. The rest is cast out and abandoned to oblivion and boredom. As Benjamin writes in The Storyteller: "Boredom is the dream-bird that hatches the egg of experience" (Illuminations, p. 91), noting that the attention required for traditional oral narrative forms depends on the rhythms of repetitive crafts which in themselves are conducive only to self-forgetfulness. The decline of this factor, however, the dream-bird boredom of which Benjamin observes: "His nesting places—the activities that are intimately associated with boredom—are already extinct in the cities and are declining in the country as well" (ibid.), can scarcely be because productive work has become less monotonous in the industrial economy.

I would take the position here that it is the consciousness that such work, or rather its conditions, are watched over and recorded by media which forget nothing, that changes all attitudes to it, both the resentment and the acquiescence. It takes on meanings and becomes the focus of attention along channels which did not exist for the traditional activities of the world from which the storyteller comes. This labor is now a political issue for the same reason that Schlegel calls prose a political medium—it is caught up and interwoven with all other represented modes of life, whereas once there was no space available to redeem more than the narrow range of matters which were the accepted concern of wisdom.

The form of attention given by Romantic prose, which represents all of human existence, has no special criteria of significance by which time must be filled up if it is not to vanish as boredom. Because everything is set at an equal level, no activity is trivial in itself, and none important in itself. That would be a denial of the very basis of the universal historical and political reality which prose brings to all existence without discrimination. The sense of value attached to diligence in general tends to be a virtue which produces self-forgetfulness and therefore drives out the consciousness of freedom which is essential to the novel. Wisdom permits thought only of what has exemplary status—what reflects the eternal verities of mythic counsel. A life must struggle to the particular point of righteousness for it to earn entry into the illuminated landscape of a story. The novel, on the other hand, seeks out just that area of life which is otherwise most easily lost to history because it is outside the traditional claims of privilege, being either too subtle, or perhaps too unseemly. The goal of political totality means that nothing is abandoned to the shadows, and each aspect of life is rendered into its own particular significance. "Here 'meaning of life'—there the 'moral of the story,'" writes Benjamin, "with these slogans novel and story confront each other, and from them the totally different historical co-ordinates of these art forms may be discerned" (Illuminations, p. 99).

For Schlegel, consequently, activity itself only obscures the issue of the novel. Idleness is the condition in which the function of attention is at its clearest and most potent: "Müßiggang ist die hohe Schule der Selbstkenntniß . . . durch sie wird die Welt erhalten" (LN 1524, 'Idleness is the noble school of self-knowledge . . . through it, the world is sustained'). It is for this reason that Lucinde is filled from end to end with the praise of idleness. The novel as a form altogether is described in the notebooks as the natural state of literature which develops where there is idleness and a written record, for one "kann . . . den Roman, die Erzählung in Prosa zur Naturpoesie zählen, überall wo es Müßiggang und Lektüre giebt" (LN 2088, 'can consider the novel, the narrative in prose, to be the natural form of poetic literature wherever there is idleness and reading').

Purposeful activity, as a narrowing and distorting perspective, is inimical to the Bildung of consciousness which may be associated with the universality of New Mythology. It is, rather, an expression of that fundamental error and inversion he calls the evil principle: "Alle Nützlichkeit und Thätigkeit ist höllisch und teuflisch" (LN 1524, 'All usefulness and activity is hellish and devilish'), whereas "Die Begeisterung der Langeweile ist die erste Regung der Philosophie" (KA XVIII p. 87 #689, 'The inspiration of boredom is the first stirring of philosophy'). The special demand for action which springs from any mythical intrinsic division of life into the significant and the insignificant, is identified here as the Fall itself by Schlegel: "Man muß mit Bewußtseyn müßig gehn. Jeder hat ein Paradieß; Thätigkeit heißt der Engel der uns daraus vertrieb" (LN 1524, 'One must be consciously idle. Everyone has a Paradise; activity is the name of the angel who drove us from it').

But since the Fall is here transformed from a theological category to a quite easily penetrable historical one, the redemptive elements of New Mythology and New History remain similarly removed from any shadow of Messianism. New History is in the first instance a quantitative change, its reconstructed adequacy is therefore in principle one which may be imagined and described from the vantage point of what is already known and familiar.

The equilibrium which occurs when the variety of historical images becomes commensurate with the variety of historical phenomena, or the variety of experience, renders the restrictive privilege of previous outlooks redundant. Myth augmented the status of the outnumbered few, and built a stable world out of only such aspects as could be accomodated within its close confines. Those limits have also generated unphilosophical distortions in the possiblities of signification which are simply without foundation in the new superabundance of representation. Just as the anarchist epistemolgist in Feyerabend's account of scientific knowledge is able to match the plethora of possible theories, observations and experimental results with an equal prodigality of interpretive interest, the New Historian may acknowledge that there is a promise in any text he might read. Boredom is not an immanent quality of any text, but a limitation of reading. Nothing need be declared void, irrational, meaningless or beyond the pale. There is, on the contrary, endless hope for everything. New History is merely the form of reading in which, so to speak, there is enough meaning to go round.

This does not indicate that all texts are equal in significance, or in value. What distinguishes a textual object from any other is the mark it carries of another moment, of an act in which another existence has produced the legible signs of its unique presence. The extent of that existence, and the degree to which it has impressed itself on the text, are obviously not always the same. There is power in a work that flows from the author's awareness of the resources of the medium in which he writes it, and a "great" work is produced when an exceptional sense of that potential is realized. But that also implies an image of the reader and the interpretive principles he will bring to his reading. A great literary artist is one for whom a particular readership can discover the fluid spirit of its own vitality filling the lines of the text like blood filling the veins of the shades from the underworld. The reading is a labor, a test, and a discovery of its own life relived.

Achievement of such a book is not a matter of chance, but not a matter of velleities either. In something so complex as systems of language and traditions of representation, not even the highest degree of consciousness in the artist will be enough to either explain, or even guarantee, the way all this is mediated into the text, nor will it reveal how a work acquires the elaborate stamp of all these worlds which leave their trace for others to reenact and bring back. Nothing of what is serious and of real value is predictable or controllable here. The writing is a single moment through which many agencies flow to the potential revolutions in which that product may be caught up. The appearance and disappearance of audiences is unpredictable, their energy and insights, their motivations and wounds beyond the author's control. Similarly no judgement can reach outside its own moment. Nonetheless, there is a sense in which the potential in a work is put there, and reaches out across time for the right connection to find its charge.

This is the non-Messianic redemption of the past by which I would like to re-interpret Benjamin. It is not final, but always subject to change, and yet it is the medium of life without end:

> The past carries with it a temporal index by which it is referred to redemption. There is a secret agreement between past generations and the present one. Our coming was expected on earth. Like every generation that preceded us, we have been endowed with a _weak_ Messianic power, a power to which the past has a claim. That claim cannot be settled cheaply. (Thesis II).

The most important philosophical contribution in Walter Benjamin's conception of the Marxist revolution is the contradictory character of historical change itself. Where change flows out of the narrow, intentional consciousness of the present, it is not really change. In the form of progress, it is bound to reproduce the criteria of the present the way a machine is modified and improved by advancing technology. The performance of the machine is a quantifiable set of qualities, and every quantity always implies it should be increased, if its triumph is to be large, or decreased, if its achievment is in having already been reduced. The design improves, everything advances, everything gets better and better, except that this "everything" no longer includes what is most important to human life. And those forgotten things, too obscure to grasp, too disruptive to contend with, too dangerous to admit into the discussion of where we are going, or why, are abandoned as irrational and impossible concerns. Any agreement made which does not give that side of life its due, is indeed settled too cheaply.

Development within those rigid determinants is life on an endless train journey between high ghetto walls. Revolution, as Benjamin saw most clearly, has to be more than the continuation of an advance already long conducted by the technical and purposeful tradition of bourgeois enlightenment. In that tradition a bourgeois class has used the capital resources of the community to pursue the public purpose of rational development in economic forces by nourishing its private interests. Marxist revolution in the twentieth century has turned out to be the replacement of that class in the attempt at a more direct, more 'rational' and transparent, organization of the community's resources by state and party. Benjamin refused to accept that this technocratic shift in itself meant much more than the same journey guided by charts drawn in a new projection. It would certainly not arrive outside the same dramatic spiral to nowhere. He absorbed supplementary ideas to expand Marxist philosophy beyond this constrained, pinched vision from many quarters, largely from Friedrich Schlegel's Romanticism, though from other areas too. In so doing, he frequently scandalized materialist orthodoxy.

But however the purists who find security only in a single high road of rationalist advance may object, history which attempts to produce its unitary order by exclusion of the most fundamental tracts of its own substance, is not history at all. It is an arithmetical rigidity masking chaos. The field of true history must resemble the novel Nadja in having a "banging door." What results from that open access may be more demanding and more complex, but will not be more chaotic than technocracy. As Benjamin noted very early on, Romanticism was the last movement to undertake the philosophical project of mediating the entirety of the past and its inheritance into the present. In our age, the means and the enterprise have taken a different form, but the task is in no way less pressing.

Historical existence itself is identical with and indissoluble from its reponsibility to the past, and to the future. The historical subject lives only where there is history—which is renewed and increased, where the terms are understood in an extended sense, by reading and by writing. The theory of New History is drawn about the desire for historical life in abundance. It looks for changes which, however unforeseeable, will not be altogether astonishing. The sweetness of that life emanates from the desire burning in every fragment of every existence, whose claim it would acknowledge and settle in full.

NOTES

[1] Thirteen Epistles of Plato, translation and notes by L. A. Post (London: Oxford University Press, 1925), 341 C, p. 94. I am indebted to Professor Paul Feyerabend for drawing my attention to the material from Plato used in this chapter, and also for his encouraging response to the project of this book.

[2] Walter Benjamin, Berliner Kindheit um Neunzehnhundert (Frankfurt am Main: Suhrkamp, 1966), p. 46-47.

[3] Plato's Phaedrus, translation and commentary by R. Hackforth (Cambridge: Cambridge University Press, 1952), 275 E, p. 158. Further quotations from this edition indicated as Phaedrus.

BIBLIOGRAPHY

Behler, Ernst. _Die Zeitschriften der Brüder Schlegel_.
    Darmstadt: Wissenschaftliche Buchgesellschaft, 1983.

Belgardt, Raimund. _Romantische Poesie_. The Hague: Mouton,
    1969.

Benjamin, Walter. _Briefe_. 2 Bde. Hrsg. Gershom Scholem u.
    W. Adorno. Frankfurt am Main: Suhrkamp, 1966.

---------- _Gesammelte Schriften_. 3 Bde Hrsg. Rolf Tiedemann
    u. Hermann Schweppenhauser. Frankfurt am Main:
    Suhrkamp, 1977.

---------- _Illuminations_. Trans. Harry Zohn. Ed. Hannah
    Arendt. New York: Schocken Books, 1969.

---------- _Reflections_. Trans. Edmund Jephcott. Ed. Peter
    Demetz. New york: Harcourt, Brace and Jovanovich, 1978.

---------- _Schriften_. 2 Bde Hrsg. Th. W. Adorno u. Gretl
    Adorno. Frankfurt am Main: Suhrkamp, 1955.

Bulthaupt, Peter, Hrsg. _Materialien zu Walter Benjamins
    Thesen Über den Begriff der Geschichte_. Frankfurt am
    Main: Suhrkamp, 1975.

Dischner, Gisela, Friedrich Schlegels Lucinde und
    Materialien zu einer Theorie des Müßiggangs.
    Hildesheim: Gerstenberg Verlag, 1980.

Eagleton, Terry. Walter Benjamin, or Towards a Revolutionary
    Criticism. London: NLB, 1981.

Feyerabend, Paul. Against Method. London: NLB, 1975.

Goethe, J. W. Wilhelm Meisters Lehrjahre. Bd. VII.
    Gedenkausgabe der Werke, Briefe und Gedanken. Hrsg.
    Ernst Beutler. Zürich: Artemis Verlag, 1949.

Gomperz, Heinrich, "The Limits of Cognition and Exigencies
    of Action." University of California Publications in
    Philosophy, 16, 1938), p. 57-75.

Haven, Richard. Patterns of Consciousness. Amherst:
    University of Massachusetts Press, 1969.

Hermann, Armin. Die Begründung der Elektrochemie und
    Entdeckung der ultravioletten Strahlen. Frankfurt am
    Main: Akademische Verlagsgesellschaft, 1968.

Lakatos, Imre and Alan Musgrave. Eds. Criticism and the
    Growth of Knowledge. London: Cambridge University
    Press, 1970.

Lawrence, D. H. Letters. Selected by Richard Aldington.
    London: Heinemann, 1950.

Lohner, Edgar, Hrsg. Ludwig Tieck und die Brüder Schlegel.
    München: Winkler Verlag, 1972.

Nietzsche, Friedrich. Vom Nutzen und Nachteil der Historie
    für das Leben in Werke Bd. III: Hrsg. Giorgio Colli
    und Mazzino Montinori Berlin: De Gruyter, 1972.

Novalis. Schriften. IV Bde. Hrsg. Paul Kluckhohn u.
    Richard Samuel. Stuttgart: Kohlhammer Verlag, 1975.

Plato. Thirteen Epistles. Trans. L. A. Post. London:
    Oxford University Press, 1925.

---------- Phaedrus. Trans. R. Hackforth. Cambridge:
    Cambridge University Press, 1952.

Pohlheim, K. K. Die Arabeske. München: Ferdinand
    Schöningh, 1966.

Preitz, Max. Hrsg. Friedrich Schlegel und Novalis,
    Biographie einer Romantikerfreundschaft in ihren
    Briefen. Darmstadt: Hermann Gentner Verlag, 1957.

Rexroth, Tillman, Hrsg. Walter Benjamin über Haschisch.
    Frankfurt am Main: Suhrkamp, 1972.

Rilke, R. M. Letters of R. M. Rilke. vol II. Eds. Jane
    Banner Greene and M. D. Herter Norton. New York:
    Norton, 1969.

Ritter, Johann Wilhelm. Fragmente aus dem Nachlasse eines
    jungen Physikers. Hrsg. Arthur Henkel. Heidelberg:
    Verlag Lambert Schneider, 1969.

Schlegel, Friedrich. Kritische Friedrich-Schlegel-Ausgabe,
    Bde. II, V, XII, XIII, XVIII, XIX. Hrsg. Ernst Behler
    unter Mitwirkung von Jean-Jacques Anstett und Hans Eichner.
    München: Verlag Ferdinand Schöningh, 1962-1970.

---------- Literary Notebooks 1797-1801. Ed. Hans Eichner.
    Toronto: University of Toronto Press, 1957.

---------- Prosaische Jugendschriften, II Bde. Hrsg. J.
    Minor. Wien: Verlagsbuchhandlung Carl Konegen, 1906.

Steiner, T. R. English Translation Theory 1650-1800.
    Assen: Van Gorcum, 1975.

Valéry, Paul, Variété III. Paris: Gallimard, 1936.

Witte, Bernd. Walter Benjamin mit Selbstzeugnissen und
    Bilddokumentationen. Reinbeck bei Hamburg: Rowolt,
    1985.

Wolin, Richard. Walter Benjamin. New York: Columbia
    University Press, 1982.

Woolf, Virginia. Letters of Virginia Woolf, Vol. III. Eds.
    Nigel Nicholson and Joanne Trautmann. New York:
    Harcourt, Brace and Jovanovich, 1978.

Steven E. Alford

IRONY AND THE LOGIC OF THE ROMANTIC IMAGINATION

American University Studies: Series III (Comparative Literature), Vol.13
ISBN 0-8204-0110-2   184 pp. paperback   US $ 19,45

Recommended price — alterations reserved

This study examines romantic irony as a principle of style in the work of Friedrich Schlegel and William Blake. The first half traces Schlegel's critique of the principles of identity and noncontradiction, his development of a *romantic* logic, his view of dialectic and rhetoric, and how romantic irony is a stylistic mirror of the results of his critique of formal logic. These findings are tested in a close reading of his essay *Über die Unverständlichkeit* (1800). The second part examines the suggestive relation between Blake and Schlegel's views on logic, dialectic, and rhetoric, and uses these views as the basis for a reading of *The Marriage of Heaven and Hell* (1794). Both thinkers support the conclusion that romantic irony as a principle of style has two moments which can be characterized hermeneutically as negative dialectical and performative.

Contents: This study examines romantic irony as a principle of style in the work of Friedrich Schlegel and William Blake, using Schlegel's «Über die Unverständlichkeit» and Blake's «The Marriage of Heaven and Hell.»

PETER LANG PUBLISHING, INC.
62 West 45th Street
USA - New York, NY 10036

Richard Hoffpauir

ROMANTIC FALLACIES

American University Studies: Series IV (English Language and Literature), Vol. 31

ISBN 0-8204-0257-5   218 pp.   hardback   US $ 30,50

Recommended price - alterations reserved

As a contribution to a critical debate, this study is an attack, in the tradition of Yvor Winters and F.R. Leavis, on Romanticism in English poetry and criticism. It begins with an outline of the movement in eighteenth-century aesthetic thougt that gave rise to several fallacious literary notions, doctrines, and procedures: mythic form, individual authority, inspiration, and dramatic immediacy. The argument moves from an extended critique of Meyer Abrams' *Natural Supernaturalism,* through an evaluative comparison of William Wordsworth and George Crabbe, to intensive analyses of the critical reputations and poetic weaknesses of those two most definitive of Romantic poems, Coleridge's «Kubla Khan» and Keats's «Ode to a Nightingale.»

Contents: *Romantic Fallacies* is a critical study of the tradition of romanticism in English poetry and criticism, surveying the persistence of several fallacious notions: mythic form, individual authority, inspiration, and dramatic immediacy.

PETER LANG PUBLISHING, INC.
62 West 45th Street
USA - New York, NY 10036